THE NEXT AMERICAN CIVIL WAR

PREVIOUS WORKS BY LEE HARRIS

Civilization and Its Enemies: The Next Stage of History

The Suicide of Reason: Radical Islam's Threat to the West

THE NEXT AMERICAN CIVIL WAR

THE POPULIST REVOLT AGAINST THE LIBERAL ELITE

LEE HARRIS

palgrave
macmillan

First published in 2010 by PALGRAVE MACMILLAN® in the United States—a
division of St. Martin's Press LLC, 175 Fifth Avenue, New York, NY 10010.

Where this book is distributed in the UK, Europe and the rest of the world, this is
by Palgrave Macmillan, a division of Macmillan Publishers Limited, registered in
England, company number 785998, of Houndmills, Basingstoke, Hampshire RG21
6XS.

Palgrave Macmillan is the global academic imprint of the above companies and has
companies and representatives throughout the world.

Palgrave® and Macmillan® are registered trademarks in the United States, the
United Kingdom, Europe and other countries.

ISBN: 978-0-230-10271-2

Library of Congress Cataloging-in-Publication Data
Harris, Lee, 1948–
    The next American Civil War : the populist revolt against the liberal elite/ Lee
Harris.
      p. cm.
    ISBN 978-0-230-10271-2
    1. Liberty—United States. 2. United States—Politics and government. 3.
United States—Social policy. 4. National characteristics, American. I. Title.
JC559.U5H37 2010
323.440973—dc22

                                                                    2009047356

A catalogue record of the book is available from the British Library.

Design by Letra Libre

First edition: May 2010
10 9 8 7 6 5 4 3 2 1
Printed in the United States of America.

For Andy Fuson,

Thanks for always being there.

Those who profess to favor freedom, and yet depreciate agitation, are men who want crops without plowing up the ground. They want rain without thunder and lightning. They want the ocean without the awful roar of its many waters. This struggle may be a moral one; or it may be a physical one; or it may be both moral and physical; but it must be a struggle. Power concedes nothing without a demand. It never did and it never will.

—Frederick Douglass
An Address on West India Emancipation, 1857

CONTENTS

INTRODUCTION

WELCOME TO THE POPULIST REVOLT

I t wasn't supposed to happen this way. In the special election called to fill the Senate seat left vacant by the death of Ted Kennedy, everyone naturally expected the voters of Massachusetts to cast their ballots for another liberal Democrat, Martha Coakley. Massachusetts, widely regarded as the most liberal state in the union, had not elected a Republican to the Senate since 1972. Yet in the week running up to the election, the pollsters began to notice something odd. Their initial surveys had indicated that Coakley, state attorney general, was running far ahead of her Republican rival, Scott Brown, a relatively obscure member of the Massachusetts House of Representatives. In the last week before the election, however, the trend was suddenly reversed. Brown had not only caught up with Coakley in the polls, but he was now several points ahead of her. Alarmed by this unexpected development, President Obama went to Boston to campaign on behalf of Coakley. The president was willing to risk his prestige because he knew what was at stake for his party: Coakley's defeat would mean the end of the Democratic Party's filibuster-proof sixty-man majority in the Senate. Yet Obama's support was to no avail and on January 19, 2010, the nation and the world were stunned to learn that Scott Brown had trounced his Democratic opponent by a five-point spread.

People do not rush to explain the obvious, and if Coakley had won the special election, no one would have felt the need to offer reasons for her victory. But the shock of Brown's stunning electoral triumph produced an outpouring of plausible explanations. An AP byline declared: "Obama Gets Voters' Message: It's Jobs, Jobs, Jobs."[1] But was this really the message of the Massachusetts' voters? If Martha Coakley had vociferously campaigned against creating new jobs, this interpretation might make sense, but presumably Coakley was no less concerned with solving the problem of unemployment than her Republican rival. A more persuasive interpretation of the voters' message was offered by *USA Today* in its byline "Scott Brown drives his GMC pickup to U.S. Senate victory." With more than 200,000 miles on its odometer, Brown had driven his 2005 Canyon truck around his home state during his intensive campaign, transforming the pickup into what *USA Today* dubbed "a symbol of humility, hard work and rugged ideals,"[2] while simultaneously revealing himself to be a regular guy no different from the average working-class voters of his state. On this reading, Scott Brown did not win the election because he offered more in the way of "jobs, jobs, jobs," but because he made it clear to the voters that he understood what it was like to have a regular job and to drive a pickup to work, like many of them did.

The most striking take on the election upset came from the *Boston Herald*. In a lead editorial entitled, "A Revolution Begins," Brown's victory was compared to the famous "shot heard round the world"[3] that launched the American War of Independence when the British opened fire on Americans at Concord, Massachusetts on April 19, 1775. In offering an explanation for why the voters of Massachusetts chose Scott Brown, the editorial board of the *Boston Herald* offered several reasons, but concluded that "most of all, they [i.e., the people] are simply tired of the kind of Washington arrogance that says 'don't worry, we know what's best for you.'" Furthermore, the election of Brown was not seen simply as a fluke that had no bearing on the future course of American politics. Instead, "like that battle in Concord more than two centuries ago, this is only the opening round."[4]

In fact, Brown's election was not the opening round. That had already occurred in the summer of 2009, when, as in January of 2010, something happened that wasn't supposed to happen. A series of town hall meetings had been planned at which local congressmen would have the opportunity of letting ordinary people express their own points of view on the issue of health care. Polls showed that Americans were generally in favor of some kind of health care reform,[5] and President Barack Obama had vowed to make it the first priority of his new administration. The town hall format was deliberately chosen because it was expected to offer a classic, Norman Rockwell tableau of good old-fashioned American participatory democracy. Then, suddenly, it all went up in smoke.

In one town hall meeting after another, congressmen who had come expecting a well-mannered and well-informed public debate were confronted by angry and unruly crowds. Instead of calmly discussing the host of complicated issues relating to health care reform, the congressmen found themselves struggling to combat rumors of an insidious plan to establish death panels manned by government bureaucrats who would heartlessly terminate the life of senior citizens and order euthanasia for children born with Down syndrome. Those who attempted to debunk these allegations by rational arguments found that their appeals fell on deaf ears. So what if there was not a word about euthanasia or death panels in Obama's plans for health care reform? That proved nothing. Of course, the proponents of "Obama-care" would deny the inevitability of death panels—what else would you expect from the hardened Marxists who had seized control of the federal government?

Paul Krugman, the Nobel Prize–winning economist and columnist for the *New York Times*, was among the first prominent American liberals to register his shock at the mayhem at the town hall meetings. Dubbing the crowds "mobs," Krugman argued that they were symptomatic of a profoundly disturbing transformation in the way Americans have normally negotiated and settled their political differences. After reviewing well-mannered protests of the recent past, Krugman concluded that the town hall debacle signified "something new and ugly" on the American political scene.[6]

There was certainly something ugly about American politics in the summer of 2009, but it had been simmering ever since the previous November when Americans elected a new president. For many people, both in the United States and around the world, the election of Barack Obama was a moment of euphoria to be savored. But not all Americans shared their bliss. Many of them did something that they had never done after a presidential election: They ran out to stock up on guns and ammo. Those who behaved this way saw no reason to wait to see what kind of president Barack Obama would be. Like the fiery South Carolinians who began the process of secession only four days after Lincoln's election in 1860, they had already made up their minds. That man, Barack *Hussein* Obama, is not "our" president. This government is no longer "our" government—it has been taken over by a sinister conspiracy of radicals—which was precisely how Civil War secessionists felt about the election of Lincoln. Only, this time the sinister conspiracy was made up not of radical Republicans but of radical Marxists out to impose socialism on our nation.

It is true, of course, that no state seceded from the union after Obama's election; but a quasi-secessionist sentiment instantly swept over large swaths of our country, the depth and virulence of which was largely ignored by the mainstream media. Many liberals assumed such irrational and paranoid fears would give way once Obama actually became president. The new president's good sense, prudence, and moderation, they argued, would surely relieve such fears, so any remaining paranoia would be restricted to the tiny minority of the lunatic fringe—and who can really take them seriously? Yet, by the middle of the summer of 2009 it had become overwhelmingly evident that the "lunatics" were not a tiny and negligible factor operating in the shadows of American politics. On the contrary, they represented a formidable chunk of American public opinion. Two Rasmussen polls taken in early August of 2009 found that 41% of Americans viewed the town hall protestors favorably,[7] while 49% of Americans believed that protestors were "genuinely expressing the views of their neighbors."[8]

The liberal commentators who expressed shock and astonishment at the town hall protestors often asked, Who were these people? Where did they come from? Were they potential terrorists like Timothy McVeigh, or neo-Nazi extremists? Unlike these commentators, I did not need to ask myself these questions, because I already knew the answer. For most of my life I have lived in Georgia, and I have known many men and women who might have attended the town hall meetings, including some who might have shown up toting guns. I have talked with people who believe that Barack Obama is a Muslim and with others who are convinced that he is a radical socialist bent on the destruction of everything of value in the America that they love so passionately. I know some people who stockpiled weapons in order to prepare for the coming second American Revolution. I know people who, when Sarah Palin talked about "real Americans," believed that she was talking about them, and who look forward to voting for her in the next election. I know people who pulled their kids out of school when President Obama gave his address to the schoolchildren of America on September 8, 2009.

The easiest answer to why so much paranoia persisted after the election would be to conclude that people like those I had talked with were merely hopeless basket cases and crackpots, dangerous fanatics and deluded stooges. This, after all, was the explanation that many liberal commentators found most appealing. Perhaps if I had come to know these people only through conducting a formal interview with them, as a journalist for example, I too might be satisfied with this easy answer, because then I would see them not as living human beings but as mere ideological specimens. But these people are my friends, neighbors, and acquaintances. They are not lunatics or nutcases. They don't want to blow up anything. They are thoroughly decent and law-abiding people, many of whom would happily go far out of their way to lend both friends and strangers a helping hand. Many of them have lent their helping hands to me and have been there when I needed them the most, whether coming to my rescue when my car broke down or fixing something around my house that I could not figure out for myself.

By and large, the attitude of these people is that of live and let live. But they all have one highly conspicuous quality in common. They don't like other people telling them what to do. They don't like being bossed around. They insist on retaining control of their own lives and affairs. They are quick to display the proverbial "Don't tread on me!" attitude whenever they feel that their own traditional rights and liberties are in danger. These are people that might be best dubbed natural libertarians. They may never have read a single piece of the classic libertarian literature. They may never have even heard of John Locke or John Stuart Mill, but they have instinctively adopted Thomas Paine's maxim that "government, even in its best state, is but a necessary evil."9 To such people, there is nothing more odious or obnoxious than a government whose attitude is "Don't worry, we know what is best for you."

America's natural libertarians share two features that have characterized the natural libertarians of every historical epoch, from the Englishmen who rebelled against King Charles I in 1640 to the British colonials living in America who rebelled against King George III in 1775. First, they often fall prey to paranoid fears, attributing the ills of the world to sinister conspiracies of wicked men intent on robbing them of their freedom and turning them into slaves. Second, when confronted with any power that they see as a threat to their precious independence and autonomy, they will rise up to resist its encroachments, often resorting to behavior that makes the recent town hall mayhem look quite tame in comparison.

In the past, many of these outbreaks of defiance and resistance have reflected irrational fears and have been directed at the wrong targets, pursuing phantom solutions to genuine grievances. The same thing is true today. Talk of death panels, for example, is sheer collective paranoia—and yet, it is a paranoia that must be seen in perspective. It is rooted in the average American's healthy fear that concentrations of power will be used to rob them of control over their own lives and destinies and, in the case of the death panel, to decide which of them will live and which will die. In fact, if the state is called upon to ration health care, then it will inevitably be forced to decide who gets care and who doesn't. This does not mean that there will be death panels; it may simply mean that faceless bureaucrats will apply a complicated mathematical formula for deciding who receives medical treatment and who doesn't, an impersonal mechanism that would operate without the need for real human beings to agonize over the death sentences that they pass down on real human beings standing in front of them.

The Obama death panel is a myth—but it is a myth that expresses a genuine anxiety that decisions over our lives and deaths could one day end up being made *for* us and not *by* us. It is not enough simply to discredit the myth, which is relatively easy; it is necessary to address the underlying anxiety, which is much more difficult, since the source of this anxiety is the well-founded fear of the little guy that those who wield power over him will not be inclined to use it for his benefit. Those who dismiss this anxiety as shrill or alarmist are also misguided. For history has repeatedly shown that the little guy is right to entertain these fears. Power breeds arrogance. It has done so in the past, and those who believe that our modern liberal societies have tamed power to the point where it can never again grow despotic are simply deluding themselves. Power must always be watched and feared, and, when necessary, resisted.

In American history, this resistance has most frequently taken the form of popular rebellion. Traditionally, American populists have championed the rights and liberties of ordinary men and women like themselves, and have attacked what they have seen as a dangerous accumulation of power in the hands of an overbearing elite. In the early days of the American Republic, Thomas Jefferson saw the Federalist party as a power-hungry oligarchy, intent on bullying and exploiting the average man and woman, while the Federalists deemed Jefferson to be a dangerous demagogue, set on reducing the wealthy and educated to the same level as the masses. Jefferson eventually

won this particular battle—by getting elected president—but the struggle between the elite and the masses would continue to be a central theme of
American history down to our own day.

Most Americans will agree that our home-grown populism has played an
invaluable role in shaping our nation precisely because it has made ordinary
men and women wary of allowing any single group to amass too much power
over them. Yet all too frequently American populists have undermined the
strength of their case by espousing an overly simplistic understanding of how
the world works. They turn to populist demagogues and charlatans. They listen to conspiracy mongers. They become convinced that the ills of their
world can be solved by some quick fix. In short, they are often their own
worst enemy. This is unfortunate, because the freedom enjoyed by any society
rests ultimately not on a constitution or a Bill of Rights, but on the willingness of ordinary people to stand up for themselves and to resist those who
have the power to trample on their liberty.[10] They may rebel for reasons that
others find bizarre and incomprehensible, and their resistance can take on
forms that others see as grossly disproportionate to the real threat to their
freedom. Yet both this paranoia and this quickness to rebel have played an indispensable role in the creation of those rare and exceptional societies that
provide liberty for all, not just the lucky few.

The strong, the powerful, and the rich—they have always been free. But
in only a few societies have ordinary people managed to obtain their freedom,
often against great odds. A long-range view of history makes it clear that if
the so-called lower classes had waited around until the ruling class decided to
give them their liberty, they would have never had any liberty at all. What
liberty they have managed to create and maintain for themselves has been the
product of their own acts of defiance and rebellion, some bloody and violent,
others relatively peaceful, but all inevitably rowdy and unruly. The champions
of liberty have not always been knights in shining armor—more frequently
they were rebellious peasants, riotous apprentices, outraged artisans, thwarted
smugglers, unruly mobs, and lawless vigilantes.[11]

Just as there are far too many liberal intellectuals who were caught clueless by the latest populist revolt and who see it only as a frightening outbreak of mass lunacy, so there are those on the right who are prepared to shamelessly manipulate and exploit populist anxiety to serve their selfish purposes. The incomprehension of the liberal elite is dangerous because it underestimates the potential explosiveness of the current populist upheaval—those who ignore it, or prefer to wish it or explain it away, do so at their peril—and at the peril of their society. The opportunism of the populist demagogue is equally dangerous, however, because the demagogue all too often calls into being demonic forces that take on a life of their own, beyond his control, creating havoc in the body politic. It is easy to shout, "We are mad as hell and we aren't going to take it anymore,"[12] but it is much more difficult to channel popular anger and frustration into politically constructive purposes. There is an inherent danger in all populist revolts: Once resistance against authority has reached a certain point, it becomes increasingly difficult to keep it in check. Eventually a point of no return is reached, when all efforts to govern the society are baffled, so that no other options remain except revolution and civil war. Many other societies, including our own, have reached this point in the past. Ours may well reach this point in the future.

IN OUR CURRENT SEASON of confusion, it is of the utmost imperative to think—to think seriously, deeply, and searchingly—without the onerous constraints of political correctness or partisan bias. We must do as our forefathers did: We must scrutinize the lessons of the past for clues that can help us through the current crisis that is so rapidly and, to all appearances, so irreversibly breaking us apart. Those who are entirely caught up in the present moment, in the bright, glittering ephemera of the hour, cannot see what is before them because they have forgotten what is behind them. They are in the pitiful condition of the victims of Korsakoff's syndrome, a neurological disorder that renders its sufferers incapable of retaining any memory for more than five or six minutes, so that no matter how many times they are introduced to the same person, they will invariably greet him as a total stranger. Similarly, those who suffer from historical amnesia will be shocked by events that they take to be new and unprecedented, when in fact they are seeing a historical pattern that has repeated itself over and over. Krugman's verdict on the town hall riots as "something new and ugly" betrays more than a hint of this amnesia. Yes, the mobs were ugly, but ugly mobs are hardly new in either American history or in the history of other free societies, including those of the English, the French, and the Dutch. The Sons of Liberty were a very ugly mob, as were the mobs that demanded freedom for the serfs in the Peasants' Revolt of 1381.

The stunning election upset of Scott Brown cannot be understood apart from the town hall revolts. What was remarkable about January 19, 2010 was not the revelation of voter anger and frustration, but the realization that not even the nation's most liberal state was immune. The "revolution" did not begin in Massachusetts, but in the town hall meetings that took place all over our nation. They signaled the stirrings of a genuine populist revolt against the liberal elite—a highly educated elite that many ordinary Americans see as arrogant know-it-alls who are grossly out of touch with the fundamental values and visceral convictions of "real Americans." What was most significant about the town hall uprising was not the unruly defiance of the protestors, but the shock with which this defiance was greeted by the liberal opinion-makers whose opinions the protestors most despise. It was a moment that illuminated, like a lightning flash, just how vast the chasm is that separates the populist conservative from the liberal elite. The future, as always, remains in the lap of the gods. Yet, it is possible that the town hall revolts may turn out to be precisely the kind of event that people look back to and reflect on and say, "This was the first sign of trouble," similar to the way that Americans looked back on John Brown's ill-fated raid on Harpers Ferry as a harbinger of the Civil War. This, they might well say, is where we all began to fall apart.

CHAPTER 1

FREEDOM AND
ITS AMBIGUITIES

Today's populist conservatives are up in arms about freedom. In their political narratives they see themselves as champions of a liberty that they are convinced is under attack, and they are quick to invoke memories of our nation's early struggles over freedom in order to justify their glorious cause. They are the true patriots, the real Americans, threatened by the sinister force of America-hating, godless liberalism. To many liberals, needless to say, this attitude is more than a little annoying, since they would argue that they are the real champions of freedom and that the populist conservatives are simply the unwitting stooges of greedy and sinister corporate interests. The same Rasmussen poll that showed that almost half of America thought the protestors were genuinely expressing their own grievances also indicated that 37 percent of Americans believed that the protestors were being manipulated by "special interest groups and lobbyists."[1] At first glance, two such radically different interpretations of the spirit of the town hall protests would seem to indicate that either one or both of these interpretations must be the product of stupidity or bad faith. But there is another way of explaining the violent contrast in the two perspectives, which is to point out that the very idea of freedom is inherently ambiguous, and that it lends itself to radically conflicting interpretations.

If we survey some of the burning issues of our day, it quickly becomes apparent that while Americans may all agree that freedom is of great value as an *abstract* ideal, they do not agree about how this ideal relates to the concrete social and political issues of the day. In addition, even a brief review of these issues will confirm the astute observation made by the British economist John Maynard Keynes: "The ideas of economists and political philosophers, both when they are right and when they are wrong, are more powerful than is commonly understood. Indeed the world is ruled by little else. Practical men, who believe themselves to be quite exempt from any intellectual influence, are usually the slaves of some defunct economist." Or of some defunct political philosopher, Keynes should have added.[2] The "hard facts" that practical men of our era offer up in their PowerPoint presentations are frequently only "hard" in the eyes of those who unwittingly share their same unexamined philosophic assumptions—a truth that American foreign policy has repeatedly demonstrated in the last half century as "the best and the brightest" of each generation have amassed mountains of hard facts to justify the most quixotic and self-defeating adventures.

Prior to the invasion of Iraq, for example, American neoconservatives argued that the freedom our people enjoyed could be extended to other nations across the globe—even to a country like Iraq that had no indigenous tradition of democracy or free institutions. The Bush administration acted on the principle that one nation can literally bestow liberty on another nation. The recipe was quite simple really. Topple the tyrannical regime of Saddam Hussein and a free society will spontaneously emerge, like mushrooms cropping up in a shady glade.

Behind this optimism lies a long philosophical tradition that looks upon liberty as the natural birthright of all mankind, a tradition most closely associated with the seventeenth century's John Locke and the eighteenth century's Thomas Jefferson, one that has been enormously influential among English-speaking people, especially in America. When President George W. Bush argued that we all want the same things—among which he included liberty—he was echoing this philosophy of freedom. But there is another English tradition about liberty that takes a radically different view of the subject.

The eighteenth-century Anglo-Irish orator and political thinker Edmund Burke gave the classic formulation of a rival philosophy of liberty when he argued that the unparalleled rights and liberties enjoyed by the English people of his time were not the result of any vague or abstract natural right but were an inheritance from their ancestors. Against those who saw liberty as a universal right of all men, Burke argued that liberty could only flourish among those whose ancestors had fought for it, and who were themselves determined to preserve and cherish the rights and privileges that had been won for them by earlier generations. Liberty was not to be found in bold experimentation, which often destroyed it, but in a kind of political conservationism—that is to say, a careful and alert stewardship over those cultural, political, and religious traditions that were the indispensable condition of the preservation of a free society.

In the nineteenth and early twentieth centuries, the American conservationist movement sought to protect America's great natural treasures, such as Yosemite Valley and Yellowstone Park, from destruction through pollution and exploitation. A century earlier, Burke's political conservationism aimed to protect Britain's great national institutions, such as Parliament and the Church of England, from reformers who wished to tinker and tamper with them. Behind both conservationist movements, however, was the same insight. Great things that are the work of time, that have arisen organically and through the interplay of many contending and conflicting forces, must be conserved, because once they are gone there is no way of replacing them. For Burke, English liberty was like the Grand Canyon—a serendipitous gift of Providence that no amount of human contrivance could hope to recreate once human folly had allowed it to perish.

At first sight, these two conflicting paradigms of liberty—Locke's and Burke's—may appear to be two sides of a purely speculative dispute, without any serious consequences for the real world. Yet it was the triumph of Locke's concept of liberty over Burke's that was ultimately responsible for one of the longest, costliest, and most controversial of all the wars that the United States has ever fought. Had Burke's view of liberty been dominant in White House circles, Saddam Hussein might still have been overthrown, but there would have been far less extravagant rhetoric about bringing democracy to the Middle East. Indeed, one might argue that the dampening of expectations for democracy in the Middle East reflects a revival of Burke's emphasis on liberty as a specific cultural tradition prized by some societies but not by others.

In 2008, with the election of Barack Obama, popular conservative pundits like Sean Hannity took to the airwaves to argue that under the new administration our liberties were again being threatened, just as in the days of the American Revolution. Suddenly Thomas Paine was a hero again. Self-styled patriots, such as Glenn Beck, began quoting from the feisty Englishman who, after failing in several businesses, had sailed to America in order to use his nimble pen in defense of our war for independence. Yes, they asserted, Paine was right when he wrote in his famous pamphlet *Common Sense* that "government, even in its best state, is but a necessary evil; in its worst state an intolerable one."[3] If the people found their government too intolerable, they had every right to overthrow it and to replace it, just as John Locke argued in his *Second Treatise on Government*. By the same logic, if the nation under an Obama administration were to become too intolerable, then the people would have a right to rebel against the government, although under such circumstances only these "true-blue patriots" could be relied upon to take the appropriate action. Other Americans might be appalled and even frightened by this attitude, but the patriotic extremists they deplore could quote chapter and verse from the Declaration of Independence to justify their right to rebel.

In the past, Americans have found ways to overturn the status quo without the need for violent revolution. The populist rebellion that made Andrew Jackson president in 1828 was entirely peaceful, yet it transformed the political culture of the United States forever. Could our current populist revolt end up catapulting a new populist hero—or heroine—into the White House?

Mention the name Sarah Palin and you will immediately have a fight on your hands. When John McCain chose Palin to be his running mate in 2008, there was a natural desire on the part of the electorate and the press to know more about this hitherto relatively unknown governor of Alaska and former mayor of the small town of Wasilla. Who exactly was she, and what kind of record had she acquired during her brief career in politics? These were certainly reasonable questions that required forthright answers. Yet far too much of the controversy that surrounded her sudden rise to political prominence was superficial, reflecting cultural biases and focusing on the irrelevant minutiae of her personal life. Even here, buried deeply beneath the blather of the blogosphere, pro and con, lies a genuine philosophic issue. Who should speak for the people? Should it be someone who shares their own values and ideals, including their own prejudices and their own blind spots? Or should the people be represented by someone who is prepared to champion their real interests even if the people do not see where their real interests lie, and even if they disagree emphatically with the person who is claiming to act on their behalf?

This is a debate that goes back a long way. Thomas Paine thought that the job of the representative was simply to speak the people's mind, not to try to improve on it. How could anyone improve on the people's common sense? On the other hand, when Edmund Burke ran for Parliament in the city of Bristol, he frankly told the voters that he would represent whatever views he thought were best for the people of England, and not just the views of those in Bristol who were sending him to the House of Commons. He would do what he thought was right whether or not it reflected the position of his constituency. Surprisingly, Burke was elected despite this bold announcement.

How concerned should we be about the contemporary explosion of populist conservatism? Is a political scourge to be fought tooth and nail? Or should we look upon it as a completely understandable reaction on the part of those Americans who feel that their ideals and values—traditional to the core—are under siege by godless liberals intent on teaching their children about natural selection and unnatural sex? At the very least, the populist revival may be a helpful hint to the enlightened elite that it is always dangerous to push people too far into a corner, since you can never tell when they might decide to fight back. Even when you cannot see why other people venerate their traditions, you cannot hope to curry their favor by making an open display of contempt toward them. A society that claims to be a democracy should show some minimal regard for the will of the common man, at the very least.

GAY MARRIAGE poses another riddle. Its proponents argue that it is a matter of fundamental human rights. For some, a moral right, for others, a natural right. In any case, the defenders of gay marriage draw on a philosophical tradition that asserts the existence of a higher order of rights than those that happened to be written down in the law books of a society. Because these rights attach to individuals outside of, and even prior to, society, no society can legitimately take them away or withhold them. Even if ninety-nine out of one hundred Americans were violently opposed to gay marriage, it would make no difference. No majority vote, no matter how overwhelming, can rob people of those rights assigned to them by nature or by transcendent moral law.

John Locke might well be appalled by this application of his theory of natural rights, but he would have to acknowledge that the line of argument is recognizably his own. The eighteenth-century German philosopher Immanuel Kant would have felt the same horror, but he too would have been familiar with the concept of moral rights that trump all other considerations of the general will or of public utility. On the other hand, during roughly that same century, both Samuel Johnson, the Tory reactionary, and Jeremy Bentham, the radical reformer, would have considered all such talk as rubbish.

Johnson, for one, dismissed all chatter about natural rights as sheer cant—one of his favorite words of opprobrium—by which he meant lofty but insincere language designed to masquerade the genuine but ignoble selfish motives of those who employed it. When a man claimed something as his natural right, all he was really saying, shorn of its vague metaphysical abstraction, was: "I want what I want. Give it to me." Take those rebellious Americans, for example. When they declaimed about their natural right to be exempt from taxation, they were simply using pretentious language to justify their basic stinginess and lack of political responsibility.

Jeremy Bentham, the father of utilitarianism, had the same attitude. He thought we Americans, with our highly touted love of liberty, were appalling hypocrites. The whole theory of natural rights and moral rights was an unnecessary fiction. Bentham, like Johnson, would have seen the debate over gay marriage as simply another political contest, or naked power struggle, between two contending parties. The proponents of gay marriage want to change their society to suit them; the opponents want to keep the traditional society that they are accustomed to. Liberty, in the abstract, has nothing to do with it. It is all merely a question of which party gets its way. Instead of being concerned with finding the greatest happiness for the greatest number—the maxim of utilitarianism—both parties are only interested in pushing their own agendas. While Johnson would no doubt have come down on the side of traditional marriage, Bentham, who was no friend to tradition, might well have come down on the other side.

IMMIGRATION CAN be added to the list of burning issues deeply implicated in two contrasting concepts of freedom. To one side are those Americans who recall that we are a nation of immigrants and who are prepared to welcome all those who wish to come here, seeking to enjoy the freedoms that ordinary American citizens too often take for granted. On the other side are those who insist that an essential aspect of freedom is the freedom to decide who else will become members of your community. A country club, a university, or a business corporation that is not free to select and reject applicants would thereby lose all claims of autonomy and self-government, and the same logic can easily be extended to an entire society.

You cannot ask an individual to care about the fate of everyone in his community and then deny him the right to decide who gets to join it. Or, more accurately, you can try, but you are bound to fail. A genuine community can only exist when the people in it have something they share in common—values and traditions that define their identity, and by so doing, separate them from those whose values and traditions differ from theirs. If a community cannot maintain its borders, it will inevitably lose its established character—a shattering experience for those who are happy with their time-honored way of life. From the perspective of the outsider, this loss of cultural identity may be a good or an indifferent thing. But to those on the inside, it will invariably be perceived as a threat to their core values and traditions, generating bitterness and often violent resentment. One may, of course, regret this fact about human nature, but it would be dangerous to ignore it. Liberal cosmopolitans, while yearning to embrace all mankind, frequently find themselves the bitter enemies of their next-door neighbors.

OTHER ISSUES COULD be added, but these examples should be sufficient to show that Americans are deeply divided over our shared heritage of freedom. It is of supreme importance to grasp that this conflict over liberty is not the result of either bad faith or stupidity on the part of the various antagonists. Each side is genuinely championing freedom—but only as they see it, which is simply another way of saying that the concept of freedom is complex, multi-faceted, and even at times disturbingly self-contradictory.

In the American Civil War, both sides were profoundly convinced that they were fighting for freedom. We take this for granted today when we think about Lincoln and the North, who fought to bring liberty to the slaves. But those who sided with the Confederacy were no less certain that they too were fighting for freedom, in this case the freedom to create a government of their own choice and to preserve their traditional way of life. They saw themselves as the new Sons of Liberty, prepared to struggle against the tyranny of the vastly richer and more powerful North.

The disquieting truth is that there are many different kinds of freedom, and that not all of them are compatible with one another. In order to free the slaves, the North was forced to impose military rule on much of the defeated South for over a decade. On the other hand, if the Confederacy had won and had established its independence and autonomy, it would have meant the continuing enslavement of millions of men, women, and children—and their children's children as well.

MEN HAVE been willing to kill each other over their different definitions of freedom and liberty. They have done so in the past and they may well do so again in the future. Liberty, as an ideal, can unite. But it can also divide, and divide very bitterly. Indeed, the political question that has divided men most often throughout history has been the question, Who should be free? For some, like the ancient Greek philosopher Aristotle, it was self-evident that only a small elite of superior human beings—all males and all Greek—were entitled to freedom since they alone had the capacity for self-control that allowed them to achieve and preserve their political independence. They were the natural masters. On the other hand, those who lacked the ability to control their impulses and appetites could not be free. Their lot in life had been decided by fate. They were destined to be governed and ruled over by the elite; they were the natural slaves. It was only right and just for the natural masters to rule and govern the masses, because if the masses were free to make decisions about their own lives and the affairs of their society, they would shortly make a mess of everything due to their ignorance, incompetence, and impulsiveness. Therefore, the most humane and decent method of governing the common people is to teach them to obey unquestioningly the commands of their natural superiors.[4]

All populist revolts in history, including the one underway today in America, have seen themselves as engaged in justified rebellion against an arrogant ruling elite. It does not matter to the populist rebels on what grounds the elite claims to be entitled to govern the rest of society. The elite may boast of their greater self-control, their superiority in arms, their noble blood, or their high IQs, but these self-serving arguments do not impress the defiant populists. They are familiar with the facts that all ruling classes will inevitably find a justification for why they should rule and that the only way to keep a self-appointed elite from abusing its power is by uniting to-gether to resist such abuse from the very first moment it's felt. Otherwise, the abuse of power will inevitably increase to the point at which resistance against it is no longer feasible.

Today's populist revolt is different from earlier populist revolts because it is a rebellion against a new kind of elite. It is an elite that is a product of the modern system of education-based meritocracy that has come to dominate not only the United States but all the advanced nations of the world. As today's populist conservatives see it, the problem with this new elite is that it aims to subvert America's messy tradition of popular democracy and to re-place it with an efficiently operated utopia, managed and planned out to the smallest detail by intellectuals who, like all elites of the past, do not trust av-erage people to make the right decisions about their lives or the welfare of their society.

CHAPTER 2

THE REVOLT
AGAINST UTOPIA

If you ask most Americans what freedom is, they will no doubt reply, "It is what we have here in the U.S.A." Or, at the very least, they will say, "It's what we used to have in America." If you push a bit further and ask them why they are free, they will probably say it is because they live (or lived) under a democratic form of government. Yet it is entirely possible for a society to have all the paraphernalia that we commonly associate with our democratic system—beautifully written constitutions, elections, legislatures, courts—and yet still trample on the liberties that Americans have long taken for granted. Joseph Stalin wrote an exemplary constitution for the Soviet Union in 1936, but the millions imprisoned in the forced labor camps of the Gulag found little consolation in its generous Bill of Rights, despite the fact that Article 127 clearly states: "Citizens of the U.S.S.R. are guaranteed inviolability of the person. No person may be placed under arrest except by decision of a court or with the sanction of a procurator." Since the time of the American Revolution, dozens of other nations have written constitutions for themselves, largely inspired by ours, but the vast majority of them proved to be of less worth than the paper they were written on. Elections can be rigged. Legislatures can be corrupted. Judges can be bribed. The rich and strong can still bully and exploit the poor and the weak, and no Bill of Rights, however eloquent its rhetoric, has ever been able to prevent the gross abuse of power by those who possessed too much of it.

When the United States attempted to bring democracy to Iraq, it acted on the assumption that our style of democracy could be exported as easily as our cell phones and blue jeans. This assumption proved to be naïve, yet there is still debate about why democracy does not seem to work for certain cultures, and why many in these cultures show so little interest in making it work. Some critics of American policy have argued that the Middle East simply isn't "ready" for democracy, though it is not at all obvious how a society goes about getting ready for its advent. Many argue that education is the answer; but the education they are talking about is our style of education, resolutely secular and equally available to men and women. This solution too poses a new question, since much of the Middle East seems no more ready for our style of education than it is for our style of democracy. So how does a society get ready for democracy?

THE WORD *democracy* was first coined by the Greeks, and their experiment in democratic government has exercised a profound influence on the Western political tradition. Somehow or other, the Greeks—or more precisely, the Athenians—managed to get themselves ready for democracy, and they were able to achieve this without availing themselves of existing democratic models of government, for there were none to imitate. Athenian democracy was a do-it-ourselves project. But to understand how this new form of government came into existence, we must first discard our modern idea of democracy as government by the people. To us, the majestic phrase "we the People" in the preamble to our Constitution refers to all the members of our society, rich and poor, the great and the insignificant. But the Greek word *demos,* which we translate as "people," did not mean everyone in the society but only those ordinary individuals who were not members of the ruling elite—the multitude of little guys whose counsel was neither sought nor heeded by the governing aristocrats who called all the shots.

Greek democracy was government under the control of the common man, who had to work for a living in contrast to the aristocrats who lived off the labor of others. But the common man,[1] whom the aristocrats looked upon as rabble, could only obtain control over his society by rebelling against the aristocratic elite, often resulting in a very vicious power struggle. The common people of Athens made themselves "ready" for democracy by insisting, quite forcefully, that they should play the dominant role in the collective life of their city. They got ready by becoming uppity—at least in the eyes of those they rose up against.

From the time of the great Athenian experiment, its populist style of democracy has had bitter critics, including such distinguished ancient Athenians as the philosopher Plato and the historian Thucydides. Both blamed Athens's unbridled democracy for the catastrophes that left the great city state divided, prostrate, and helpless before its various enemies at the end of the Peloponnesian Wars early in the fourth century B.C. Many centuries later, when the American Founding Fathers referred to democracy, the word still reverberated with this negative appraisal of popular government. For most of the Founding Fathers, democracy simply meant misrule by the vulgar masses, a political pathology to be avoided at all costs. Many of the Constitution's famous checks and balances were precisely designed to prevent the unwashed multitude from overriding the better sense of the wiser few. Although the Constitution's framers believed the ordinary man could manage his own affairs well enough and pass competent judgments on those matters that closely concerned him, they also believed that he lacked the leisure to study and to reflect, to gain the kind of specialized knowledge that is required by those who have the onerous task of directing the course of state.

Over two thousand years earlier, the Greek philosopher Socrates had made the same point by comparing the state to a ship. Modernizing Socrates' analogy somewhat, let us imagine a ship carrying a large number of passengers, none of whom know anything about sailing, but all of whom are at risk if their ship should sink. When a storm comes up, the passengers can face the danger in several ways. Each of them can propose a course of action, and then they can all debate it, though by the time a decision has been reached their ship will have sunk. Or they could entrust their life-or-death decisions to the man who has devoted himself to mastering the art of navigation, namely, the captain of the ship.[2]

Here was one powerful argument against populist democracy: Sometimes you need experts and not the idle opinion of uninformed men. Otherwise you face shipwreck and disaster, as happened in Athens. An even more compelling argument against rule by the common man, however, was provided by the life—or rather death—of Socrates. In Athens, the majority ruled; but the majority often ruled badly, as when a 500-man jury of his peers condemned Socrates to death on the charge of seducing their young from the traditional Greek religion. Athenian populist democracy had given ordinary men more power over the affairs of their own society than they had ever had before, but they used this power to crush precisely the kind of freedom that the modern liberal West has championed above all others, namely, the freedom of thought and expression. Since that time, critics of populist democracy have repeatedly pointed out that the tyranny of the majority can be far more oppressive and invasive than the tyranny of a single man. The majority always has more eyes and ears.

There remains one classic argument against popular democracy, and this asserts that such a system of government would inevitably endanger property. Because the masses are generally poor, they will use their political clout to redistribute wealth in their own favor, robbing from the rich to give to themselves. Because the well-to-do have a higher stake in the affairs of their community, having literally more to lose, they alone should be entrusted with the governance of the commonwealth, just as it is reasonable that the fate of a business corporation should be decided exclusively by its shareholders. Popular democracy is dangerous because the masses cannot be trusted to preserve the economic status quo, in which the rich are on the top and the poor on the bottom. The leveling tendency of popular democracy, the argument goes, will leave no one's property safe, and without security of property, no society can ever hope to become either stable or prosperous.

A profound distrust of popular democracy is written into the United States Constitution, but it also appears to exist in the nation today. In poll after poll, Americans indicate their lack of respect, often bordering on contempt, for precisely the institution that was originally designed to reflect, in theory, the will of the people—namely, Congress. On the other hand, the same polls show that the institutions Americans respect and trust are those that are most exempt from democratic control: the Supreme Court, the Federal Reserve, and the various branches of the military. For some observers, there is an obvious lesson to be drawn from these polls: Ordinary people would be happier and better off if there were more institutions similarly free from democratic control. Let the experts make the decisions, and not the people. Socrates was right, after all.

Those who subscribe to this view today represent a long and venerable tradition. In Plato's ideal society as sketched in *The Republic,* power would be placed in the hands of a ruling elite whom he identified as the philosopher kings. The members of this group would be selected for their superior intelligence and would then be subjected to a long process of educational training and ethical cultivation designed to suit them for their job. The guardians would constitute the ruling class, but they would behave in a manner that was radically different from all traditional ruling classes.

Normally, the only interest the ancient ruling classes had in the masses was to exploit their labor and to use them as pawns in their various power struggles with one another. But unlike these predatory ruling elites, Plato's guardians would be raised to have zero interest in furthering their own selfish goals and objectives, having been brought up from childhood to feel contempt for mere sensual pleasure and worldly wealth. Instead, they would be instilled in a strict discipline that made them think only of what was best for their community. They would constantly look for what was good, not what was merely popular or expedient. They would scout out the long-term interests of their republic and would not be swayed by the passions and caprice of the moment. They would be benefactors, not exploiters, and they would educate the people to pursue the good. In short, they would be dedicated to creating and preserving an ideal state that would be free from all the ills that plagued most human societies.

Plato's *Republic* was the first great utopian project, but it did not just pop out of thin air. Rather, it was a response to what Plato and many of his fellow citizens saw as the dangerous excesses of their own populist government. The fate of Athens, according to Plato's pupil Aristotle, had exactly traced out the fate destined for all popular democracies. Too much freedom given to too many people will inevitably end in discord. They will bicker and argue endlessly, unable to reach a critical decision on a life-or-death question facing them, such as in time of war. This discord will inevitably set off a violent power struggle, producing the dreaded state of anarchy in which civilized life collapses back to the rule of brute force. Anarchy, in its turn, creates the desire for a restoration of order and stability. When this point is reached, the people will happily welcome the advent of the strong man, the dictator who eliminates anarchy by crushing out freedom altogether. The tyrants will return, and the experiment in popular democracy will have once more revealed itself as a suicide mission. The only alternative, as Plato saw it, was for wise men, like his guardians, to guide the ship of state.

Plato's spirit is alive and well in America today. It is reflected by such influential political commentators as Fareed Zakaria when he argues that "the deregulation of democracy has . . . gone too far"[3]—an appeal made all the more persuasive in the wake of the town hall meetings, with their telling reminder of just how messy and rowdy deregulated democracy can get. A regulated democracy, however, obviously requires regulators, and if the masses cannot be entrusted to regulate themselves, then this task must be assigned to those who are competent to manage and govern society for them. In other societies in other epochs, a ruling class, who based their claims to govern on their aristocratic descent, was always available to do this job. But this was a solution that Plato rejected and that Americans reject as well.[4] We have to because we have never had a formal aristocracy—titles of nobility were banned by the Constitution itself. Instead, American elitists, both conservative and liberal, have put their faith in the ideal of a meritocracy. Society should not be governed by the masses but by elites chosen on the basis of their merit, that is to say, their intelligence, their competency, their breadth of education, their outstanding skills and capacities. This certainly sounds like a reasonable idea, and for most Americans the concept of a meritocracy carries none of the insidious implications of an inherited aristocracy. A meritocracy is fair and open to all who can make the grade. Yet if we examine the concept of a meritocracy we discover that it is a high-tech variation of an old political ideal, an ideal that at first glance seems to have little in common with our American tradition of practical-minded, hard-nosed politics. This is the ideal that has fascinated and beguiled thinkers from the time of Plato—the ideal of a perfectly ordered and administered society, otherwise known as a utopia.

THE WORD *utopia* was coined in 1516 by Thomas More, who used it as the title of his own version of the ideal commonwealth. A pun on two Greek words, a utopia can mean both "good place" and "no place." Put these two meanings together and you get an imaginary land that it is literally too good to be true. Actually, an imaginary island—for that was where More set his utopia, as did Plato. Other famous utopias would also be set on islands. That is where Tommaso Campanella put his ideal community in his 1603 book *The City of the Sun,* as did Francis Bacon in his 1623 book *The New Atlantis.* These three influential visions of a perfect society also had something else in common: They would all be ruled by men selected for their superior intelligence and general enlightenment, those whom today we might call intellectuals. Unlike societies languishing under the exploitative thumb of kings or despots or commercial oligarchies, the classical utopia promises to flourish under the benevolent control of men exactly like the intellectuals who conceived them—men like More, Campanella, and Bacon.

Aristotle classified different political systems in terms of who ruled and governed them, and this tradition has been handed down to us. A monarchy is governed by a king, an aristocracy by those who have inherited their status and position from their ancestors. A plutocracy is in the hands of those with money, while a democracy is ruled by the common people. A utopia is none of the above. It is a society governed solely by those with superior intellects, that is to say, by a cognitive elite.[5]

For centuries, the empire of China was governed by the class of literati. These were individuals, often of humble origin, who thanks to their brain power were able to master the difficult classical texts that were the foundation of the Chinese educational system. The next step on their upward path was to take the rigorous competitive examinations that tested their knowledge of these texts. If successful, the candidate became part of the bureaucratic administration of the empire. The mastery of the art of letters was the key to power and influence in China. To coin a word, the government of classical China was a *literatocracy,* that is, rule by men of letters. And the same can be said of all the influential utopias devised in the West.

A utopia, defined in this way, is not a never-never land where the sun always shines and no one ever cries, although the word *utopia* is often used in this indiscriminate manner. A utopia is a society in which everything is harmonious *because* of the intelligent design imposed on it by the intellectuals who act as its guardians. It is a consciously elaborated work of art, not a land flowing with milk and honey from the bounty of nature. Utopias are constructed in the brain, not stumbled upon in the wild. Like democracy or plutocracy or aristocracy, utopias represent a specific form of social and political organization.

Utopias are not democratic. Indeed, they are profoundly antidemocratic. As Plato astutely recognized, the cognitive elite cannot always explain to the dim-witted masses what is in their best interests, just as a parent cannot always get his child to understand why he must do some things and avoid doing others. Therefore, just as clever parents learn to handle their kids by subtle methods of psychological manipulation (such as tricking them into eating their spinach), so the cognitive elite, whom Plato called the guardians, must learn to trick the people into doing what is best for them. These methods of popular deception Plato called "the noble lie."

For example, Plato's philosopher kings naturally wanted intelligent women to mate with intelligent men, in order to assure a healthy supply of good minds in the future. They didn't want a smart girl to fall for the not-so-bright jock no matter how dashing or handsome he was—indeed, no matter how much they loved each other. Yet the philosopher kings also knew that they couldn't hope to get away with simply telling people whom they had to marry—if they tried such a thing, they would have had a mutiny on their hands. Therefore, they had to concoct a bizarre cover-up. Marriages were to be arranged by a lottery system. People would reach into a hat and draw out a number. If a man and a woman got the same number, then they would become husband and wife. But it was all a charade. The lottery was rigged. The philosopher kings had played matchmaker based on their own dispassionate examination of the two individuals' merits and defects.

This systematic practice of deception was deemed to be noble because it was not undertaken to exploit the people for the self-serving purposes of those who were deceiving them. Instead, Plato's guardians were acting in the spirit of benign paternalism, behaving the same way a wise and loving father will naturally behave toward his own children. They were tricking young people into making the kind of marriages that the couples would themselves elect to make if they were only as mature, disinterested, and farsighted as their guardians.

Paternalism always involves a curtailment of the personal freedom of those who are the objects of its benevolent intentions. This is obvious in the case of a father who insists that his fourteen-year-old daughter not be allowed to experiment with heroin, or the mother who refuses to let her eight-year-old son do wheelies on his bicycle at the edge of a cliff. True, the child's freedom of action is limited by the parent's protective measures, but these measures are obviously taken for the child's own good. Yet there is a different form that paternalism can take, and this occurs whenever one group of adults decides to limit the freedom of other adults in their community. Such groups may spring from a church, a state, an institution, or even a business corporation,[6] but they all have in common a sense of duty to improve the lives of ordinary men and women by limiting their freedom of choice. When the great humanitarian General James Oglethorpe founded the colony of Georgia in 1733 as a refuge for imprisoned debtors, his benevolent paternalism was displayed in a set of laws that, in addition to prohibiting slavery, forbid the importation of rum. The consumption of alcohol was bad for people; therefore, by taking away the freedom to get drunk on rum, Oglethorpe was convinced that he was improving the welfare of his fledgling colony.

Oglethorpe was exercising hard paternalism, which works simply by making certain actions illegal and subject to punishment. Drink rum and we will put you in jail. But there is another kind of paternalism that works by subtler and less directly intrusive methods. For example, when a modern up-to-date parent "uses psychology" to coax his child into proper behavior, he is engaged in the practice of soft paternalism.

Recently two economists, Richard H. Thaler and Cass R. Sunstein, have argued that the government should adopt the soft paternalism practiced by the modern parent. In their book *Nudge: Improving Decisions about Health, Wealth, and Happiness,* they reject the kind of hard paternalism to which Oglethorpe resorted, arguing instead that the government should play the role of the savvy parent who is well versed in the psychological techniques of subtle persuasion. The father knows that his eleven-year-old son lacks the maturity to make the right decision about how late to stay out at night, so he must make this decision for him. Yet if the father is psychologically astute, he may be able to nudge his boy into accepting the decision as the correct one. Later in life the boy will undoubtedly thank his father for curtailing his liberty to stay out all night. By the same analogy, the government could nudge citizens into making better choices in their lifestyles. It could nudge them away from cigarettes, from fattening foods, from excessive alcohol consumption—not by outlawing them in the ham-fisted manner of Oglethorpe, but by adopting the methods of the contemporary behavioral sciences. These methods, according to Thaler and Sunstein, could be carefully designed by psychologists to give citizens the illusion of free choice while subtly and subliminally directing them to make the "right" decision.

For the soft paternalists, there is no moral ambiguity to the idea of the "right" decision that they have in mind. The right decision is one that will optimize such objectively measurable values as wealth and health, while at the same time increasing your happiness—your happiness as measured not by others but by you yourself. It is true that the state, acting as your guardian, is psychologically manipulating you to make decisions that you otherwise might not make; but as a result of these subliminally guided decisions, you will become a happier person than you would have become if you were left solely to your own devices—and you, and no one else, will be the judge of whether you are indeed happier. The attitude of the professional soft paternalist is, "You will come to thank us later," just as, in fact, we do often come to thank our parents for the often quite strict discipline they imposed.

If the government can devise psychological techniques that will manipulate us into becoming wealthier, healthier, happier people, without robbing us of our illusion of free choice or openly insulting our dignity, who could possibly complain about that? Furthermore, if our belief in our ability to make free choices is nothing more than an illusion in the first place, then those who are fearful that soft paternalism will rob us of our liberty are simply refusing to face facts.

AS SCIENCE reveals more and more about the true springs of human action, it becomes increasingly obvious that what many of us look upon as our free choice is in truth no such thing. Normally we think we know what we mean when we say that we can choose freely between two different boxes of cereal on a shelf, and we feel confident that we can contrast this example of free choice with a choice that is not free, as when a man is holding a gun to our head. Yet are we really any freer in the first case than in the second case? The eighteenth-century French physicist Pierre Laplace argued that we are not.

Suppose we know all the laws that govern the universe, and suppose we have complete knowledge of the state of the universe at any given moment. Armed with this knowledge we could predict all future occurrences, including the most trivial actions on the part of human beings. We could predict, for example, which box of cereal you would end up "choosing"—though, of course, what appeared to you as your free choice was simply an illusion. The choice had been made for you long before you were born.

Now what is important here is not the metaphysical debate over the reality of our free will—that we can leave aside. What matters, for our purposes, is the practical consequence of this debate on society in general. Does the belief in determinism really make a difference in our lives? It has often been argued that this belief cannot make any difference. When facing a row of cereal boxes, it may well be true that an omniscient observer could accurately predict which box we would choose, but we ourselves are not in that position. We cannot predict what we will buy based on a complete knowledge of the laws of the universe. Thus, we must act *as if* we are free, even while knowing, in the philosophic part of our minds, that our action is really not free at all. But imagine, for a moment, that we are not considering our own decisions about which box of cereal to choose. Suppose we are considering the decision being made by someone else—a child, for example. The child will naturally think that he is really deciding for himself what cereal he wants to eat. But we who are observing him in the act of making the decision are not under the same illusion. To us it is obvious that the child is being subliminally guided to buy the cereal with the colorful happy dinosaurs on the box, with an orange plastic submarine hidden inside, and coated with layers of fattening sugar. He is acting exactly like a robot that has been programmed to respond mindlessly and automatically to certain stimuli presented before his eyes. Because we think that the child is not exercising his free will, we do not hesitate to inter-fere with his pseudodecision if we think that our intervention will keep his teeth from prematurely rotting out of his head. Indeed, under these circum-stances, we might well think that it is our duty to interfere—and most par-ents would agree.

Now, suppose we are dealing not with a child but with an adult about to buy the same box of cereal. Like the child, the adult too thinks he is exercis-ing his free will. If we subscribe to the doctrine of determinism, we will see his choice of cereal as a pseudodecision no different from the child's. He has been programmed to buy a cereal that is bad for him, just as the child has been. In this case, our belief in determinism can make a practical difference. Because we do not believe that the adult is really making a free choice, we will be only slightly more hesitant to nudge him away from the bad cereal and toward a cereal that has solid nutritional value. In doing this, we will not think of ourselves as interfering with his freedom of choice, because we don't believe he has any. Instead, we will think that we are doing him a favor, just as the mom who insists that her kids eat a healthy breakfast is convinced that she is acting in her children's best interests. To the philosophical determinist, the common sense division ordinarily made between the pseudochoice of a child and the free choice of the adult simply does not hold up. The one choice deserves no more respect than the other, so that it becomes just as per-missible to interfere with the adult's decision—for his own good—as it is to interfere with the child's decision—for his own good.

The recent advances of neuroscience, along with more sophisticated techniques of behavior modification, have only strengthened the determin-ist's case for treating adults as we treat children. If both adults and children are equally the product of external forces acting on us, for good or bad, then why shouldn't benevolently inclined scientists try to get control over these forces, to channel and program them in order to produce human beings that rise to a higher standard than the course of nature generally produces? After all, the nudge given by soft paternalism is nothing in comparison with the shoves given us by our family, by our religious upbringing, by our friends, by our ethnic traditions—not to mention the jolts and jostles to which we are subjected by the blitzkrieg of the media, seducing us into believing that we genuinely desire to buy whatever advertisers want to sell. If our universal fate is to be psychologically manipulated by other people, surely it is better that those who are pulling the strings should be genuinely concerned with improving our health, wealth, and happiness, as opposed to those who are only interested in exploiting our weakness for their own benefit, either for the purpose of obtaining more power for themselves or simply lining their pockets with our hard-earned cash. Guardians with good intentions must obviously be preferable to predators with bad ones.

BUT JUST how far are we willing to go in the direction of soft paternalism? Let us assume that behavioral science advances to the point at which parents can program their children to refrain from making any of the normal mistakes of infancy and childhood, without, of course, robbing them of their illusion of freedom—perhaps by means of brain implants? Would you want this device implanted in the brains of your kids, even if it involved no risk to your child's health? The device, after all, would not turn them into robots. It would only nudge them away from the wrong choices and toward the right ones. Properly programmed, you could guarantee a remarkable improvement in your child's spending habits, health, and even happiness. You could be sure that your teenagers would never think of lighting up that first cigarette or taking that initial toke of pot. You would never have to worry if they were out driving drunk in the wee hours of the morning. You could even trust them with your credit cards. Teen pregnancies would become a thing of the past, like smallpox, while the average SAT score would soar since kids would be nudged to hit the books instead of ruining their brains by watching too much TV or playing too many video games or surfing the Internet for porn. Does the vague, abstract noun *freedom* really mean so much to us that we would jeopardize our children's future out of our irrational reverence for a concept that none of us is really terribly clear about? Isn't it time that we consign the illusion of human freedom to the museum of outmoded ideas, alongside a belief in witchcraft and elves?

This was precisely the position taken by the behavioral psychologist B. F. Skinner in his best-selling book *Walden Two*. Written in 1948, Skinner's novel depicts an ideal community composed of a thousand people, whose life is under the guidance and care of its small elite of Planners and Managers. The Planners decide on the overall direction of the community, while the Managers are in control of everyone's daily life. All decisions are made on the basis of the scientific principles revealed by Skinner's own brand of behavioral psychology. The family has been abolished, as has religion. The customs and traditions that prevail in the outside world have no place in Skinner's utopia. But none of the inhabitants of Walden Two miss any of this. They live in a Golden Age of peace and harmony, enjoying the cultivation of the arts and sciences and unselfishly sharing their income. In short, life in Skinner's utopia is not much different from life in the classical utopias. Perhaps the only significant deviation from the classical model is that Skinner does not locate his utopia on an uncharted island in a distant sea. You can get to his by bus.

Skinner regarded our continuing belief in the reality of freedom as an obstacle to the genuine progress that ordinary people could make if they discarded these unscientific and antiquated notions. Indeed, it is the obstinate conviction that they have free will and moral autonomy that keeps ordinary people from recognizing how easily they could obtain true happiness through the magic of "cultural engineering"—Skinner's phrase for reshaping the human personality through the techniques made available by behavioral science.

Skinner should be admired for having the courage of his fanaticism. He spells out with startling clarity what others prefer to conceal beneath inno-cent-sounding euphemisms. But a brief glimpse of Skinner's utopia should be enough to make us wonder if even the tiniest baby steps in this direction should be encouraged or even tolerated. And the trouble is not just restricted to Skinner's particular brand of utopia—the trouble arises from the very idea of utopia. For disguise it as much as you please, the essence of every utopia, from Plato's *Republic* to Skinner's *Walden Two*, is the same: namely, the dictatorship of the intellectual—far less brutal than the dictatorship of ruthless thugs to be sure, but potentially far more deadly to human freedom.

This might sound like an extravagant claim. But let us consider the main selling point of the soft paternalists: They are nudging others into making choices that the soft paternalists have already made for them. They are playing the role of the utopian Planners and Managers, but they are doing it so subtly and cleverly that no one even recognizes that he is being psychologically manipulated. The very objective of their soft paternalism is to make people believe that they are really acting freely and making their own choices. The advanced techniques of behavioral modification they employ are simply a much more sophisticated version of Plato's "noble lie," explicitly designed to preserve the illusion of freedom while taking away its substance.

General Oglethorpe's experiment in hard paternalism failed abysmally. The population of the colony of Georgia dwindled away, resentful of the well-intentioned ban on rum and slaves, and set up new homes in the neighboring colonies where rum and slaves could be had in abundance. The Georgia experiment in utopianism all too clearly revealed that hard paternalism has a dangerous tendency to spark rebellion. When adults are positively told what they can and cannot do, they will naturally resent those who are arrogantly setting themselves up as their guardians. But a soft paternalism that is so sophisticated that we remain unaware of its influence on our decisions will not be resented, simply because it won't be noticed. Furthermore, precisely because our new high-tech guardians are sincerely convinced that they know what is best for us, their deployment of this awesome new power of mind control will not seem to them to be a naked bid for dominance over society, but rather an unselfish act of the purest altruism. Thus, as they are manipulating others, they are simultaneously deceiving themselves. They sincerely believe that they are simply doing what these others would do if they were only as bright and sharp as the soft paternalists themselves. In short, they are pursuing the same old utopian dream, only with a dangerously high-tech twist.

IF RELIGION is the opium of the people, utopianism is the methamphetamine of the intellectual. Religion, it is often claimed, makes the humble content with their lot in life: It resigns them to their inevitable fate. The utopian's drug of choice has the opposite effect: It offers intellectuals a vision of a world in which they are omnipotent. Convinced that their superior intelligence provides them with superior ideas, they want to see their ideas implemented in the real world and show scant respect for the traditions to which ordinary people blindly and tenaciously cling. They want to improve society, which, in their minds, means redesigning it according to their own ideals. But the ideals of the intellectuals invariably clash with the cherished traditions of the ordinary men and women whose society they are eager to overhaul. That is in the nature of things. If intellectuals shared the ideas and values of the average person, they wouldn't be intellectuals in the first place. Thus, the intellectuals' chief value to society—a critical attitude toward the status quo—is also their chief disadvantage in trying to win over the masses who are happy with the way things have always been. This is why utopian intellectuals are so easily persuaded to resort to the policy of the noble lie. It is perceived as the quickest path to the realization of their vision of a perfected social order.

Today's advocates of soft paternalism share the goal of earlier utopian thinkers. They simply think they have discovered a better and more effective method of reaching this goal than those who came before them. Perhaps they are right. But the psychologically sophisticated approach of our modern soft paternalists, if successful, would extinguish liberty more effectively, because more subtly, than any tyrant of the past could ever hope to do. Theirs will be an invisible dictatorship of men and women who do not think of themselves as dictators, while they control the lives of people who are unaware that they are being controlled. No form of dictatorship has ever been a more insidious threat to human freedom than that.

To regard soft paternalism as a threat to liberty there is no need to assume that its practitioners are villains aspiring to be brutal tyrants on the order of a Nero or a Hitler or a Stalin. On the contrary, let us imagine them to be the most benevolently disposed people in the world, anxious to improve the human condition as they find it, and working tirelessly to achieve their goal—the goal of a society made up of prosperous, healthy, and happy men and women. Yet, if they are making all the real decisions for other people—however cleverly they disguise their methods of subliminal persuasion—they will not be creating prosperous, healthy, and happy adults, but prosperous, healthy, and happy infants who just happen to inhabit adult bodies. And once this cognitive elite has reduced the citizenry to the status of manipulated babies, who will be able to stand up to the elite in defense of even the most minimal rights? Seen in this light, even the softest paternalism potentially poses a genuine menace to the liberty that Americans of all political persuasions value the most—namely, the right to be in charge of their own lives and to make their own choices as they see fit.

The whole point of the paternalism exercised by parents toward their children is to make sure that one day their kids will be able to take charge of their own lives and will learn how to make the right decisions for themselves. Its goal is to turn infants into adults. But the paternalism of the modern liberal state, often dubbed the nanny-state by its critics, reverses this pattern. Its goal is to turn adults into infants. It treats the masses as if they are congenitally incapable of making the right choices for themselves, so that the state must continually act as their guardian. Because it never expects ordinary people to be able to make intelligent decisions about their own lives, it will always feel itself entitled to make these decisions for them. Indeed, it will feel that it has a duty to make them.

Some of us, it is true, may not mind in the least being governed and managed by a well-qualified cognitive elite: It might indeed improve the quality of our lives in many ways, making us healthier, wealthier, and happier. But there is an American political tradition that vehemently rejects the very idea that ordinary American men and women need to be managed and controlled by a superior elite. It is the tradition embraced by those people for whom any kind of paternalism, however much softened, is completely unacceptable. This tradition long preceded the establishment of the United States. It was already quite evident in the attitude of those early inhabitants of Oglethorpe's paternalistic colony who left it because it robbed them of control over their own lives. They wanted to make their own choices, for better or for worse, and they refused to let anyone else make those decisions for them. That same spirit animates the natural libertarians who are at the heart of today's populist revolt, perhaps receiving its most boisterous expression in the growing Tea Party movement.

In the past, the violent anti-elitism of American populism invariably put it in bitter conflict with the American conservative tradition. Populism was radical, as befits a movement whose motto is "Power to the people!" Populism aimed at overthrowing a corrupt and predatory elite that was alleged to have grown rich off the exploited labor of the working man. Conservatives, in contrast, have been fond of social stability. They do not like to rock the boat. In America, as in Europe, the conservative tradition has always been wary of the dangerous excess of populist democracy and has sought to keep it in check through a government of well-qualified and propertied elites. But today's populist revolt rejects all forms of elitism while aggressively asserting its conservative credentials.

For the conservative thinkers of the past and many of today, the very idea of a political movement that is simultaneously populist and conservative is a contradiction in terms. Yet in today's political landscape, key players like Sarah Palin and Glenn Beck, both of whom have large and devoted followings, have managed to combine immense populist appeal with conservative agendas. It is this fact that gives our current populist revolt its unique flavor. It also explains why it poses a serious dilemma for both the Republican and Democratic parties—neither of which relishes the prospect of a populist movement that refuses to play by the rules of the game, rules that have been set down by the party establishments themselves. The title of Sarah Palin's memoir, *Going Rogue,* is symbolic of the populist conservative's contempt for the current political status quo. Establishments have never been enthusiastic about those who choose to go rogue, because rogues represent a threat to their dominance. This is especially true today when there are millions of American voters who are delighted to follow Sarah Palin's footsteps in going rogue, perhaps right into the White House.

The populist conservative is a new kind of political animal. Unlike the neoconservatives who dominated American conservatism in the latter part of the last century, the populist conservatives are not particularly interested in honing beautifully crafted logical arguments directed at other intellectuals. They proudly address their appeals to Joe Six-Pack and feel no shame in vulgar rebel-rousing. In the eyes of populist conservatives, neoconservatives are no less elitist than their favorite target of scorn, the liberal elitist. The neocon has made his peace with too many of those sinister forces that are eroding America's traditional values and ethos. His pact with the devil can be traced back to the Republican Party's decision to accept the consequences of the New Deal in the aftermath of Eisenhower's election in 1952. Since then, the neocon has been far more concerned with establishing America's global supremacy than in protecting and preserving our precious heritage of liberty here at home.

What most agitates the populist conservative is a conviction that America is losing its historical uniqueness, rapidly becoming more and more like those European nations managed from the top down by a well-trained cognitive elite, whose attitude toward ordinary men and women is not so very different from that of the Planners and Managers in *Walden Two.* Skinner and others may look upon human liberty as an illusion, but the populist conservatives regard it as the supreme value in life, and their heroes are those American patriots whose rebellious passion for liberty made our country a shining exception among the nations of the world.

CHAPTER 3

THE WANING OF AMERICAN EXCEPTIONALISM

American exceptionalism is the conviction that America is unique among nations, or, at the very least, that it *was* unique at some point in our past. For many Americans, our nation was, is, and will always remain exceptional because it was chosen by Divine Providence to play a uniquely benevolent role in the general history of mankind. For the Puritans who came here in the early seventeenth century, America was the shining city on the hill. For Abraham Lincoln, it was the last best hope of the human race. For Woodrow Wilson, America provided a model of how a free and democratic society could actually work in practice. The other nations of the world had only to copy us to become free and democratic themselves.

This relatively benign version of American exceptionalism had an ugly cousin that found expression in such jingoist notions as Manifest Destiny. Early American settlers were an exceptional people, busily creating a radically new kind of society on the shores of *their* New World. They were white, Anglo-Saxon, and Protestant. These characteristics made them not only statistical anomalies in both the Old World and the New World—a fact that no one can argue with—but were also alleged to make them a superior race. They were rugged individuals who had separated themselves forever from the political tyrannies and ecclesiastic despotisms that prevailed in the Old World. Because of their inherent superiority, Americans felt justified in their westward expansion across the wilderness of the North American continent, even if this required the conquest of large parts of Mexico and the annihilation or forced removal of tribe after tribe of native Americans. To the proponents of Manifest Destiny, our acquisition of a great continental empire at the expense of "inferior" races was simply the price that had to be paid for the advance of a higher form of civilization.

Today, critics on the left often dismiss the doctrine of American exceptionalism as a myth propagated by neoconservatives to justify a foreign policy that aims at achieving global dominance and superiority over all the other nations of the world. These critics have a point, up to a point. The phrase "American exceptionalism" was indeed coined by neoconservatives, and it has frequently been used to justify a kinder, gentler form of Manifest Destiny by which America, as the world's single, great superpower, has the obligation to act as the world's policeman. But the belief in America's exceptional status preceded the advent of the neoconservative movement by many centuries, and it was shared by those who hated us as well as by those who admired us in both Europe and America.

Early visitors to America from foreign lands left with the uniform conviction that America really was different, often shockingly different, from their homelands. Many were struck by the great beauty of our natural landscape, like the Scottish naturalist John Muir who stayed and devoted his life to preserving it. Others marveled at our skyscrapers and our railroads, canals, and bridges. Some chuckled at our foibles, like our obsession with ice water. There was one aspect of our national life, however, that struck all the travelers who visited us in the eighteenth and nineteenth centuries. When giving a general overview of the American character, foreigners repeatedly offered the same assessment: Americans were a people who were fiercely jealous of their liberties.

This interpretation of American exceptionalism rests on solid historical evidence. America really did start out as a country largely made up of natural libertarians, people who did not want anyone telling them what to do or giving them orders, or even demanding deference from them. As the failure of Oglethorpe's utopian experiment in the Georgia colony demonstrated, the original settlers on our shores insisted on making their own choices, even if those choices were not as good as the ones their "betters" wanted to make for them. Some early observers of America found our passion for liberty—our own liberty, that is—to be truly admirable and a sign of our noble contempt for slavery. But there were many others who were convinced that the early Americans carried their passion for liberty to the verge of barbarism. When every man thinks he is as good as any other man, regardless of his intelligence, his education, or his cultural attainments, the result is bound to be a society that is uncouth, unpolished, and uncivilized—which is precisely how many cultivated European visitors saw us, and, indeed, often the way that today's cultured Europeans continue to see us.

THE POPULIST revolt underway in today's America, symbolized by, but not restricted to, the Tea Party movement, is based on the deeply held conviction that the United States is rapidly losing its exceptional status as the land of the free. It is this anxiety that explains the seemingly paradoxical nature of an avowedly populist movement that simultaneously claims to be conservative. It is a demand for more liberty, a demand historically associated with liberalism. Yet, at the same time it is genuinely conservative, because the liberty that is being demanded is not some newfangled kind of liberty that no society has ever enjoyed before. What is being demanded is the restoration of those liberties our forefathers once enjoyed, but which are now under attack by a central government that has obtained a degree of power over our lives that our Founding Fathers never envisioned.

As a matter of course, every political movement will develop its own peculiar reading of history, and populist conservatism is no exception to this rule. The English Whigs, for example, offered a reading of history that explained why they were right to chase the lawful king of England, James II, from the throne in the so-called Glorious Revolution of 1688. They justified their rebellion by arguing that James, in collaboration with the Jesuits, was on the verge of forcing England's Protestants to abandon their religion for James's own beloved Roman Catholicism. Both during and after the American Civil War, apologists for the Confederacy argued that they had the constitutional right to secede from the Union, just as their forefathers had the natural right to rebel against English tyranny.[1] Nineteenth-century socialist movements inspired by Karl Marx offered a sweeping interpretation of human history in order to prove the inevitable collapse of capitalism and the certainty of a happy ending to the violence and bloodshed of all previous epochs.

In the reading of history offered by today's populist conservatives, the erosion of our traditional liberties is traced back to 1933, when a new attitude toward the federal government came into being under the administration of President Franklin D. Roosevelt. This profound change was signaled by a critical shift in the meaning of the word "liberal." Unlike the liberals of the nineteenth century who championed the liberty of the individual against the tyrannical tendencies of the state, what would become the New Deal school of liberalism looked to the state as the remedy for society's ills. Not only would the New Deal state fix the economy by trying to pull it out of the Great Depression, it would guarantee its citizens a set of hitherto unheard-of freedoms—not just the traditional freedoms of speech and religion, but freedom from want and fear. Thus, modern liberalism was born, a political movement characterized by two basic principles. First, the state should be used in order to improve the lives of ordinary people, even if ordinary people did not wish to have their lives improved in this particular manner. Second, the control of the state should be entrusted to intellectuals who were experts and specialists in their fields, like FDR's famous Brain Trust, made up of distinguished members of the American academic community who were assigned to advise the president on the host of issues facing the nation during its most severe period of economic crisis.[2]

In this interpretation of American history, modern liberalism is a betrayal of the cherished ideal of individual liberty for which our ancestors fought the American Revolution. Indeed, in the eyes of populist conservatives, modern liberals have no right to call themselves liberals at all. The individual liberty historically championed by the liberals of an earlier epoch, the classical liberals, is of little or no interest to these moderns. On the contrary, modern liberals look upon the desire of people to manage and control their own lives as an obstacle to achieving the construction of the utopian state. As the populist conservatives see it, modern liberalism is a dangerous new form of authoritarianism in which the state uses its immense power to manipulate and control its citizens. The modern liberal is not a liberal at all, but a statist, that is, someone who puts his faith in "the supremacy of the state."[3]

Deeply troubled by the enormous expansion of the federal government since the New Deal, populist conservatives are frustrated by the seemingly unstoppable tendency toward statism, a process that neither past Democratic nor past Republican administrations have been able to check despite a host of campaign promises by the presidential candidates of both parties. To many of them, the election of Barack Obama in 2008 was simply the last straw. His administration is seen as a "superduper New Deal" that would give the federal government more power to do mischief than ever before. Under Obama, legions of "godless liberals" would attempt to achieve the utopian state of their demented dreams. Arrogant and out-of-touch intellectuals would try to fix the inevitable defects of a free society by curtailing ordinary Americans' traditional freedoms, such as their right to bear arms or their right to listen to Rush Limbaugh. A new Brain Trust, armed with superior means of mind control, would attempt to nudge Americans into desiring whatever the members of the Brain Trust want them to desire. A new high-tech Big Brother would be watching us—not to see if we have been bad but to make sure that we have been good. Once more, the road to utopia would reveal itself to be the road to serfdom.

Against this dire vision of the future, populist conservatives harken back to simpler virtues of the American past. They desire to return to the minimalist state envisioned by the Founding Fathers. Living in the twenty-first century, the populist conservative dreams of returning to the ideals and values that came naturally to the yeoman farmer of the good old days.

There is much to be said in favor of Jefferson's ideal citizen, the yeoman farmer. He was stubbornly independent, a man who insisted on making up his own mind and on exercising his personal liberty. No one bossed him around or told him what to think. He was an admirable model of the self-governing citizen and worthy of imitation by his descendants. But in the world of today, imitating the yeoman farmer has become a challenge. The political ideals of the yeoman farmer were deeply rooted, both literally and figuratively, in the soil that he owned and from which he earned his daily bread. He could be an independent individual because he did not really need other people. He grew his own food. He built his own house. He distilled his own whiskey. He made his own furniture. His wife made the family's clothes. There were no gigantic farming consortiums to compete against. There was no TV or Internet to seduce his children into wanting things that the yeoman farmer and his wife could never have imagined, from iPods to Xboxes.

Jefferson's yeoman farmer still has spiritual descendants living in America. But it is a telling fact that, by and large, their way of making a living is similar to that of the yeoman farmer, which is to say they are relatively independent and self-reliant. They don't work for Big Business or Big Government or Big Universities. Instead, they are individuals who own and operate small businesses, and who are justified in thinking of themselves as their own boss. No one tells them what to do or when to show up for work. The decisions they make about their businesses are their own. They suffer the folly of their mistakes. They gather in the rewards of their prudence or, at times, their sheer dumb luck. Their business is their own creation—frequently, like the God of Genesis, it is a creation *ex nihilo*—that is to say, a creation out of nothing but their own imagination, enterprise, and industry. In short, they think of themselves—and not without reason—as self-made men and self-made women.

To the self-made man of today, who has often made a tidy sum while running his small business, the American tradition of rugged individualism is not a quaint myth—it is the realization of his dreams and aspirations. A little reflection will show that there is a logical connection between today's populist revolt and the self-made man's anxiety over losing hard-won independence and self-determination. Those who work for enormous corporations forfeit the satisfaction of being their own boss, but they are compensated with a high degree of security and peace of mind. In addition, a huge company has political clout. The government cannot push it around. Indeed, as the recent bailout shows, if a company is huge enough, the government will run to its rescue in order to keep its collapse from creating havoc in the overall economy. But small business proprietors do not see the federal government as their benefactor. On the contrary, the state, with its power to interfere and to regulate, to command and order around, to tax and to redistribute, will inevitably appear to them as exploitative and oppressive—a sinister force to escape from rather than a benign power to appeal to.

Yet the American small business owner did not always view the federal government as the enemy. When the Progressive movement began in America over a century ago, the self-made little guy looked to the state to protect him and his small enterprise from the gigantic corporations that threatened his economic independence and survival. When the muckraking journalist Ida Tarbell published her *History of the Standard Oil Corporation* in 1904, her aim was to encourage the federal government to check the monopolistic and predatory practices of Big Business, as exemplified by John D. Rockefeller's mammoth company, Standard Oil. Tarbell's book was partly inspired by the fate of her own father—who operated a small oil company made extinct by the cutthroat competition Standard Oil engaged in. By virtue of its enormous size, Standard Oil could easily undersell the various little, local oil companies, forcing them either to declare bankruptcy or to offer themselves for sale on the cheap to Rockefeller's vast conglomerate.

In both the Republican and the Democratic parties of Ida Tarbell's time, the spirit of progressivism manifested itself in the mania for trust-busting, the effort to level the economic playing field so that gigantic corporations could not use their economies of scale to absorb or vanquish small businesses. The only player around big and strong enough to level the field was the federal government, to which the little guy appealed for protection from the rapacious trusts that threatened his independent livelihood. Ultimately, however, this appeal was made in vain. In this one respect at least, Karl Marx's crystal ball got it right. The earlier epoch in which the economy was simply an aggregation of small family businesses was destined to pass away, to be replaced by huge megacorporations. As Big Business came to dominate more and more of American life, it was perhaps inevitable that the state, instead of trying to turn back the clock, decided to join the club.

Today, and for some time now, the higher echelons of the American federal government have been filled with men and women who either worked their way up through gigantic corporations, or who expect to work for them when they leave their government jobs with a salary naturally proportionate to the inevitably helpful connections they have made within their former government circles. Given this cheek-to-jowl, buddy-buddy relationship between Big Business and Big Government, it should come as no surprise that the small business owner long ago ceased to see the federal government as a protector. By an ultimate irony of fate, today's self-described progressives usually display nothing but contempt for the Chamber of Commerce mentality of America's small-business people, unlike the progressives of Ida Tarbell's time who championed their interests. In October 2009, for example, the progressive administration of President Obama, who rode to the presidency on a platform of economic populism, made a deliberately calculated decision to marginalize and ignore the Chamber of Commerce in the health care debate, and to court the favor of the CEOs of American mammoth corporations such as IBM, Wal-Mart Stores, Time Warner, Eastman Kodak, Starbucks, Amazon.com, and Coca-Cola.[4]

Napoleon may have been wrong when he said that "God was on the side of the big battalions," but Karl Marx was certainly right when he argued that history was on the side of Big Business. The predatory expansionism of Rockefeller's Standard Oil revealed the general direction of capitalism's movement as it headed into the twentieth century. Any corporation that was big enough could employ the same methods as Rockefeller to undersell the little guy, and over time capitalist societies became dominated by huge corporations. Classical economists of the nineteenth century thought Marx was wrong, but the twentieth century proved that he was right. Marx, however, did not regret this development. On the contrary, Marx thought that the rise of Big Business represented progress.[5] The Austrian economist Joseph Schumpeter, an ardent proponent of capitalism, agreed with Marx on this point. The enormous wealth of America did not come from the labor of the individualist businessman, but from the team players, those organization men who staffed the committees that guided the fate of the gigantic and globally sprawling megacorporations. It was not Josey the Plumber sweating in her little shop that made America the dominant economic power in the world; it was the huge assembly lines of General Motors and Ford, the global networks of IBM, Coca-Cola, and Microsoft—colossal enterprises whose operations were far too intricate and complex to be understood by any single individual. As Karl Marx might have put, the "material conditions" of the early republic supported an economic environment favorable to rugged individualism. The yeoman farmer could live happily in his rural retreat, cut off from the world; but few of us can live that way today unless we are prepared to move to the Arctic Circle and live in an igloo. We are all too intertwined, interconnected, interdependent. In every aspect of our lives, complexity has replaced simplicity as big has triumphed over little. The result is what we call modern progress, and it has lifted individual Americans to their unprecedented level of affluence and elevated their nation into the status of supreme global superpower.

The truth is that very few of us today would be willing to trade our prosperous and toy-filled lifestyles for the arduous struggle of our pioneer ancestors scraping out a bare subsistence on the prairies—and it is this fact that makes the populist conservative's appeal to the American tradition of rugged individualism often seem more like an exercise in political nostalgia than a genuine solution for the myriad problems facing the United States in the twenty-first century. Those who listen to right-wing radio may devoutly wish to return to days of yore, when every man was free to do what he wanted, so long as he didn't kill anyone, but as the country boy once said to the stranger who asked for directions to a distant village, "You can't get there from here."

THE EXCEPTIONAL degree of liberty that once flourished in early America was a product of a set of exceptional historical, geographical, and cultural circumstances—but these circumstances have changed dramatically. America started out as a weird and improbable mixture of an economy made up of self-sufficient farmers and small merchants, the Anglo-Saxon tradition of local government, the European peasant's tradition of hard work, the Calvinist tradition of the self-governing congregation, the Lutheran tradition of priesthood of every man, the absence of feudal institutions, the expanse and freshness and plentitude of a colossal continent located in a new world. All these factors combined to produce a country overflowing with natural libertarians, and it was this fact that led the Founding Fathers to devise a severely limited government for their new nation. They did not choose to have a limited government—they simply recognized that this was the only form of government that would be tolerated by America's natural libertarians, who instinctively resented any kind of interference in their own affairs by outsiders.

The Founding Fathers were quite right to tread carefully. When the United States Constitution, which had been composed in a shroud of secrecy, was first offered for public inspection, it faced lively and vociferous opposition from a large segment of the American people who saw it as a threat to the freewheeling freedoms that they had enjoyed under the Articles of Confederation that it replaced. America's natural libertarians preferred the weak government to which they had become accustomed, and were suspicious of the stronger central government proposed by the men who met in Philadelphia in 1787 to create "a more perfect union." The anti-Federalists, as they came to be called, looked upon the Constitution's more perfect union as a pretext for reviving the despotic form of government that they thought they had left behind in the Old World, and they fought against its ratification heart and soul.

In the populist conservative reading of American history, it was Roosevelt's New Deal that marked the moment when the United States began losing its exceptional status as the sweet land of liberty. But the anti-Federalists of the early republic displayed the same attitude to the new political arrangement provided by the United States Constitution as FDR's critics displayed toward the New Deal: It was a dangerous and unnecessary innovation that would ultimately give the central government far too much power. For the anti-Federalists, the ratification of the United States Constitution endangered the very liberties for which Americans had bravely fought during their revolt against English tyranny, and marked the beginning of the end of America's libertarian exceptionalism. Nor were they entirely wrong, as the suppression of the Whiskey Rebellion of 1794 clearly showed.

The first treasury secretary of the United States, Alexander Hamilton, was a firm believer in a strong central government. He wanted to tax the whiskey that frontier farmers had previously been free to produce and sell without any kind of government interference. Hamilton's intent was to use this unprecedented tax to pay off the national debt, which was mainly owed to men of wealth and property. When the poor farmers of western Pennsylvania rebelled in 1794, federal troops were dispatched to put down their revolt. Like the despotic forms of government prevalent in the Old World, the new American government had resorted to military force to compel unwilling citizens to pay a tax that they thought was unfair, and on a product that they had been making for generations without paying anyone else a dime for the privilege. Here was an obvious and painful loss of a traditional liberty.

Statism scored its first triumph over America's natural libertarians under the administration not of Franklin Delano Roosevelt but of our first president, George Washington.

The truth of the matter is that America has been in a gradual process of losing its libertarian exceptionalism ever since the Puritans landed on Plymouth Rock. The native Americans were far freer than the Puritans, who immediately set about curtailing people's liberty in order to create their New Jerusalem. As urban civilization expanded along the Atlantic coast of America, those who preferred to live free of its constraints began to move farther inland, into the wilderness, where they would be at liberty to live more or less as they pleased.

In the 1820s, some European observers began to speculate that our apparent libertarian exceptionalism might simply be a passing phase, a temporary function of our unlimited frontier. As long as Americans were free to move to virgin soil and to create from scratch their own communities, their liberty was assured. They could have as much personal freedom as their hearts desired simply by moving into the wilderness. Under such circumstances, there was no need for a powerful state. But when later generations reached the last frontier, their situation would begin to resemble that of the Old World, in which limited resources produced a zero-sum-game mentality: I can only get what I want by taking it from you. Class and regional conflicts would emerge and there would be a need for a strong state to keep these conflicts from tearing America part—like the strong state that emerged out of the devastation of the Civil War.

In addition, in the nineteenth century and well into the twentieth, America was protected from all external enemies by two great oceans. What would happen to our fundamentally pacific nature if we suddenly found ourselves in the midst of a catastrophic global war? It was simply not possible for the minimalist state envisioned by the Founding Fathers to wage a war against a mighty state that had no qualms about conscripting its citizens and taxing them heavily to build up its arsenal of weapons. Jefferson's solution during the Napoleonic wars was to refuse to fight. Instead he hoped—rather wistfully—to bring both England and France to sue for peace by refusing to sell them our goods. It didn't work. Over a century later, in the face of the First World War, Woodrow Wilson initially announced that America was too proud to fight, but he was eventually driven to enter the conflict because of Germany's refusal to stop sinking neutral America's ships on the high seas. When other nations use the state as the ultimate weapon of mass destruction, there is no equally formidable weapon available to those who distrust and fear the state. Historically minded libertarians reflecting on our past wars invariably explain that they were not really necessary. We could have stayed out of them. We could have let the conflicting megastates fight it out among themselves, while we stayed on the sidelines. But if American libertarians have good reason to fear the power of their own state, they surely have a much better reason to fear the power of hostile foreign states bent on self-aggrandizement and the achievement of global domination. Here again the impersonal forces that move history came down on the side of the statists: America had to become more like the powerful European states if it hoped to defend itself against their bullying and aggression. But a state powerful enough to hold its own on the global stage costs a lot of money, and the only way to raise this money is through increased taxation.

During America's first seventy-odd years, it was possible to pay for our limited government primarily by a tariff on imported goods. Of course, in one sense, this was a tax—a means by which the government raised revenues from its citizens. But no citizen was forced to buy imported goods. Those who did not feel the need for such European frippery and finery could do without, and not pay a cent to support their government. Significantly, the first American income tax was an emergency measure taken by Lincoln to pay for the costs of waging the Civil War. After the war, the income tax was abandoned and even declared unconstitutional by the Supreme Court in 1895.[6] It required the Sixteenth Amendment to the United States Constitution, ratified in 1913, to establish the legal basis for a federal income tax. The first personal income tax was extraordinarily modest and fell only on the very rich.[7] But over the course of the twentieth century, the burden would grow constantly greater and it would fall on the working man as well as the wealthy. While there were many protests and much grumbling, there was no violent rebellion—a fact that would have greatly astonished and disturbed our revolutionary ancestors.

In 1775, commenting on the rebellion underway in the British Colonies of North America, Edmund Burke observed that the "fierce spirit of Liberty is stronger in the English Colonies probably than in any other people of the earth," but he went on to explain that the American "love of liberty" was "fixed and attached on this specific point of taxing. Liberty might be safe, or might be endangered in twenty other particulars, without their being much pleased or alarmed. Here they felt its pulse; and as they found that beat, they thought themselves sick or sound."[8] At the original Boston Tea Party, the American patriots expressed their outrage at the British attempt to impose a trifling tax by deliberately destroying private property in a flagrant act of vandalism that shocked even those Englishmen who had been most devoted to the American cause. At today's revival of the Tea Party, tax-hating Americans sit around sipping tea. Here, too, we are no longer quite so exceptional—in this case, exceptionally rowdy and unruly—as we were in Burke's day, though our tax burden is vastly greater than that of our colonial ancestors. The triumph of statism in the form of heavy taxation was not the work of evil conspirators but the product of impersonal historical forces. Superpower status is not cheap, and someone must pay for it.

OPPONENTS OF statism can argue that America's ascent to superpower status was not inevitable, and they can point to many in our past who warned against it. The populist movement that began in the 1890s among the farmers of the American Midwest, for example, was fiercely isolationist and pacifist. The farmers saw no reason why America should meddle with European affairs or send its sons to fight their wars. They didn't even see much need for foreign trade. In their reading of history, it was the sinister eastern states' conspiracy of Big Business and Big Finance that insisted the United States play a grand role on the world stage—for their own selfish economic benefit, of course. The so-called peerless leader of agrarian populism, William Jennings Bryan, was so deeply convinced that America should stay out of the First World War that he resigned his post as secretary of state after he failed to dissuade President Wilson from firing off a stern note of protest to Germany after one of its U-boats sank the British ocean liner *Lusitania* on May 7, 1915. For Bryan, the only way of avoiding entry into the European bloodbath was for the president to issue a frank and sensible warning to the American people: If they stayed at home, they were safe; but if they elected to travel the high seas during the war, they might well suffer the same fate as the 128 Americans who had died on the *Lusitania*. To Bryan's faithful followers, the midwestern farmers, such advice made perfect sense. They certainly weren't planning trips to Europe any time soon.[9]

America's convulsive intervention in the First World War was followed by a rapid return to our national tradition of pacifism and isolationism. The general consensus among ordinary Americans after the war was that we had been suckered into joining a fight that was really no business of ours. Those who felt this way emphatically rejected the idea that America should play a leading role in world affairs. They did not want the United States to become a member of the League of Nations, the pet project of Woodrow Wilson, the archetype of the liberal internationalist. The isolationists of this period were not moronic reactionaries, as they are often portrayed. On the contrary, they included leading progressive figures, like Robert M. La Follette and George W. Norris, intelligent men who were sincerely convinced that only a strict and unswerving policy of isolationism could keep our nation from succumbing to the European mania for statism. If the United States could keep itself aloof from the bloody wars of the Europeans, it could continue to have a limited government with only a very modest military establishment. After the First

World War, the isolationist sentiment in America was so strong that at the commencement of the Second World War our army was rated inferior to the armies of Poland and Czechoslovakia.

Up to the very eve of the attack on Pearl Harbor in 1941, most Americans saw nothing in Europe worth spilling American blood for. It was Hitler's impulsive and foolish decision to declare war on the United States along with his ally Japan that brought American troops back to Europe for the second time in the twentieth century. Since then, American troops have never left. As the menace of Soviet totalitarianism began to loom after World War Two, the once powerful tradition of American isolationism, with its dream of returning to the small and limited government of our forefathers, was banished to the museum of outmoded ideas by those who had once been its ardent supporters.[10]

Today's populist conservatives are neither isolationists nor pacifists. None wants to reduce the American army to the size of Slovakia's. All want America to remain the dominant military superpower on the planet. Many of them have supported sending our sons and daughters (often their own sons and daughters) not just to Europe but to remote corners of the world such as Iraq and Afghanistan. To the populists of America's past, contemporary populist conservatives would be an enigma. Fervid champions of America's status as a superpower, they refuse to recognize the simple fact that superpower status requires a superstate. You can't have one without the other. Earlier populists did not want America to be a superpower; they wanted their nation to mind its own business. They didn't want a state big and powerful enough to send their sons to fight expensive wars halfway around the world. Despite these differences, however, today's populist conservatives do share one important sentiment with American populists of the past: They are not terribly fond of Europe or Europeans. Indeed, the mere fact that Barack Obama was Europe's enthusiastic choice for America's next president indelibly tainted him in the eyes of many populist conservatives, who figured that if the Europeans liked him, there had to be something wrong with him.

CHAPTER 4

A POST-AMERICAN AMERICA

To most Americans in the early republic, Europe represented a hopeless basket case, in which all men lived under tyrannical systems of government, and most under even more despotic religious creeds. Thomas Jefferson, one of the most cosmopolitan men of his day, despised prerevolutionary Europe and found little good to say about it, while the average American citizen of the day often expressed his conviction of his superiority by drawing invidious comparisons between his country and those of the Old World. In America, ordinary people were free and didn't need to grovel before anyone. Servility was neither part of their nature nor part of their society. They were capable of directing their own fate. Often this contrast between the New and Old Worlds was overblown, at least in the opinion of those Englishmen who were equally proud to boast that they had been "free-born." By and large, however, there was much truth to the proud conviction of early Americans that they were living in a land where the average man was freer and enjoyed greater equality than he had ever possessed before. The Old World represented a house of bondage from which the oppressed had managed to escape in order to establish their own community in the promised land of the New World.

This view of the contrast between America and Europe was not limited to the ordinary American of the Revolutionary period. It was shared by a host of brilliant nineteenth-century writers and thinkers such as James Fenimore Cooper, Walt Whitman, and Ralph Waldo Emerson. But today there are many Americans, especially among liberal intellectuals, who are firmly convinced that the path of salvation for America is to reform its institutions and its politics, both foreign and domestic, based on European models. Give greater control of our society to the professionals. Reject the populist temptation to return to simpler days that are long gone. Adopt the kind of soft paternalism favored by the European intellectual elites as the only realistic solution to the challenges of the new century. Embrace multilateralism and discard the "cowboy style" of foreign policymaking—after all, the American frontier, along with the rugged individualism appropriate to it, is long gone. We are now more like everyone else and far less like we were in our hallowed and often highly romanticized past. It is high time for Americans to face the fact that we live not only in a post-American world but in a post-American America.

For the populist conservative, such counsel smacks of treason. The explosive quality of today's populist revolt arises from a pervasive fear that we are rapidly and irreversibly hurtling in the direction of a post-American America. The populist conservatives' instinct is to turn back the clock, but they fail to recognize just how far back they will need to turn it. It is in this particular respect that today's populist revolt displays the chief defects of all populist revolts throughout history.

Populism has always displayed a pronounced tendency to blame all social ills on a conspiracy of wicked men, who, though few in number, wield immense power over the society they are manipulating behind the scenes. The popularity of conspiracy theories arises from the fact that a conspiracy theory is almost invariably a good story, and everyone likes a good story. To begin with, a story is about people, not ponderous abstractions and boring statistics. It has good guys and bad guys. The good guys fight the bad guys. Sometimes they win, at other times they lose. But no one ever confuses the good side with the bad. When populist conservatives read history, they tend to regard it as a struggle between the good guys who act out of the purest noble aims and the bad guys who are consumed with an unquenchable desire to do evil purely for kicks. In their story line, the good guys are the true patriots, Sarah Palin's "real Americans," while the bad guys are the "godless liberals," the arrogant statists who are out to destroy the good guys' sweet land of liberty. For many of them, the solution to America's problem is obvious: Remove the godless wicked statists from their positions of power and influence, fill their positions with "real Americans" like Sarah Palin and the devoted admirers of Glenn Beck, and America will be saved.

A simple story line like this can be immensely helpful in mobilizing the masses behind a political movement.[1] You need to think about an ideology, but a story grabs your attention and holds your interest without the need for much reflection. Indeed, its direct appeal to the imagination often does an end run around our rational faculties, and we see no need to examine why we have instinctively chosen this side over the other. This is not to deny that story lines often contain a great deal of truth, offered up one-sidedly and too simplistically no doubt but still raising valid issues. The story line of today's populist revolt, however, while containing a kernel of truth, undermines its own validity by focusing too much on a sinister conspiracy of godless liberals intent on destroying America, instead of recognizing that our drift toward a post-American America has been largely the result of impersonal forces far beyond the control of even the most cunning and ingenious cabal of villains.

Bashing liberals has become an enjoyable recreation for many, and for a select few it has become a highly remunerative occupation. But ultimately liberal-bashing solves nothing, because, at their very worst, the much decried godless liberals are only symptomatic of the waning of American exceptionalism—they have not brought it about. The causes of our "de-exceptionalization" go deep, and are the result of vast historical forces over which individual human beings have precious little control. Indeed, even the populist conservative has conflicting feelings about the way he thinks America should go. For example, he wants a simple homespun America that is also the dominant military, cultural, and economic power on the planet. He wants to return to the old-fashioned traditions of the past, but he doesn't want to miss out on the latest hi-tech gizmos of the future. On a whole host of issues the populist conservative is torn and divided, but instead of recognizing the contradictions that exist within his own mind, he does what most human beings do under the same circumstances: He finds someone to blame all his problems on. Get rid of the rascals (that is, the godless liberals) who are currently in charge of things, and replace them with good, decent, honest folks like us, and all will be well.

The political maxim "Throw the bums out!" is the quintessence of all populist revolts, but it is most often heard when the people have become extremely unhappy with the direction their society is taking. When the managerial class is competently handling the great affairs of state, winning wars or avoiding them while providing prosperity all around, then you hear little grumbling from the people. But when things begin to fall apart, those in charge will inevitably lose the confidence of the public. As the situation worsens, this loss of confidence spreads until it discredits virtually the entire managerial class, the competent and the diligent along with the incompetent and reckless. Seen in this light, the populist revolt against Bush's bailout plan in 2008 played a role in igniting the town hall revolts of 2009—and perhaps the second revolt cannot really be understood separately from the first. The urgent request for the bailout revealed to ordinary people that those who were managing the economy had inexplicably fallen asleep at the wheel. The embarrassing fact that the federal government had done nothing to protect our economy and then had to turn to the people to pay for the bailout of huge financial institutions did not inspire confidence that it could handle the much-needed overhaul of our health care system.

During such a crisis of confidence, the people will often simply throw the bums out and demand a new managerial group to replace them. The men and women who have been misgoverning and mismanaging our affairs so wretchedly need to be replaced with people who can be trusted to handle complicated challenges honestly, intelligently, and competently. But in today's America, we will inevitably recruit our new managerial class from the same place as our old one. We will select them from those who have been most successful in earning a high place for themselves in our meritocracy. Not even the most populist-minded conservative will want his hunting buddy to become the new secretary of defense simply because he can shoot a gun. He will naturally want someone with expertise and good credentials, preferably the graduate of a good university, intelligent and sharp enough to deal with the awesome complexities of a demanding job—just as Sarah Palin's most devoted admirers would be scandalized if she picked her high school and college chums to fill her cabinet. We have all been brought up to accept nothing less than "the best and brightest" in positions of leadership, no matter how many times in the past the best and the brightest have led us to disaster, both at home and abroad.

Herein lies the predicament facing the populist conservative. He dreams of returning to the world of Thomas Paine, in which common sense was all a person—or even a whole society—needed to get by. But the populist conservative of today lives in a society far too complicated to be governed by ordinary citizens selected at random—the system used by early Greek democracies to prevent any single man from gaining too much power and prestige. Even the most passionately populist conservative acknowledges the need for experts and technocrats who have highly specialized education and training. Like all other contemporary Americans, populist conservatives are also emphatically keen on educating their children and sending them to college. They are ardent champions of the American system of meritocracy, which to them seems fair and just. Yet our system of meritocracy, based primarily on education and high-ranking scores on standardized tests, inevitably tends to put college-educated people into positions of power and influence. Therein lies the rub, for people with higher education will tend to separate themselves ideologically from ordinary men and women. They will be less traditionalist in their outlook, and, by and large, they will also be more liberal.

Opinion polls customarily divide people into different groups depending on their level of education. There are sound reasons for this procedure. For example, a recent Pew Poll surveying attitudes on gay marriage showed that "college graduates age 65 and older are more than three times as likely to favor gay marriage than are seniors with less education (33 percent to 9 percent). Among those age 50 to 64, college grads are twice as likely to favor gay marriage as their less educated counterparts (43 percent to 21 percent). By comparison, education makes relatively little difference among those under age 30, where support for gay marriage runs highest. Since younger generations are more likely to have college degrees than older, this education gap contributes to the overall size of the generation gap on gay marriage."[2]

The term "education gap" was coined by two Democratic pollsters, Stan and Anna Greenberg, whose work revealed that in the election of 2004 Bush led among men with only a high school education, and Kerry led among men with college degrees.[3] A similar education gap showed up in the polls taken during the 2008 Democratic primaries, which showed Hillary Clinton leading among those with only high school education and Barack Obama leading among those with college educations.[4]

Generally speaking, people who have only a high school education or less will be inclined to have more conservative or traditionalist views on all sorts of contemporary issues than people with a college education or advanced degrees. These two groups will normally tend to disagree on immigration, gay marriage, the war on terror, the threat of socialism under the Obama administration, and a host of other questions. It does not matter in the least which group is right or wrong—all that matters for the purpose of my argument is that there will be substantial disagreement between the two groups. It is obviously true that there will be a certain amount of crossovers from either side. There will be college professors who oppose gay marriage, and high school dropouts who approve of an ultraliberal immigration policy, but they will tend to be the statistical outliers.

At this point we are only dealing with a sociological phenomenon, namely, that better educated people in the United States today tend to be liberals, and that liberals tend to be better educated. But this phenomenon is open to two radically conflicting interpretations. One way of interpreting it would be to argue that better educated people will obviously have the right answers on the issues of the day, because they are smarter and see things more clearly. Needless to say, this interpretation of "the education gap" tends to be favored by educated liberals. Yet there is another way of interpreting this phenomenon, which is to argue that the so called education gap is really an "indoctrination gap." The wide consensus among the better educated on different questions is not proof that they have been taught to think for themselves, but irrefutable evidence that they have been programmed to think alike.

To most of us, education is good, while indoctrination is bad. But how exactly can we tell when a program of education has in effect become a program of re-education? The underlying metaphor of education starts with a blank slate that represents the student's fresh and open mind, so that the teacher's mission is simply to fill him full of knowledge and information. But the premise of re-education is quite different. It assumes that the student's mind is already cluttered with ignorance and prejudices, normally those he has picked up from his family's inherited traditions. This means that the first task of the re-educator is to cleanse and purge the student's mind of those traditions he has been taught to accept by his family. Only then can the re-educator fill his student's mind with the right ideas and opinions—namely, the ideas and opinions to which the re-educator subscribes. But this kind of re-education seems suspiciously like straightforward indoctrination.

The slippery slope between education and indoctrination is an ambiguous heritage from the European Enlightenment of the eighteenth century. It is a direct result of the new way of looking at the world adopted by the enlightened elite of that time. Before the Enlightenment, European intellectuals most often saw their job as defending the status quo. After the Enlightenment, they came to see their mission as improving the world in accordance with their own values and ideals. These improvements, however, came at a cost. They required the abolition of traditions and customs that ordinary—that is, unenlightened—people dearly cherished. But this abolition could not take place without a power struggle: The average person did not want his traditional world turned upside down. The unenlightened fought back and resisted, and this required the enlightened elite to enter more forcefully into the political arena. Hitherto the intellectual had contemplated the world. Now he was determined to reform it. Thus the enlightened intellectual began his struggle to achieve cultural hegemony and domination—a struggle he inevitably justified in the name of human progress, often employing the standard argument that the end justifies the means. This was his fall from grace, for the intellectual, by committing to the implementation of his utopian visions of a perfect world, deliberately risked his most precious asset—his reputation for being reliably objective and disinterested about all the questions that came to his attention. But the enlightened intellectual is willing to take this risk because he is convinced that he has a world to win, and ever since the European Enlightenment, he has been trying to win it. And today he is succeeding, which is precisely what is driving the populist conservatives nuts.

It is part of the legacy of the Enlightenment that the American intellectual community of today, like other modern intellectual groups, will invariably hold to ideas and values that clash radically with those of most ordinary people—indeed, that often shock and scandalize them—like gay marriage or the insistence on removing the Ten Commandments from American courthouses. This clash is the result of the attitude toward tradition handed down from the Enlightenment. Ordinary people tend to routinely accept the traditions they have been raised in simply because these are the traditions their family has always honored. They do not seek to find a higher court of appeal before which they can justify their adherence to the traditional ideas and values of their ancestors. But intellectuals, precisely insofar as they are enlightened intellectuals, can never be content with inherited traditions merely because they have been passed down from their predecessors (and, in their opinion, passed down quite arbitrarily). They may choose to remain faithful to family or ethnic traditions, but they will need to find an intellectually respectable argument to explain both to themselves and others why they refuse to abandon these traditions for more up-to-date ideas. But the intellectual who attempts to justify an inherited tradition by means of logical argumentation walks into an inescapable trap. Those who must have a reason in order to accept a tradition are demonstrating that their ultimate loyalty is not to their community's tradition but to reason itself. Because of their compulsion to find and offer explanations for their beliefs, intellectuals can never become members in good standing of any community, religious or political, that is based on unquestioning faith, while the blindly devout members of these communities will always regard the intellectual with suspicion and mistrust. Most modern intellectuals have recognized their inevitable alienation from the majority of individuals who are quite happy to live and die holding on to the same ideas and values as their ancestors. Our contemporary liberal elite's alienation is simply the dark legacy of the European Enlightenment to which they are the spiritual and philosophical heirs.

IN 1784 the German philosopher Immanuel Kant offered the briefest and most accurate summary of the Enlightenment when he wrote that its operating maxim was, "Dare to think for yourself! (*Sapere aude!*)"[5] In practice, of course, this meant: Dare to think differently from what your parents, your people, your community have taught you to think. Dare to discard their traditions and to adopt the new ideas being offered to the world by the rising elite of secular intellectuals, such as Kant himself.

For intelligent men and women during the Age of Reason, there was no escaping the influence of the Enlightenment. It was all-pervasive. You could support it enthusiastically or you could hate it passionately, but eventually everyone had to deal with its impact. There were several significant nineteenth-century intellectuals who rejected the Enlightenment's cult of reason as shallow and absurdly overly optimistic, among them the Danish theologian and philosopher Søren Kierkegaard and the Russian novelist Fyodor Dostoyevsky. But the majority of intellectuals did not follow their path. They shrewdly recognized that attacking the premises of the Enlightenment was the swiftest way to undermine the source of their own authority and influence within society. Their mission was to enlighten, and not to conserve. If inherited tradition was good enough, there was no point in thinking for yourself. Even worse, if tradition was right, then those who were looking to develop their own original ideas were certain to go wrong. Samuel Johnson wittily caricatured the position of those enlightened intellectuals who spurned tradition in a search for new ideas when he remarked: "Truth will not afford sufficient food for their vanity; so they have betaken themselves to error. Truth, Sir, is a cow that will yield such people no more milk, and so they are gone to milk the bull."[6]

Yet milking the bull had some obvious advantages to the intellectual aspiring for more control over society. Any idiot could milk the cow. Truths within the reach of the merest simpleton did not require geniuses to discern them. If a man wanted to get ahead in the world solely on the basis of his superior intellect, he had to convince both himself and others that his greater intelligence allowed him to perceive truths—and important truths—hidden from the view of the ordinary man. He needed to reveal new and unsuspected insights unknown to the inherited traditions that had previously satisfied everyone else, from the most ignorant peasant to a walking encyclopedia like Samuel Johnson. No wonder those intellectuals who were ambitious for power naturally turned away from the cow, and went after the bull. If the world were to be remade in accordance with the light of reason, then maximum power would be entrusted to those in whom the light of reason shone most brightly.

The enlightened intellectual has a self-flattering ideology: He claims he is only interested in getting at the truth and disseminating it to the people. Yet his behavior too frequently indicates that he is also interested in gaining power—power to do good, he assures us, but power all the same. In the eighteenth century, a number of celebrated French *philosophes,* the embodiment of the European Enlightenment, brazenly pursued the goal of obtaining maximum power by shamelessly courting the high and the mighty, in the belief that this was the quickest way to cure the world of all that ailed it. Voltaire grossly flattered Frederick the Great, while Diderot buttered up Catherine, Empress of Russia (also called "the Great"). Neither Voltaire nor Diderot had any moral reservations about encouraging their respective "enlightened despots" to use their full armory of dictatorial power to suppress superstition and ignorance, and to impose on the peasants and the servile classes the ideals and values that reason had revealed to their superior intellects.

The eighteenth-century intellectual's flirtation with enlightened despotism ended badly. The despots enjoyed the witty conservations of their ingenious philosophical companions, but they were not about to take their utopian notions seriously. Much can be said against despots but they usually have a rather firm grasp on reality, otherwise they would quickly forfeit their firm grasp on power. Yet, just when it looked like Enlightenment was doomed to remain limited only to a select elite, a world-shattering event convinced many advanced-thinking intellectuals that the age-old dream of a utopian society entirely designed and managed by men like themselves might at last be within the realm of possibility—indeed, that it might in fact turn out to be the wave of the future.

CHAPTER 5

ENLIGHTENMENT
IN POWER

The world-shattering event that promised the creation of a more egalitarian society was the French Revolution in 1789. Among the many waves of the future that it set in motion was the idea of public education provided free of charge to the children of every French citizen, rich or poor. From this moment on, intellectuals stopped trying to persuade enlightened despots to implement their utopian schemes. Instead, they pinned their high hopes for world regeneration on the comprehensive system of public education that would be firmly under their own control.

In *The Republic* Plato had argued that there were only two possible routes by which a society could be perfected. Either kings would have to become philosophers or philosophers would have to become kings. Voltaire and Diderot had tried to make kings and queens into philosophers but had failed. The advent of the idea of universal public education, however, offered philosophers an unsuspected path to power. By fashioning the minds of the rising generation in accordance with their own enlightened ideals and values, they would in effect become the dominant power in their society. Kings and queens might retain their titles, but real authority over the people would pass imperceptibly into the hands of philosophers, who would bring enlightenment to the masses. They would usher in an era in which utopia would at last be realized on earth, beginning naturally in France, the epicenter of the revolution that would soon change the world—and America along with it.

The idea of universal public education provided by the state was first popularized by the French mathematician and polymath the Marquise de Condorcet, who immediately grasped its enormous potential to reshape and reform the corrupt old order. Condorcet had joyfully greeted the coming of the French Revolution, but he immediately grasped the drawback to the promise of universal equality. It was all too easy to declare that everyone, including the lowliest peasant, was now an equal citizen of the French Republic, but the peasant could hardly be expected to make intelligent decisions about great affairs of state. A peasant knew enough to raise and harvest crops, but his knowledge of the world seldom went beyond his own fields. There was no way to prepare the peasant to assume the responsibilities of citizenship in the new French Republic, but, Condorcet argued, there was a way to prepare his children.

Condorcet's solution was universal education. If all were to be citizens, free and equal, all would have to be educated. The French government would need to launch a program of universal and compulsory education, undertaken at state expense, which would guarantee the children of the most humble peasant the same educational opportunities as those of the wealthiest aristocrat. All French children would receive the same education, which, in theory at least, would level the playing field. Only in this way could the promise of equality be translated into reality. A French philosopher, not George W. Bush, initiated the first "no child left behind" program.[1] It changed the world then, and it is still changing it today—in ways that are seldom fully grasped.

TODAY MOST of us simply regard the American system of public education as part of who we are, but it played no role in the Founding Fathers' vision for our future—and it played an even more marginal role in the mind of the average American of their time. Two years after America proclaimed its independence, Thomas Jefferson, often cited for his interest in promoting education, introduced his "Bill for the More General Diffusion of Knowledge" to the Virginia legislature and later proposed a new system of public education for his native state. Elementary school education would be provided for all free children, male and female, but it was limited to only three years. Grammar schools were for free boys only, and no girls. There would be a limited number of scholarships provided to poor boys, but otherwise the students would have to pay their own tuition. Significantly, even this extraordinarily modest innovation was voted down by the Virginia assembly.

Halfway through the nineteenth century, many Americans continued to be appalled at the very idea of universal and compulsory education, regarding it as a utopian flight of fantasy that positively reeked of the fanaticism spawned by the French Revolution. To them, it was as outrageous as socialism, the abolition of slavery, or the emancipation of women. To make matters even worse, the youngsters of the early republic were not terribly keen on going even to the private academies of the time. According to educational historian Merle Curti, "in 1837 some three hundred teachers were driven out of their schools by the unruly and riotous pupils over whom, in spite of the prevalent use of the whip, they were unable to keep any semblance of order."[2] And this was in the civilized state of Massachusetts, not in the wilds of Ohio or Missouri. Perhaps most importantly, average Americans just didn't think that book-learning was relevant to their affairs. If they could read the Bible, that was enough book-learning for them. Otherwise, everyone could get by on what no one ever complained to be lacking in—namely, common sense.

America started out as the promised land of common sense. When Thomas Paine took up the cause of the American Revolution, he had no doubt that the common sense of the ordinary man could serve as the foundation for a flourishing democracy. The American spirit of cognitive egalitarianism—the belief that my opinions are just as good as yours or anyone else's—would keep the common people from being manipulated by intellectual charlatans of every ilk. But not everyone in the early republic shared

Paine's optimism. John Adams and Alexander Hamilton, for example, were sincerely convinced that the operation and management of government should be left up to "the better sort," namely men like themselves. These patriotic elitists were in thorough agreement with the ancient critics of democracy, such as Plato and Aristotle, who had warned of the dangers of entrusting the people with too much power.

Up until the populist explosion of 1828, when Andrew Jackson was elected president, America had been entirely in the hands of "the better sort," such as Jefferson, Madison, Monroe, and John Quincy Adams, and no one gave any attention to the idea of mass education. But overnight, with Jackson's election sweep, the political landscape changed. The people didn't want to be ruled by the better sort but by their own kind. They wanted to see men in office who would support and govern for the good of ordinary individuals like themselves—farmers, laborers, backwoodsmen, and mechanics. In addition, immigrants flocking to America brought with them alien political customs and traditions, most of them dangerous to the established order. The question for the better sort was how to respond to this grave threat to their own security.

The answer offered by some was to adopt Condorcet's revolutionary idea, but to apply it to counterrevolutionary purposes. The people would be exposed to universal and compulsory education supervised by the state. Public education would be used not only to teach the children of the people reading, writing, and arithmetic, but also to instill in them morally uplifting and resolutely middle class messages aimed at their self-improvement. Thanks to the edifying lessons of McGuffey Readers, the standard primer used in virtually all nineteenth-century American schools, the people would be transformed from an ignorant and potentially dangerous mob into an educated and intelligent electorate, who would naturally turn to the elites to guide and lead their nation. In short, mass education would be the cure for what ailed democracy.[3]

But like many cures, this one had an unexpected side effect. The American principle of the separation of church and state meant that public education would have to be both a civic and a secular education centered upon and emanating from the state, not the church. With the clergy cast out of their teaching jobs, there was no one else who could be entrusted with the promotion of secular education other than enlightened intellectuals—or at least those who had learned from them. Thus, as public education became the foundation of the newly emergent popular democracy, more power was turned over to the enlightened elite whose job was to manage and guide the powerful engine of mass education.

In 1852 when the state of Massachusetts pioneered the first program of public education in America, it decided to borrow as its model the Prussian educational system, the then reigning paradigm of educational discipline and efficiency. The designers of the Prussian system did not share Condorcet's concern with teaching children to think for themselves. The German philosopher Johann Gottlieb Fichte, an enthusiastic supporter of the Jacobins during the French Revolution, had been one of the spiritual architects of the Prussian system. Fichte summed up his philosophy of public education by saying: "If you want to influence [the pupil] at all, you must do more than merely talk to him; you must fashion him, and fashion him in such a way that he simply cannot will otherwise than what you wish him to will. . . . The new education must produce this stable and unhesitating will according to a sure and infallible rule."[4] This method of teaching no doubt produces the kind of orderly discipline necessary for mass education to work at all, and yet it is also the doctrine of education embraced by all subsequent forms of totalitarian government and eerily prophetic of George Orwell's Newspeak.

With Massachusetts leading the way, the other states in the union would also turn to the European model of mass education, some moving much faster toward that goal than others. Thus midway into the nineteenth century, Americans began to turn their backs on their traditional reliance on common sense and began to plunge headlong into the business of mass-producing consensus, based on the educational ideals directly derived from the European Enlightenment. We were becoming less like us, and more like the French and the Prussians—and at the level that ultimately mattered most in the long run, namely, how we educate the next generation.

AS THE twentieth century progressed, it became obvious to the average man that the welfare of his society depended increasingly on the mastery of science and technology. By devising weapons to defend ourselves against our enemies, science and technology protected the lives of all citizens; they worked together to transform the daily existence of every man in a thousand different ways. Even those who lacked any serious knowledge of science and technology recognized the enormous positive contribution that both made to their own lives. Yet, built into the very nature of science and technology is a principle that was profoundly antidemocratic and elitist. Those who excelled in these fields were inevitably the best and the brightest. They had to be.

This outcome was not the product of a sinister conspiracy. It was an inevitable result of the bell curve that governs the distribution of human intelligence. Some people are a lot smarter than others, and they will naturally rise to the top of any meritocracy that is based on the kind of intelligence necessary to master modern science and technology. The complexities of modern science and technology require more than common sense, so that even the average Joe and Josie will want their rockets designed by rocket scientists and their brains operated on by brain surgeons. Thus, by an ineluctable and irreversible process, all modern liberal democracies by their very commitment to promoting education, science, and technology must increasingly turn over power and control to the intellectual elites that specialize in these fields. In this respect, the United States is no exception to the rule.

When rumors began to circulate early in the Second World War that the Germans were at work on a nuclear device, the president of the United States turned to the most brilliant scientists he could find to staff the Manhattan Project. The crisis he faced could not be resolved by common sense, but by equations too boggling for the average man even to begin to comprehend.

Only a scientific elite of the very highest caliber could make the bomb to end all bombs. And they succeeded.

Following the Second World War, as education, science, and technology played a greater role in the life of the individual and of the society, more decisions about more things had to be made by experts, leaving fewer decisions to be made by citizens lacking the relevant expertise. Today, when our economy spins out of control, we don't take a poll of American barbers to decide what to do about the crisis; we turn to those who have doctorates in economics, though we are naturally more confident if they have also won a Nobel Prize in the subject. When a new epidemic of flu threatens, we don't run to the local shaman and solicit his advice, nor do we ask Granny for her traditional nostrums—we turn to those who are accredited experts in epidemiology. Indeed, for most of us, our very idea of modern progress is intimately linked with a society in which brains not brawn, education not inheritance, is the path to power and worldly success.

But there is a drawback to any cognitive elite: Ordinary people do not get to decide who will be a member of it and who will be excluded from it. That is entirely the prerogative of the elite, as it has to be in order for the elite to maintain its high standards—a cognitive elite must accede to the demands of the bell curve if it wishes to maintain the intellectual superiority of its ranks. To that extent it is self-selecting and self-perpetuating. If the cognitive elite played no serious role in our affairs, there would be little reason to be concerned about the undemocratic principles on which it thrives. Most of us are willing to let others decide who should be the next chair of the Greek department at Stanford University. But the greater the role the cognitive elite plays in the lives of ordinary people, the more this role becomes an object of interest, attention, and even anxiety. When members of the cognitive elite begin to argue that they should be permitted to nudge the masses in directions that they think would be suitable, then we begin to worry. Are they overstepping their proper bounds? We don't mind having people with high IQ's design our computers, but we don't want anyone, no matter how brilliant, to tell us how we may use them. We can't live without our cognitive elite, but we certainly don't want to live under them. This is especially true when the cognitive elite promotes innovative ideas that dramatically clash with the inherited traditions of the ordinary men and women they have set out to enlighten. In the modern liberal West such clashes have occurred ever since Enlightenment thought took hold in the eighteenth century.

KARL MARX thought of history as a series of class conflicts based entirely on economics, but history has been no less a series of cultural conflicts. These arise whenever there are two competing camps within a society. In America today, one camp is determined to hold on to the old ways of life—or what they imagine those ways to have been—while the other camp is determined to vanquish what they see as outmoded traditions and replace them with their own superior and enlightened wisdom. Both camps are deeply convinced that they are fighting for what is right, but because they speak entirely different languages, neither camp can ever hope to persuade the opposition to change its mind. The inevitable result is a power struggle to determine which camp gets to teach and instill its values in the next generation. The Greek philosopher Socrates was a victim of such a struggle in the Athens of his day. His enemies charged him with seducing the young into discarding ancient traditions in order to teach them his newfangled nonsense called philosophy. The same power struggle occurred during the European Enlightenment. Condorcet obviously represented the camp of enlightenment and radical reform; but he was bitterly opposed by those who wanted their children to be educated to respect their own traditional faith and values, and certainly not educated to repudiate them.

When populist conservatives speak of godless liberals, oppose gay marriage, and worry about the teaching of evolution in public schools, they are engaging in a battle about the future of American culture. They do not want their children "educated"—or, in their eyes, brainwashed—by a cognitive elite that has nothing but contempt for their traditional ways of life. When they foam at the mouth about the villainy of modern liberals, they are in part displaying the standard populist paranoia that explains all that is wrong with the world by blaming an evil conspiracy of sinister men operating behind the scenes. But the populist conservative, in this case, has a valid point. There really *are* godless atheists who want to destroy his Christian religion—just ask Richard Dawkins and he will proudly tell you that he is one of them. Nor is he alone. Today there is an influential group that has dubbed themselves The Brights, with a website on the Internet called The Brights' Net. In the words of one of its eminent spokesmen: "A bright is a person with a naturalist as opposed to a supernaturalist world view. We brights don't believe in ghosts or elves or the Easter Bunny—or God."[5] But today's Brights are not simply atheists. They are evangelical atheists.[6]

In the past, there were atheists who had no interest in disseminating their infidelity among the masses. On the contrary, while disbelieving in God personally, they thought it was better if ordinary people continued to believe in him—belief in God was a useful fiction that promoted social stability. For the ignorant masses, a revealed religion whose ethical commandments they simply took on blind faith was necessary.[7] But evangelical atheists do not share this point of view. Their ultimate aim is to convert the rest of society to their own persuasion.

The same evangelical spirit is characteristic of the liberal elite in general, and to spread their gospel they have no qualms using every means of persuasion at their disposal, including the powerful vehicles of modern mass communication. Populist conservatives who grew up watching the apolitical antics of Daffy Duck now find that their kids are watching a different kind of cartoon. Through a skillful combination of entertainment and propaganda, their children are being gently nudged into accepting the agenda of the liberal elite. On the television show *Family Guy* kids can learn that gay marriage is cool. On *South Street* they can learn that Christianity isn't. Those who write these shows are perfectly convinced that they are disseminating enlightened values to the next generation, and perhaps they are. But this is not how the populist conservatives see it. When the populist conservatives are confronted with a cognitive elite that controls much of what their children learn in school, hear on the radio, watch on TV, or surf on the Internet, they naturally come to the conclusion, "They're out to get me." And they are out to get them—or, at least, their children. But the members of the liberal elite do not see themselves as conspiring to take away all that populist conservatives love in life. They are trying to teach them to love the right things, like the things they love, and to hate the right things, like the things they hate.

The populist conservatives intuitively reject many of the ideas embraced by the cognitive elite that is trying to enlighten them and their children. Yet, paradoxically, they have no intention of rising up to chase the cognitive elite from the temples of higher education. Instead, they busily save up money in the hopes that they can send their kids to one of those temples, preferably one that is highly ranked.

Those who are leery of populist conservatism often characterize its adherents as simple-minded clowns. Yet the problem with America's current crop of populists may be that they are not nearly simple-minded enough. They have far too much faith in the modern progress that is shared by the "godless liberals" they deplore. They believe in salvation through education. Some of the more rigorous of them may insist on home schooling their kids, but they still want them to be as sharp and as knowledgeable as possible. Even if the populist doesn't have much education himself, he will still want his sons and daughters to go to college, preferably a good one. (And he will know which are the good ones.) He will champion the meritocracy to the extent that he would be outraged to think that his sons and daughters were not given a chance to excel in the world because of their father's lack of education.

Today you would be hard pressed to find anywhere in America a man who is proud to argue that book-learning and schooling are complete wastes of time, although back in the good old days of the early American republic, such men were quite plentiful. That is why education had to be compulsory—ordinary people seldom saw any point in sending off perfectly good workers in the form of their own kids to fiddle away their valuable time with McGuffey Readers. We may dismiss these old codgers as benighted buffoons, but in the nineteenth century, their view was shared by many men who were by no means stupid.

In the England of 1820, William Cobbett—one of the most successful writers of his era and a reformer deeply committed to the welfare of ordinary people (as long as they were English)—could not condemn enough the dangerous idea inspired by the French Revolution that the sons of working men and common laborers should be exposed to bookish education courtesy of the national government. He argued that "some people must remain to labor; all men cannot attain to eminence in the world; and, therefore, that which is laudable in individuals [*i.e.,* the acquisition of book-learning], is, to say the least of it, foolish upon a national scale."[8]

More remarkably, John Stuart Mill, perhaps the best educated Englishman of his time, also had serious reservations about public education offered free of charge by the state. Despite his credentials as the leading liberal thinker of his day, Mill argued that a state-operated school system inevitably becomes "a mere contrivance for molding people to be exactly like one another . . . in proportion as it is efficient and successful, it establishes a despotism over the mind, leading by natural tendency to one over the body."[9]

It says much about the quandary faced by modern democracy that one of its foremost champions, John Stuart Mill, was convinced that universal and compulsory education undertaken by the state would inevitably lead not only to "a despotism over the mind," but ultimately to a cultural totalitarianism that mandated conformity of conduct as well as conformity of thought. For Mill himself had argued, like Condorcet before him, that the people must be educated prior to being given the right to vote. Like many other progressives of his era, Mill looked upon education as the panacea that would spare democracy from the threat of populist demagoguery.

Yet, unlike Condorcet, Mill did not want the education of the masses to be concentrated in the hands of the state. He insisted that people be taught to think for themselves and not to parrot the opinions of their intellectual superiors. Yet he was not at all sure how this could be accomplished. How do you *teach* people to think independently? Certainly not by telling them what to think. Can such cognitive self-confidence even be taught in a schoolroom, or does it require the wider scope of experiential opportunity provided by the rough-and-tumble interactions with the real-world school of hard knocks?

For a time, Mill toyed with a system in which education would be handled by private schools, allowing parents to decide which schools to send their own children to—a precursor of what we now call the voucher system. At the same time, Mill had no doubt that popular education should mainly concern itself with disseminating objective knowledge and scientific truth, and this conviction naturally made him wary of permitting private schools to set their own standards and curriculum. But if the private schools could not be allowed to decide what to teach, then the task of imposing standards and deciding what subjects should be taught would naturally fall to the state. Even if the state operated only behind the scenes, its impact would be decisive, once again raising the very specter of mental despotism that Mill found so disturbing.

John Stuart Mill began his intellectual career as the champion of Jeremy Bentham's philosophy of utilitarianism, with its emphasis on hard facts and logical inferences, its contempt for tradition, and its adamant insistence on radical and systematic reform to attain the goal of the greatest happiness for the greatest number of people. Later in his life, Mill came under the influence of the writings of the English poet Samuel Taylor Coleridge. Like many of his English contemporaries, Coleridge had been flush with enthusiasm for the new dawn promised by the French Revolution, only to see his high utopian hopes dashed by the grim reality of the Reign of Terror. In response to these traumatic events, Coleridge became a political reactionary, seeking to revive the traditional institutional safeguards that the French Revolution had swept away. The stupendous rise of Napoleon to supreme power in France once more demonstrated that popular democracy inevitably ends in a new form of despotism. To Coleridge, the lesson was clear: The people could not be trusted to determine their own best interests. They needed to be watched over and guarded by a cultivated elite.

Coleridge coined the word *clerisy* to describe his ideal elite, which would be composed not of the rich and the property-owning class but of those with outstanding intellectual gifts—what later came to be termed the intelligentsia. Unlike the Roman Catholic clerics who had controlled European education during the Middle Ages and up to the very eve of the French Revolution in France, Coleridge's clerisy would have no interest in passing on any specific religious doctrines and dogmas to the next generation. Their job would be to preserve and transmit the very highest ideals of their culture. Instead of acting as defenders of the faith, they would be defenders of reason and culture—of great art, great poetry, great music, rationality, and scientific discipline.

From Coleridge, John Stuart Mill adopted a vision of society in which the clerisy—of which he would naturally be a leading member—should play a privileged role in the social order. It would be their job to provide a new creed for the masses, which Mill dubbed the Religion of Humanity. Needless to say, there would not be much religion in this new Religion of Humanity—at least not by orthodox standards. Instead, the Religion of Humanity would emphasize all the themes that appealed to men like Mill himself. It would extol healthy skepticism and the paramount importance of science. It would encourage men to challenge religious dogmas and political doctrines based on privilege and prescription. It would wean the common people from the hoary traditions that they had been raised to take on faith, and it would promote the virtues of rational analysis. It would teach humanitarian values and provide a secular foundation for the exercise of what were once quaintly known as Christian virtues, such as charity and acts of mercy.

In return for the blessings bestowed by the clerisy in the form of this new rational religion, the common people were asked only to believe in it—a modest demand, it might appear. Unfortunately for Mill's Religion of Humanity, however, real human beings simply refused to get excited about a creed so coolly rational that not even a hardened skeptic could find much in it to complain about. The people, by and large, were determined to stick by their old faiths, to repeat their old creeds, and to live and die in the comfort of the traditions that they had inherited from their ancestors.

Inherent in the very concept of the clerisy lay the ticking time bomb that would explode into the culture war of our present day. The problem lay not in the elitism of Mill's clerisy, but in the fact that the values and ideals of this new elite clashed radically with those of the people whom the elite had undertaken to educate to their standards. An elite that no longer accepts the same traditions as the common people may wisely decide to leave the masses in their natural state of ignorance, but if it wishes to convert the masses to its own ideals and standards, it is courting disaster. That was the real explanation for the catastrophe of the French Revolution, at least according to the late eighteenth-century British statesman and philosopher Edmund Burke.

In his *Reflections on the French Revolution,* Burke agreed that every social order needed to be guided by a privileged elite. There was nothing novel in Burke's thesis; it was the standard position in his day, challenged only by the most radical democrats, like Thomas Paine. For most people, the question wasn't whether society should be governed and managed by an elite, but rather which elite should be entrusted with this authority. In the French Revolution, Burke saw the formation of a dangerous new kind of elite, namely, an elite entirely composed of those with "ability"—what we today might call merit or intelligence. What made the new elite a menace to society was its arrogant assurance that the values and ideals it held were superior to those of the people, an assurance that made them feel no disquiet in attacking the obsolete and outdated traditions of the masses. For example, the leading figures of the French Revolution wanted to do away with the old religion and bring in a new one—the prototype of Mill's Religion of Humanity called the Cult of Reason. Similarly, the revolutionary elite insisted on throwing out all sorts of supposedly venerable traditions, from aristocratic titles to the names of the months.

Herein lay the perilous threat posed by the new elitism. The revolutionary elite, whenever it found the people resistant to their newfangled creed and doctrines, felt they had the right and even the duty to force their own enlightened ideas on those who were simply too bigoted and benighted to grasp them for themselves. But this was not a temptation that the elites before the Age of Revolution had ever felt. The privileged classes in Burke's eighteenth-century England, for example, were social conservatives. Their status came from the great estates that they had inherited from their ancestors. They were not likely to want to rock the yacht. They were quite happy with the religion of their ancestors and had little interest in chasing after the latest intellectual fads and follies. Indeed, they took a dim view of all innovations in religion and politics. They would have felt complimented by John Stuart Mill's charge that they represented "the stupid party." They didn't want to be smart, and they certainly didn't want to hand over power to clever and cunning men who could easily outwit them. To quote Gilbert and Sullivan, the reigning elite in England would have been horrified to discover that "a Duke's exalted station" might one day be obtainable "by competitive examination."[10] They didn't want a meritocracy, and they emphatically did not want universal education. That would only stir up trouble in the inferior orders, giving the happy though humble peasant delusions of grandeur that could only make him miserable with his own lowly lot while transforming him into a potential powder keg of revolution.

The social order that Burke wished to preserve against the dangerous influences of the French Revolution was a world in which the ruling class and virtually everyone else in the society all shared the same fundamental traditions and religious outlook. Power and prestige were in the hands of men no brighter than average, and not infrequently even a little below average. Unlike Mill's clerisy, the traditional English ruling class had little interest in defending reason or great art. They shared the religious and political prejudices of the ordinary Englishman of their day—Joe the Cider Drinker. Everyone in Burke's England could equally enjoy a good afternoon of bowling, cider drinking, or bear baiting—a fact that gave Burke's England its cultural solidarity and its famous insular mentality.

English class snobbery was entirely a matter of blood. Mere smarts had nothing to do with it, which was obviously to the advantage of those who had more noble blood in the veins than brains in their head. The ruling elite came from families that had habitually been deferred to, unlike the "new man" who had to scrap and struggle to earn recognition in the world—as Burke himself had been forced to do. Yet Burke did not resent the privilege of birth and blood; he saw in it, somewhat paradoxically, the guarantee of the continued blessings of English liberty. The well born had too great a stake in their society to risk turning it upside down. The great Samuel Johnson, Burke's friend, took the same view of English politics, despite being a "new man" like Burke. Indeed, Johnson once wittily said: "I have great merit in being zealous for subordination and the honor of birth; for I can hardly tell who was my grandfather."[11] Neither Burke nor Johnson, however, were stooges of the establishment. They were both ferociously independent in their convictions and views, often to the point of great inconvenience to themselves and their own best interests. Perhaps both were so intellectually gifted that they were able to see that mere cerebral brilliance could be a danger in the wrong hands.

DESPITE BURKE'S eloquent arguments against the revolutionary ideals of the French Revolution, his nation—like ours—was inevitably influenced by them. Today, all modern liberal democracies, including ours in the United States, are actually meritocracies based on education and ability, and even those citizens least equipped to excel within the meritocratic system accept its legitimacy without serious reservations and often with immense enthusiasm. Even if they themselves have not succeeded in rising up through the meritocracy, they are confident that their children are bound to do better. To go back today and to try to reverse the immense transformations in our national life brought about by the meritocracy would necessitate a total repudiation of principles cherished by all Americans, from those who listen to right-wing talk shows to those who read the *New York Review of Books*. But the progress that we all happily embrace—progress which can be directly credited to the success of our meritocracy—has a side effect that makes a large number of us nervous. Our education-based meritocracy, while it brings much that is good to us and for us, inevitably creates an intellectual elite that confers mainly with the other members of the same club who share a consensus on how to improve the world. This consensus will be almost entirely based on the ideals of the European Enlightenment, which, by their very nature, will be invariably hostile to the traditional values and ideals of ordinary men and women, who are often far more happy with the world as it is. In the United States and the other advanced nations of the world, the meritocracy-driven cognitive elite has steadily been rising to power by virtue of the influence it has on how the rest of society thinks and feels.

As individuals, the members of America's cognitive elite may display great personal modesty, but, collectively, they are convinced that they are the bearers of enlightenment with both the right and the duty to conquer prejudice and superstition, absurd traditions and idiotic customs. The problem is that a large chunk of Americans are not only perfectly satisfied with their silly superstitions and benighted traditions, they are willing to fight tooth and nail for their preservation. The rebellious defiance of populist conservatives, when offered enlightenment secondhand, will inevitably strike their would-be enlighteners as inexplicably perverse, a product of their native ignorance and lack of education. On the other hand, to populist conservatives, the cognitive elite's attack on their traditions inevitably comes across as a deliberate attempt to subvert their cherished way of life, a treasonous assault on the very core values that made America the land of the free. Economic conflicts between two competing groups can frequently be solved, or at least eased, by splitting the difference, as when a labor strike is settled by an increase in the wages and benefits of the worker. But a cultural conflict like ours is far more difficult to resolve by compromise. Both sides are sincerely convinced they represent the forces of light and goodness, while their opponents stand for darkness and evil. Hence, the struggle between the two camps will inevitably take on a Manichean aspect, in which neither side will rest content until it has utterly vanquished its antagonist.

In a cultural struggle, all the individuals involved are committed to a cause higher than mere economic self-interest, be it the cause of humanity, or of science, or of God. This will ennoble them as individuals, in contrast to the *homo economicus* who is satisfied with merely feathering his own nest. Their loyalty to a higher cause means that they are prepared to make great personal sacrifices, often to the point of offering up their own lives. The intensity of their devotion is no doubt admirable, at least when it is observed from a safe historical distance, but when it flares up in the midst of a society like ours— one committed to moderation, rational discussion, and the spirit of compromise—it will look suspiciously like the kind of fanaticism that toppled and overwhelmed societies whose reputation for stability far exceeded our own, like the Bourbon monarchy of prerevolutionary France.

The cultural clash between the populist conservatives and the cognitive elite that is hell-bent on enlightening them underlies much of the current political tension in the United States. Indeed, this division is rapidly replacing the old distinctions of liberal and conservative, left and right, Republican and Democrat. At the basis of these older political categories was an honest appreciation that intelligent men could hold conflicting political views. During the calm and relatively untroubled periods of American history, there was a massive consensus about the goals to be pursued, so that the debates in our society were largely over the pace of progress. The liberal said, "Faster, faster." The conservative replied, "Wait a second. Slow down a bit." For other areas in which their differences were more substantive, it was still possible for the liberal to see the conservative point of view, even if he didn't agree with it, and the conservative could return the favor. In the nineteenth century, those who listened to John Calhoun as he defended slavery might have found his position morally repugnant, but no one who followed his arguments could regard him as an ignorant boob, whose ideas could be dismissed as a result of his subnormal IQ. Everyone recognized his intellectual brilliance. On the other hand, those who championed slavery might despise the abolitionist opinions of Charles Sumner, but even his bitterest enemies did not doubt his blazing intelligence. In the twentieth century no Democrat labeled Republican Robert Taft a low-grade moron, and no Republican dismissed Democrat Adlai Stevenson as a drooling cretin.

Today it is different. All too often our intellectual elite displays a disdainful contempt for those who disagree with them. They do not restrict their scorn to the artful and ingenious ridicule of a Voltaire, alternatively teasing and mocking. All too often they display the crude intellectual snobbery of the schoolboy with the high IQ, who loves to torment his inferiors by scoffing at their dullness. Our cognitive elite cannot take their opponents' arguments seriously, because they do not see them as arguments in the first place—they see merely prejudices that have been programmed into them, requiring not logical rebuttal but open derision.

For many contemporary American liberals, the fears and grievances of the populist conservatives simply cannot be taken at face value. These liberals are willing to acknowledge that the populist conservatives are genuinely upset and deeply agitated over the present state of society, but they argue that the true source of populist frustration stems from economic hard times. It is Joe Six-Pack's anxiety over job insecurity and wages that prompts him to listen to the siren songs of populist rebel-rousers like Sarah Palin and Glenn Beck. Typical of this economic reductionism was the unfortunate comment that Barack Obama made during his campaign, when he opined that many Americans—a.k.a. Joe Six-Pack—turn to "guns and religion" during a time of economic recession.[12] Presumably, by this logic, if the economy is running along smoothly, Joe Six-Pack would at once lose all interest in his gun collection, stop attending his local church, and become a member in good standing of Moveon.org. Little thought is given to the idea that Joe Six-Pack might actually treasure his gun collection, or that he might turn to religion simply because it is the religion of his fathers and has always comforted him when he has turned to it in the past—not least, because he genuinely believes in it.

While the contemporary populist revolt no doubt reflects recent economic anxieties, it is far more the result of a profound and pervasive cultural alienation that has been deepening over the past decade and which has divided America into two hostile camps, a culture war that currently shows ominous signs of degenerating into a civil war. On the one side are those who believe that they are entitled to govern by virtue of their superior knowledge and expertise. These are the highly educated men and women who represent the *crème de la crème* of the American meritocratic system, and who are genuinely convinced that they represent progress and enlightenment. It seems natural to them that they should govern simply because they know what is really best for our nation. On the other side of the cultural divide are those who resent being governed by anyone at all, and who are fully convinced that they are best equipped to manage their own affairs and to control their own lives. Often these men and women have made a place for themselves in the ·world with little help in the way of formal education. They may be blue-collar working people or the owners of small businesses. All share the same pugnacious "Don't tread on me" attitude of their revolutionary ancestors and are adamant in their insistence that no one else will govern them.

In his speech on the colonial rebellion of 1775, Burke warned his English contemporaries that Americans thought their freedom was "the only advantage worth living for."[13] Today there remains a large contingent of Americans who continue to feel the same way. For these natural libertarians, there is nothing that matters more than keeping control of their own lives and determining their own destinies. They reject paternalism in any form, and they refuse to be managed and manipulated by an intellectual elite, no matter how benevolent their intentions may be. Men much smarter than themselves, neuroscientists and behavioral psychologists with advanced degrees from impressive schools, might try to convince them that the freedom they make so much fuss about is simply an illusion. But, on this question, the natural libertarians will stick to their guns. Even if freedom is an illusion, it is an illusion that many Americans in our past have shown they are willing to die for. An illusion that can dominate the minds of so many people—to the point where they are willing to defend it with their lives—clearly poses an enigma that cries out to be unraveled.

CHAPTER 6

THE LIFE CYCLE
OF LIBERTY

Philosophers have assured us that we are born free, but the infant enduring the painful process of being born does not usually regard emergence from the mother's womb as an act of personal liberation. The infant has grown accustomed to the womb's warm security and has no desire to live outside it. Our instinctive attitude to birth is that we want no part of it. Given our own preference, we would never choose to enter so dangerous and risky a place as our world. Our first taste of freedom is thus a bitter one, which is why we have to be dragged into the world quite literally screaming and kicking. We miss the security, the certainty, and the stability of the liquid paradise we have lost. According to some psychologists, many of us remain scarred forever because of what has been called the birth trauma.

There is an analogy here with human societies. Before the unsettling dawn of the modern era, the vast majority of men, women, and children lived within their culture as snugly as the fetus lives within the womb. It is true that their material circumstances were often bleak and that their lives were frequently extraordinarily difficult, but they all shared the comfort provided by an immutable inherited tradition. All the certainty and security they could wish for was provided to them by their inherited tradition. First of all, their tradition had devised for them an elaborate code that prescribed, often in the most minute and comprehensive detail, how each of them should behave under every imaginable circumstance, according to age, gender, economic status, state of health, position in the social order, and so on. Secondly, their tradition made it a rule that this same code must be followed in exactly the same way, generation after generation, with as little variation as humanly possible. In such cultures, there was no opportunity for even the illusion of liberty to take root. In pre-modern India, if a boy was born an "untouchable," he was not at liberty to move up in the world by his own efforts. In medieval Europe, if he was born a serf, he was not free to provide more food for his family by working a little bit harder—his extra efforts would simply end up enriching the lord of the manor. Where a society's "cake of custom"[1] is highly congealed, any aberration in the direction of what we call freedom will be quickly and effectively nipped in the bud. The rebel will find himself the victim of his society's collective indignation at his disloyalty to his inherited way of life. When the enlightened thinkers of the eighteenth and nineteenth centuries attacked tradition as a barrier to human progress, this was what they were talking about, and on this point virtually all Americans are in agreement, no matter which end of the political spectrum they occupy.

But there is a different kind of tradition, one with which we are all familiar. This is the tradition that teaches us not to submit to the dictates of the bully or tyrant, but to stand up for our rights and liberties, to fight to preserve our freedom and independence. It is the tradition that tells us that we must think for ourselves, even when it makes us outcasts, and to follow the dictates of our conscience, even when it makes us heretics. This is the tradition of the rebel that, far from being an obstacle to human progress, has proven itself to be an indispensable precondition for the creation and maintenance of free and self-governing societies. Those who wish to go to war against this tradition, in the misguided belief that all inherited traditions must be discarded in the interest of progress, are not furthering the cause of liberty, but endangering it.

Herein lies the strongest argument that today's populist conservatives can make in their own defense: Yes, we are defending our inherited traditions, but these traditions are worthy of being defended because they have proven themselves to provide the cultural foundations of free and open societies. In dealing with those traditions that have held men back and denied them freedom, we are in thorough agreement with the enlightened intellectual. These traditions should be discarded. But when it comes to those traditions that have given ordinary human beings their sense of freedom and dignity, we will fight to conserve them, out of the profound conviction that once we have allowed these traditions to be perish, human freedom and dignity will perish as well.

This argument echoes the "conservationist" argument made by Edmund Burke: At the present moment we are living in a free society. Let us make sure that we can continue to live in such a society by conserving those traditions that just happen to have brought us to the present moment. But Burke's argument can be made deeper and more powerful if we stop and examine the question, How did these freedom-friendly traditions ever come about in the first place? We can understand traditions that make people docile and passive; but it is much harder to grasp the origin of a tradition that makes them rebellious, since such a tradition appears to be the absolute negation of tradition. Furthermore, it is hard to imagine why any tradition-bound society would ever voluntarily shatter its "cake of custom."

Today we have all become so accustomed to living in societies in which innovation and individualism are both prized and celebrated that it is difficult for us to understand the appeal of a monolithic tradition that automatically solves all our problems for us. But its appeal is obvious. Inherited tradition spares us the ordeal of having to think and act independently. When a tradition tells us what to do under a variety of different circumstances, it obviates the need for us to make that frightening existential commitment called a personal decision. If tradition tells a young man that his choice of bride will be determined by his parents, then he will not have to trouble himself with the anxiety of finding the right woman—tradition has settled that question for him. If tradition tells the son of a carpenter that he must become a carpenter and may not become anything else, then the boy never has to fret about what to do when he grows up—tradition has decided that for him. With equal beneficence, tradition will also decide what gods to worship, how to dispose of the dead, how to avoid the evil eye, and all sorts of other questions that would otherwise need to be decided by ignorant and confused individuals.

There have been many societies in which tradition settled all possible questions in advance, so that individuals never had to make risky decisions on their own. Indeed, over time, every reasonably stable social order will develop a set of customs and institutions that establish what is to be done under an enormous range of circumstances, so that everyone who has been properly socialized can be relied upon to follow the appropriate script. But a society, if it wishes, can go beyond this. Recognizing that unexpected change may disrupt the smooth operation of the well-oiled machine of tradition, the society can do whatever is necessary to ward off such changes. It can act to defend itself against innovation by simply forbidding it. It can close off its borders to foreigners who might import their alien ways. It can ban new ideas and punish those who introduce them. It can retreat as much as possible from the world. It can take every possible measure to prevent everyone from acting on their own individual initiatives. Under such direction, it is obvious that inherited tradition indeed becomes the enemy of progress, reason, and liberty.

RISK TAKING is an acquired taste. Human beings, by and large, do not like uncertainty. We accept it reluctantly, and if we can trade uncertainty for certitude, we eagerly agree to the transaction. Even when the certitude is illusory, the mere fact that it brazenly claims the status of certitude renders it virtually irresistible—which explains why human beings have been so willing to believe an astonishing amount of the most preposterous nonsense. Anything, it seems, is better than facing the fact that we really don't know how to deal with a crisis, which is why human societies try to avoid them. Yet, it is a curious feature of the human condition that the wonderful thing known as human creativity and innovation can only burst forth when people are most clueless—as when they are facing an unprecedented crisis.

As long as we have the traditional recipe for addressing a known problem, and as long as this recipe works, we will continue to use it, and what fools we would be if we didn't. It is only when the traditional recipe fails us that we will entertain the notion—assuming that we ever do come to entertain it—that perhaps we might be able to fix this problem ourselves. As long as a society can successfully operate according to the principle of social inertia—simply doing today whatever it did yesterday—there is no call for creative initiative on anyone's part. In fact, such outbursts of individual innovation would only get in the way.

Tradition in this sense is clearly the friend of those who have inherited their wealth, their power, or their status. It is the natural ally of the ruling elite of every age and clime, of those who are intent on keeping things just the way they are. Tradition says, "This is how it has always been around here. Therefore, this is how it should always remain." To us, this may not sound like a very convincing argument, unless of course we are the ones who have benefited from the way things have always been. But that is the beauty of normal traditions: they don't need arguments to support them. The principle of social inertia takes care of all that. People do not question that to which they have never known an alternative, and what is never questioned, never needs to be defended.

Captain James Cook learned this lesson during his third and final voyage, begun in 1776, to the Pacific Ocean. Visiting the island of Tahiti, Cook and his men were perplexed by the fact that the men of the island refused to eat meals with their women. The Tahitian men cooked meals for themselves and picked the choicest food while the women were left with the rejects. When Cook and his crew sought to discover the rationale behind this custom, so bizarre by European standards, they "could get no other answer but that it is right and necessary that it should be so."[2]

All traditions that have operated without a hitch for any long period of time will eventually come to seem "right and necessary," especially when those who follow them are ignorant of the fact that somewhere else there are human beings who practice different customs. Such unquestioned traditions obtain their powerful hold over people's minds simply because they are looked upon as a product of nature. No tyrant could ever command such complete obedience to his dictates as immemorial traditions command for theirs.

In light of these observations, we may well wonder how a tradition of rebellious independence could ever arise—a tradition that perversely tells people, "Decide this question for yourself. It is your responsibility to make up your own mind. Be sure to always keep your independence." As the children of an enlightened culture, we have come to take the desire for freedom for granted; but perhaps we should be astonished that human beings ever came to tolerate freedom, let alone desire it. So long as men and women had all the answers provided for them by a wise and omniscient tradition, what could possibly make them seek out the risk and uncertainty that are the inescapable companions of independent decision making?

The answer is that human beings would not have deliberately chosen to be free; something utterly beyond their control must have forced them to be free. Human beings would never have chosen liberty if they had had an alternative, just as none of us would have voluntarily left the security of the maternal womb for the risks and perils of living in an uncertain world. We were forcibly expelled. Human beings are not born free, nor do we achieve liberty by wanting to obtain it. Instead, liberty is thrust upon us—or, rather, some of us. Freedom can only arise when it is no longer possible for a society to operate on the automatic pilot of a monolithic tradition, and people have no choice but to play it by ear—or perish.

Here are some of the ways in which a society can experience a crash of their traditions: invasions, forced migrations, rebellions, revolutions, plagues, famines—these can all cause considerable cracks in the "cake of custom," and sometimes they shatter it completely. Less traumatically, people can voluntarily migrate from their native country and decide to make new lives for themselves on foreign soil. The Greeks did this when they sent out colonies, and such migrations also peopled North America. Frequently the colonists attempt to bring with them the inherited traditions of their native land, but the circumstances of their new homes make it difficult, or even impossible, for them to adapt these traditions to their new way of life. Whether starting over again or starting from scratch, the inhabitants of a new world are forced to improvise, to rely on their own wits. They come to depend on themselves instead of on their inherited tradition, and it is out of this enforced self-dependence that the spirit of innovation will be born.

There are many who cannot cope with altered circumstances, but some will thrive. Those will do best who are the quickest to learn the importance of self-reliance, and they will quickly win the confidence of those less quick to adapt to their new environment. Through a process of trial and error, a new leader will emerge, namely, the individual who has successfully passed through the most trials with the fewest errors. Given his track record, it is natural that others will look upon him as the man whose judgment should be trusted in the future. It is his repeated success in passing safely through stormy seas, not his official title, that gives a captain a reputation for wisdom and foresight, bestowing on him the recognized charisma that becomes a source of power over others. So it is with anyone able to help others survive under a new condition fraught with uncertainty. Still, there is always a limiting factor.

Even the wisest man can only be said to have shown foresight *up to now*. Past incidents of successful foresight do not exclude the possibility of future mistakes, which explains why so many confused and troubled human beings have earnestly hoped to find some guarantee of infallibility in their wise men. In a crisis we all want to believe that there must be someone who knows exactly what to do. It is also why we are so grateful when it turns out that someone really does. In short, the catastrophe that robs us of the security provided by our inherited tradition is the opportunity for a select individual to break from the pack and to emerge as its leader.

IN 1902 J. M. Barrie, the future author of *Peter Pan*, wrote *The Admirable Crichton*, a wildly successful stage comedy that would run for 828 performances. Barrie's play offers a rare, amusing illustration of the topsy-turvy effects of catastrophe on a hidebound traditional order. A British aristocrat, Lord Loam, sails off on his yacht, with his family, friends, and servants, including his butler named Crichton.[3] Lord Loam is a devout socialist: He believes that all men are equal. According to Lord Loam, there is no difference between him and any other man. He even condescends to say that he and his butler are brothers under the skin and therefore perfectly equal. Crichton, on the other hand, could not disagree more. Despite the fact that he is close to the bottom of the social ladder, Crichton is a staunch defender of the established hierarchy of his time. There must always be lords, and there must always be butlers who wait on them. That is the way of things, and it is beyond human power to change the natural order. (Crichton would have approved of the politics of both Samuel Johnson and Edmund Burke.)

A disaster at sea dispels Lord Loam's socialist illusion. It is Crichton's natural leadership ability that saves the shipwrecked survivors after they have scrambled onto the nearest desert island. Overnight a new inequality springs up. Lord Loam, helpless to look after himself, becomes Crichton's butler. Crichton, now the chieftain of the island colony, plans to marry Lord Loam's daughter, whom he has always loved in his heart of hearts, as she has always loved him in hers. Alas, their nuptial plans are cruelly disappointed when a ship appears out of the blue to "rescue" them. Back home, everyone returns, without much enthusiasm, to their former roles in society. The only change is the bittersweet sense of collective loss—somehow everything seemed better arranged on that island.

When a catastrophe shipwrecks a long-established social order, there will be a jolting return to the law of the jungle. This plunge back into chaos will bring down the mighty, but for others it will come as a golden opportunity. Individuals who counted for nothing before the catastrophe now find they have exactly those talents required for getting ahead in the shattered ruins of the *ancien régime*. Certainly luck will play a role, but by and large, the individuals who best adjust to the new circumstances will be those most fit to deal with these circumstances. If survival requires brute strength, then the brute will be the fittest; if cunning, then the cunning will be the fittest. The toppled aristocracy, formed by tradition and chosen by birth, will be quickly replaced by an oligarchy based on the possession of the requisite survival skills, often quite predatory and brutal skills. Nevertheless, a revolutionary new principle is at work. For in the emergent social order, success will be decided by merit and not birth status. A meritocracy always follows the shattering of the "cake of custom," though what counts as merit depends on the nature of the crisis.

BECAUSE A MONOLITHIC TRADITION is virtually inescapable as long as everything is going smoothly, freedom and independence must originate in social breakdown, in chaos, in catastrophe, in eruptions of the unknown and the unfamiliar. It is only when the principle of social inertia has failed that men are forced to improvise their own rules and routines. Only then are men compelled to take charge of their own fate—compelled simply because there is no one else to take charge of it for them.

This is the moment when reason makes its grand entrance, though much less grand than is often supposed. It is a pleasant illusion to think that, in the midst of a crisis, reason will descend from heaven like the *deus ex machina* of a Greek tragedy, bringing down to earth the Platonic forms that are glimpsed by the mind in their solitary and ethereal splendor, creating new rules and laws out of thin air. But this is not the case. Reason begins more humbly. It sneaks onto the stage, hardly noticed by anyone. The survivors of the catastrophe begin by asking each other, "What shall we do?" Looking back over their collective fund of past experience, they will begin to toss ideas around. One might say, "Perhaps we could try doing X." Another will say, "What about Y?" And a third will perhaps suggest doing Z. While plans X, Y, and Z may differ, they all have one thing in common: They have worked in the past and perhaps could work again. Each represents a tradition known to the survivors, but the survivors are not the slaves of these traditions. Instead, each plan is put forth as a living solution to the problem at hand, not as a dead relic to be dug up from the past. The survivors look on these old traditions in a new light, as temporary stopgaps devised to serve a practical function, as options to be appraised and employed to achieve certain ends. Those who tap into these traditions are free to select among them—and this is the first glimmer of something positive in the idea of freedom: the freedom to choose from a set of options. Our dependency on a monolithic tradition is then broken.

A classic example of this principle at work occurred during the debates in Philadelphia on the composition of a new American constitution. In 1787, when the convention delegates gathered in what later became Constitution Hall, Americans already had a constitution, namely, the Articles of Confederation. But not everyone was satisfied with it—though we now tend to forget how many were. The men who had been sent to Philadelphia, often called the Founding Fathers, in writing a brand new constitution for their fledgling nation technically acted without legal authority since their mandate was strictly limited to making only a few revisions in the Articles of Confederation, mainly in the sections that concerned commercial relations among the states. But most of those who assembled in Philadelphia were sincerely convinced, rightly or wrongly, that their new nation was on the verge of shipwreck, and in a fashion characteristic of independent-minded men, they quickly took matters into their own hands. They simply tossed the old constitution out of the window and began to compose a new one.

The document that they put together was not the product of pure reason operating on eternal essences: It was composed to a purpose. It had to meet certain needs, and the men assembled in Philadelphia were anxious to find ways of meeting these needs. Most wanted a stronger central government than the very weak central government allowed by the old Articles of Confederation. Nevertheless, they recognized that the new Constitution would have to win over those Americans who were suspicious of all forms of government. They knew that they had to build into their new system safeguards to prevent the central government from becoming tyrannical. Thus, they faced a complex challenge that could not be solved without a high degree of creative innovation.

If we look at the path by which they approached the future, we see that it was by a scrupulous reexamination of the past. In writing the new Constitution, the men in Philadelphia began by considering virtually all the forms of political union of which they had any historical knowledge. Some had their favorite models already in their minds. Early in the session Alexander Hamilton announced that his preference was to adopt the British system of government as much as possible, but he was too realistic to believe that this would prove acceptable to the majority of Americans— that large collection of "natural libertarians" who had just fought a war to free themselves from what they called British tyranny. Certain features of the British constitution, however, found parallels in the new system: a president instead of a king; a senate (named after the Roman institution) instead of a House of Lords; and a House of Representatives instead of a House of Commons.

The experimental approach of the Founding Fathers to tradition might be summed up as the spirit of pragmatic eclecticism. They had no desire to create a new system of government out of their own intellectual fancies. Sensible men, they began by asking, What has worked already? What forms of government had already proven their strengths, and what forms had shown their weaknesses? If something had not worked in the past, was it really any more likely to work in the future? The framers of the Constitution used and exploited a variety of traditions. All greatly appreciated the fact that history had provided them an immense fund of political experience to draw upon. None thought of arguing that this or that particular tradition should be tapped simply because it was the tradition of his ancestors. They had Burke's reverence for tradition, but it did not prevent them from wanting to improve on their inheritance.

Among Americans of later generations, there has been a tendency to treat the work done in Philadelphia as if it had been divinely inspired, and to see the Constitution as representing eternal truths. In fact, what was really most significant about this document was the spirit that it represented—the spirit of men who were suspicious of all claims to eternal truth made by any single historical tradition. What counted ultimately was not what had worked for others but what would work for them. In the final analysis, their greatest achievement was to set an example of how intelligent men should behave when they have resolved to be masters of their own fate. They would not be the slaves of tradition, but they would not be damn fools either. Rather, they would consult all the traditions they had knowledge of, would adopt whatever they found worthy of adopting and amend whatever they believed needed amending. They did not fear to innovate, nor were they afraid to imitate.

At times, such independent-minded men will innovate without quite acknowledging that they are doing so. Instead of rejecting outright an inherited tradition that does not reflect their own values and ideals, they will remake it in their own image. A classic instance of this latter phenomenon may be found in the evolution of Protestant religiosity in America. The Puritans who came to America brought along with them the theological doctrines of the Protestant reformer John Calvin, whose influence on American religion remained immense for several centuries afterward. But Americans swiftly began to reinterpret Calvin's stern doctrines to reflect their own independent temperaments. They took from him his theory that the church should be controlled by the congregation, rejecting, as he had, the idea that they should be told what to believe by a church hierarchy—they wanted to decide for themselves what they believed. They agreed with Calvin that their salvation did not depend on membership in the Roman Catholic Church, but they departed from his doctrine of predestination as rapidly and as radically as they could.

While Calvin argued that men had no control over their eternal destination because God had decided all this beforehand, American Protestants were emphatic in proclaiming that they alone were in control of their own salvation. What saved them was not God's eternal will, rather their own personal decision to accept Jesus as their eternal savior. In coming to this conclusion, American Protestants sincerely thought they were being true to the Christian faith, yet they were abandoning a cardinal doctrine accepted by both the Roman Catholic Church and mainstream European Protestant thinkers—the doctrine that men cannot save themselves but can be saved only through the grace of God. While American Protestants were flouting the Christian tradition bequeathed by history, they were nevertheless being faithful to their own values and ideals, which assured them that their destiny—even their eternal destiny—was theirs to shape. Thus, when independent-minded individuals nominally retain an inherited tradition, they will radically revise it in the spirit of pragmatic eclecticism, ignoring what is not to their tastes and overemphasizing what is.

IN ONE sense of the word, pragmatic eclecticism is a tradition, since it can be passed down and imitated. But it is an odd tradition precisely because it is eclectic, that is to say, it encourages us to pick and choose among a variety of traditions, including the traditions of other people from distant cultures. When the Puritans came to North America, for example, they did not adopt the traditional form of government of their homeland back in England, but rather elected to revive the Hebrew commonwealth as it had existed thousands of years before. Ordinary traditions, in contrast, forbid adopting the ways of strangers and foreigners, whose customs are inevitably looked upon as incomprehensible and at times unspeakable.

In addition, pragmatic eclecticism refuses to take any tradition on blind faith. If a tradition is adopted, it is expected to prove advantageous and beneficial to the community. What makes the tradition valuable is not its antiquity or venerability, but its usefulness. This is precisely the standard by which all customs, traditions, and ideas should be judged, according to the principles of American pragmatism. It has often been noted that pragmatism is the only important philosophical movement to have originated entirely on the shores of the New World, and the reasons for its emergence here should be obvious on a little reflection. In the New World, it was often simply impossible to revive the traditions of the Old World, which meant that those who came here had to improvise frequently and invent their own ways and customs, basing their innovations entirely on what worked and what didn't. Before the term *pragmatism* was coined and defined by the late nineteenth-century American philosophers Charles Sanders Peirce and William James, ordinary and often illiterate Americans had been practicing it in their everyday life for several centuries without ever suspecting it. In the New World what mattered was not the genealogy of a custom, but whether it served the purpose for which it had been adopted.

Pragmatic eclecticism is thus an anomaly among traditions. It might make more sense to call it a meta-tradition—a tradition about how to deal with traditions. At the same time pragmatic eclecticism can still act like an ordinary tradition by providing a pattern that can be taken up and used, generation after generation, by those who are confronted with an unprecedented challenge for which there is no traditional solution. It is the one tradition that men can turn to when all their other traditions fail them. And it is uniquely characteristic of the way in which Western civilization at moments of supreme crisis has confronted its most daunting and perplexing challenges—certainly not always, but frequently enough to have made it a theme, a theme with countless variations. Its makeshift, ad hoc, piecemeal quality lacks the abstract purity and mathematical precision of the products of pure reason; it is the jerry-built engine that clanks and sputters but works, as opposed to the beautifully drawn blueprint of the engine that doesn't.

Granted, there is a potential defect in pragmatic eclecticism. It may work in a crisis because it is required in a crisis, but what happens after the crisis has been resolved? Once a social order is on its feet again and there are no looming challenges to be faced, human beings will begin to lapse into old habits. Routines will become established, and the automatic pilot of social inertia will take command. Before long, everyone will go back to their old ways, doing today exactly what they did yesterday, and the "cake of custom" will again begin to harden.

Yes, there certainly is such a danger. That is why it is all the more remarkable that many of those who have managed to claim their independence from the dead hand of tradition have devised a way of passing on their own independent attitudes and ideals to future generations. But this presents a challenge, because there is only one way that human beings can effectively transmit to their children their own values and ideals, and that is by means of tradition. In the case of normal traditions, this is easy. The children are taught simply to do what their ancestors have always done and never to vary one iota from the preordained paths of their cultural traditions. But how do you pass on a tradition that says, "You must never become a slave of tradition, you must always think and act independently"?

All traditions are passed down through the visceral code of the community. This code establishes a set of do's and don'ts by which children must abide. Sometimes these rules are put into words, but more often they are expressed through actions alone. When a mother spanks a child for lying, she does not need to preach a sermon against lying—she has gotten her message across. Similarly, when she hugs and kisses her child for an act of courage, it is unnecessary for her to give a discourse on why courage is a virtue. Again, she has gotten her point across quite effectively. Lie and you will be scolded, spanked, and ostracized. Act courageously, and you will be petted, loved, and admired. But the mother, in getting her point across, is also instilling in her child the values of her community, provided that the values she is communicating to her child are those shared by others in her culture. And so, long before any of us have gained mastery of our spoken language, long before we can reason or heed the reason of others, we have all become fluent in the visceral code of our society. We feel shame at what our society wishes us to be ashamed of and take pride in what our society makes us feel proud of. But it is readily apparent that not all cultures instill the same code in their young. Some teach their children that it is better to submit to those who have power over you and that it is foolhardy to try to stand up for your rights under these circumstances. In contrast, some societies instill a radically different visceral code. From an early age, they make their children deeply ashamed to submit to bullies without putting up a fight or struggle. They will also make them feel ashamed to lose their self-control and will instill a gut-level revulsion at the very thought of becoming a slave to their base impulses and appetites. Anything that lessens self-control, such as alcohol, sex, and drugs, is viewed as a potential danger.

A people can achieve freedom and autonomy for their own generation, but the only way they can hope to pass on their own hard-won spirit of independence is by instilling in their young a visceral code that makes submission shameful, while prizing the struggle for liberty. In addition, they must also instill in their descendants the necessity for self-control and self-mastery, which will require them to prohibit certain quite natural desires. They have to protect their children from the temptations of the flesh that would undermine their independence of spirit. Like the children of Israel liberated from the house of bondage in civilized and prosperous Egypt, they must rigorously prohibit any return to the customs and traditions that might tempt them to embrace their old life. They must forbid the worship of the golden calf and shame those who hanker after the savory fleshpots of Egypt. In all possible ways, they must guard against backsliding by creating traditions to keep their children from returning to the good old bad ways for as long as humanly possible.

Traditions of independence differ most radically from most other traditions by their design: they are meant to produce a definite personality type, rather than just perpetuating customs and institutions. Ordinary traditions mold the individual to fit his culture, but the traditions of independence mold the culture to create strong and ethically autonomous individuals. Other traditions tell the individual, "These are the rules you must obey, and these are the routines to which you must bind yourself. Do not think of defying them, or rebelling against them." The traditions of independence, on the other hand, are design to maximize individuals' sense of control over their own lives.

That is why wherever you find the tradition of independence you find people who delight in telling stories that uphold shining examples of individual heroism to be admired and imitated—men and women who were resolved at all costs to be masters of their own destiny, who were willing to defy the powerful and to rebel against the status quo. The traditions of independence tell the young, "This is how you stand up for yourself. This is how you defend your dignity and protect your freedom."

THE HERO and the heroine are central figures in the traditions of independence. American Indians celebrated heroic warriors who could maintain an attitude of contemptuous defiance even in the midst of the most gruesome torture. The Greeks developed elaborate myths and stories to pass on the glory—often the tragic glory—of their pantheon of heroes, both real and imaginary, from Achilles and Prometheus to Antigone and Socrates. The Hebrews delighted in recounting the exploits of their heroes and heroines, such as Joshua, Joseph, Esther, Judith, and David, while the Roman cast of heroic characters—Lucretia, Cincinnatus, Horatio at the bridge, and Cato the Younger—similarly provided inspiration across the centuries. The literature developed by the Germanic barbarians is rich in heroes, from Beowulf to Siegfried, while the liberty-loving Swiss have their William Tell.

Typically, the traditions of independence are passed on not by philosophers and thinkers, but by storytellers. Often, to make their stories more exciting or more inspiring, the storyteller will embroider the tale, making the hero even more heroic, and the acts of defiance more noble and glamorous. From the point of view of the strict historian concerned to know only what really happened, the fables of the storyteller will inevitably be subjected to withering scrutiny and criticism. The historian will point out inconsistencies and improbable events that cast doubt on whether these heroes ever really existed. Worse, the moralists of a later age will argue that even if these heroes actually did live, there was nothing at all admirable about them. Indeed, by the more civilized standards of a later age, they will seem little more than brutish louts.

Among ancient Greeks, this process of debunking the heroes of the Homeric epics began with the tragedians Aeschylus, Sophocles, and Euripides. Men who were held up for admiration in Homer, such as Agamemnon and Ajax, were treated with ridicule and contempt. The increasing sophistication of the Greek mind made it impossible for intelligent, fifth-century B.C. Athenians in the time of Socrates to see what their more primitive and less civilized ancestors found so fascinating about a pouting, capricious psychopath like Achilles. The same process occurred with the Hebrews. The book of Joshua, for example, was composed by storytellers who intensely admired him as their great national hero. Jehovah commanded him to kill every living thing in the promised land of Canaan—men, women, children, livestock— and Joshua faithfully carried out this command. Judged by later and more civilized standards, however, Joshua's supposedly heroic actions looked suspiciously like genocide. To us, it seems obvious that Joshua should have first tried to live in a state of peaceful co-existence with his new neighbors. But this overlooks the fact that the first imperative of Joshua's people was to preserve in its simple purity the tradition of independence that they had acquired through great pain and sacrifice during their wandering in the wilderness. The unspoken command, "Thou shalt not backslide and become like unto the gentiles" took precedence over considerations of humanity.

After escaping from Egyptian bondage and learning how to live like free and independent men, the Hebrews did not want to expose themselves or their children to the culture and religion of an alien people that lacked their hard-won traditions. They recognized that they had created an exceptional culture, and they saw that its uniqueness would inevitably be jeopardized by any intermingling with the native population. Like the Puritans who came to

America, the Hebrews were looking for a new world where they could create a society all their own, from the ground up. Unfortunately, the only way of creating a new world in the land of Canaan was by liquidating those who had previously lived there.[4]

In their quest for freedom, Joshua and his people were prepared to pay this ghastly price, though there is not a shred of evidence that they felt the slightest compunction about it. Yet, despite the ferocious determination of the ancient Hebrews to remain free, to determine their own destinies for themselves, and to never again be the slaves of others, they eventually did backslide, as the Old Testament is constantly reminding us. In the process, they also lost their freedom and their national independence, becoming the subjects of a sequence of great empires. But they were by no means the only freedom-obsessed people to suffer the same fate. The ancient Greeks defied the Persian Empire's attempt to conquer and subdue them during the fifty-year-long Persian Wars of fifth-century B.C., but by 146 B.C. the Greek peninsula had fallen completely under Roman control. The Romans, in their turn, would fall prey to the barbarian invaders of the fifth and sixth centuries A.D., who dismembered the once mighty empire into a hodgepodge of fiefs and feudal domains.

Historians have offered a variety of explanations for the rise and fall of free societies. For example, the second-century B.C. Greek historian Polybius accounted for the decline of Greece and the rise of Rome by attributing it all to Fate. Today's historians tend to prefer explanations in terms of economic or environmental factors, solid and tangible things that we can quantify. Yet, the real reason why so many once free societies have lost their heritage of liberty may lie in the eternal antagonism between freedom and civilization. The more you have of one, the less you can have of the other.

As societies become more civilized, sheer animal freedom is necessarily curbed and restrained. The loss of this animal freedom is, in one sense, certainly a good thing. It makes the population more law-abiding and less inclined to violent tumult. But the civilizing process carries with it a potential risk. In his essay "The Bravery of the English Common Soldier," Samuel Johnson reminded his civilized and gentle readers that "they who complain, in peace, of the insolence of the populace, must remember, that their insolence in peace is bravery in war."[5] In other words, a society composed of men and women no longer interested in standing up insolently for their own freedom will be less likely to stand up bravely for the freedom of their society as a whole.

Another way of putting the matter is to say that freedom goes through a life-cycle. It first comes into being when humans are thrown back on themselves to solve challenges that face them, as when a group of immigrants decides to settle down in a new world and discovers that their inherited traditions and institutions are no longer adequate or even relevant to the new circumstances of their individual and collective lives. Yet as these freshly created communities grow more mature over time, they begin to exhibit the normal process of cultural sedimentation as the "cake of custom" begins to harden. Ingenious innovations that were originally made in order to survive eventually become merely routine patterns automatically followed, even when they have ceased to be adequate to new challenges thrown up by the inevitable current of history. The vast expanse of liberty enjoyed by the early pioneers—the liberty to manage their own lives and to construct and create communities according to their own needs and aspirations—is no longer available to their descendants, often, paradoxically, because of the pioneers' success in achieving prosperous, stable, and law-abiding societies.

The authors of the American Constitution had no qualms in scrapping the Articles of the Confederacy, but we, the beneficiaries of their wisdom, would be appalled if anyone dared to toss out "our" Constitution and replace it with one of their own invention. Similarly, stepping quickly from the sublime to the ridiculous, American men today lack many of the frontier freedoms their ancestors enjoyed: for example, they can't bargain away their votes at election time for hard cider and even harder whiskey, nor are they free to spit wads of chewing tobacco on the floor of saloons, restaurants, hotels, and even

Congress—the American habit that Charles Dickens found most revolting when he visited us in 1842. But surely this loss of personal freedom is more than compensated by the resultant elevation in our standards of civilization.

In the eighteenth century, thinkers as diverse as Adam Smith, David Hume, Jean-Jacques Rousseau, and Giambattista Vico were in agreement that liberty goes through a life cycle and that the blessings of civilization always come at the cost of human liberty.[6] The more civilized we become, the less freedom we have for ourselves. Thomas Jefferson, a child of the eighteenth century, was no doubt thinking of the life cycle theory of liberty when he wrote in a letter to his friend James Madison that "a little rebellion now and then is a good thing, and as necessary in the political world as storms in the physical."[7] Popular rebellion, precisely because it disrupts the routines of civilized life, is the only way that the claims of liberty can be reaffirmed against the deadening effects of social inertia. Those rebels who are most keen on preserving and reviving the freedoms enjoyed by their forefathers may at first glance appear to be acting like reactionaries, but if their rebellion is the only method by which a society is enabled to continue to enjoy liberty beyond the terms of its natural life-cycle, then even their political adversaries will have cause to thank them.

Earlier we observed that there are many reasons for thinking that today's populist conservatives are fighting a lost cause. Vast and impersonal historical forces have shaped our nation in ways that have removed it far from the halcyon days of the Founding Fathers. Yet, as I have argued in this chapter, what happened to us is simply what has happened to all other free and self-governing people over time. It is part of the life cycle of liberty. Still, history has shown that those who have fought for lost causes do not always fight in vain. In many cases, against great odds, they have been able to reclaim lost freedoms, though often at the cost of civilized values, like political order and economic stability.

Americans today may find the thesis that civilization comes at the price of freedom startling or even paradoxical, but this is largely due to our relatively high degree of success in balancing the necessary trade-offs between liberty and civilization in the past. Yet the fact remains that civilization is orderly and stable, while liberty, by its inherent nature, is volatile and explosive. Freedom most resembles the element of fire. It can provide for the amenities of civilized life, such as the warmth of a hearth and the exquisite taste of cooked food, but it can also set cities and even whole societies ablaze.

Which is precisely what the American Sons of Liberty did when they felt their precious freedom was under threat. For those who were appalled by the town hall revolts of the summer of 2009, it is helpful to recall the role that rowdiness and paranoia played in laying the foundations for the freedom and independence that Americans are so justly proud of. It is also helpful to remember that most intelligent observers of the time thought that these American rebels were surely fighting a lost cause—How could they possibly believe they could intimidate the mighty British Empire? Yet their "lost cause" turned out to be the beginning of a new era of human liberty.

CHAPTER 7

CRAZY FOR LIBERTY

In their revolt against the liberal elite, today's populist conservatives often cast themselves in the glamorous role of the new Sons of Liberty. But how well do they measure up to the original Sons of Liberty? For one thing, despite the fact that they often employ the same rhetoric as their prototypes, they are a far tamer lot. To those who champion law and order above all else, this is a good thing. But there is another way of looking at this tameness. If those who claim to be fighting in the name of liberty are not prepared to go to extremes, if they are reluctant to break either laws or windows, then perhaps it would be best if they just dropped their pointlessly inflammatory rhetoric, and got back to reality.

Most Americans are likely to have vague recollections about the Sons of Liberty from the history textbooks they read in school. But today's average American has become so accustomed to the hallowed sanctity of the rule of law that he is apt to be shocked by the lawlessness of his supposedly heroic ancestors. After reviewing even a few vignettes of their behavior, he might find himself wondering whether the Sons of Liberty might better be called the Sons of Violence, the name by which they were known to their British detractors. Indeed, he may even think that it would be more proper to simply call them terrorists.

The Sons of Liberty was a secret organization, an impromptu fraternity of self-styled patriots that sprang into existence in 1765 during the first great crisis between England and her American colonies. Their objective was to resist, by any means necessary, the Stamp Tax Act that had recently been passed by the British Parliament. The British had appointed commissioners in America to collect the tax and had sent batches of the stamps to the colonies for this purpose. These stamps were to be affixed to any legal or official documents and on various other kinds of printed material. This offended anyone who owned and operated a printing press—perhaps not the wisest thing the British could do, since the printers controlled the most conspicuous means of inflaming public sentiment of the American colonies—the printing press.

The stamp distributor appointed for Massachusetts was an American-born politician named Andrew Oliver, who had graduated from Harvard College in 1726. On August 14, 1765, a mob in Boston beheaded and burned an effigy of Oliver, then set fire to his stable house, coach, and chaise. When the sheriff of Boston and Lieutenant Governor Hutchinson tried personally to stop the mob, they were both stoned and quickly retreated. The mob then proceeded to ransack and destroy Oliver's house. Oliver escaped personal harm and, not surprisingly, promptly resigned his commission the following day. Less than two weeks later, just for good measure, the mob broke into Hutchinson's mansion, chased away his family, wrecked his furniture, knocked down the interior walls, and removed the cupola from the roof. In addition, they torched Hutchinson's great collection of manuscripts relating to the history of the Massachusetts Bay colony from its earliest days—material he needed for the history of the colony that he would later write in his post-American retirement. They also broke into Hutchinson's well-stocked wine cellar and got royally drunk. Later, when some of the leaders of the mob were arrested, they were released as a result of pressure from the merchants of Boston, amid the background threat of more mob violence.

Four days after the attack on Hutchinson's mansion, the stamp distributor for New York, James McEvers, followed Oliver's lead and resigned his commission. When the actual stamps finally arrived in New York harbor on October 24, placards mysteriously sprang up throughout the city, ominously warning that those who distributed the stamps, and even those who merely used them, should "take care of his house, person, and effects."[1] Shortly afterward the whole city went into an uproar that would last for months, the high point of which was an attack on the house of Cadwallader Colden, one of America's most distinguished intellectuals and the acting governor, in which approximately two thousand people participated. The message was loud and clear: those who tried to enforce the Stamp Act ran the risk of losing their property and, perhaps, their lives.

In hindsight, we are forced to scratch our heads and wonder what all the uproar was about. Was the Stamp Act really an insidious conspiracy to enslave Americans, to shackle them with the chains that bound men in so much of the rest of the world? By our current standards, the tax that the British hoped to impose on the colonies was far from burdensome. It would have cost the average American working man a mere third of a single day's wages to pay it off.[2] (Today Americans work nearly a third of a year to pay their taxes.) Moreover, the Stamp Act was not designed to enrich the English coffers. The money raised was to be used to defray the cost of defending the American colonies, which meant that the funds collected by the Stamp distributors would have been pumped right back into the colonies. Furthermore, the tax was not intended to pay the whole cost of colonial defense, but only a third of it—the rest would be paid by the already very hard-pressed English taxpayers. Surely the American colonies could not reasonably complain when asked simply to pay for a third of their own defense, especially in view of the heavy contribution that the British taxpayers had made during the war that had ended only two years before.

The problem was, in the aftermath of the Seven Years' War (1756–1763), the Americans didn't feel that they needed defending. England's decisive victories over France in Europe, India, and the New World had removed the standing threat to the American colonies from French territorial ambitions in North America. With no great military power threatening their borders, the American colonies were now free to pursue the peaceful paths of making money, tending their farms, and determining their affairs to their own domestic satisfaction.

The nineteenth-century Anglo-Irish historian William Lecky shrewdly observed that in some ways the British had brought the American crisis on themselves. As long as the colonists feared the French to the north, they had recognized their need for British military might and had welcomed British solicitude for their territorial security. But due to the unparalleled success of British forces at the end of the Seven Years' War, the colonies had been relieved from any anxiety on this count. British triumph over the French had resulted in a new and unexpected relationship between Great Britain and her American colonies—the mother had liberated her children from fear, and the children immediately decided that they really didn't need her anymore. They could go it alone—and they did.

By the year 1765 the American colonies actually had been going it alone for quite some time. The British had not conquered their territory in North America in the way the Spanish under Cortez had conquered Mexico. The British had merely peopled it—not as a deliberate policy of state with the intention of creating a vast empire but quite inadvertently through the private initiatives undertaken by a variety of individuals. Some colonists were motivated only by the prospect of making a quick buck, some by the nobler hope of founding communities in the New World that would reestablish the egalitarian purity of the ancient Hebrew theocratic commonwealth. Whether their motives were sacred or profane, the colonists were all animated by the same resistance to control and were equally insistent on making life on their own terms, without external interference from the world they had left behind. Indeed, over a hundred years before the Stamp Act crisis, the pious Puritans of Massachusetts had been prepared to take up arms against what they feared would be an attempt by Great Britain to impose on them the very Church of England they had escaped. Guns had been loaded but none were discharged. Though the crisis quickly passed, it was a sign of what was to come.

The legislative assemblies of the American colonies showed the same stubborn will to independence. The British had attempted to keep some degree of control over colonial affairs by appointing governors and a privy council, which in theory would function much like the king and his council back in England. But the colonial assemblies, whose members were elected by the American colonists themselves, decided to arrogate to themselves the same supremacy that the British Parliament had acquired over the crown during England's tumultuous seventeenth century. Here again the sheer will to resist, to force showdowns with royal authority, was largely triumphant, so that the American colonies had become accustomed to a degree of legislative autonomy that only made them eager for even more.

THERE WAS little sense of gratitude to England among most Americans during the colonial period because they were genuinely convinced that they had made their own little New World by their own efforts. Their attitude was that of the classic self-made man: "I got where I am through my own talents and my own hard work; by my perseverance and intelligence, by my native skill and persistent application. I am what I have made myself to be, and I owe nothing to anyone else for what I have obtained by my own hands." Besides, the American colonists were not alone in feeling that they were right not to feel any gratitude to England. Many in England shared their sentiments.

One of these was Colonel Isaac Barré, who knew the American colonies from firsthand experience. Barré had been with British General James Wolfe when Wolfe was fatally wounded on the Plains of Abraham after his victory at the Battle of Quebec in September 1759; Barré lost his right eye to a bullet wound in the same battle. Barré later became a member of the British Parliament and was present during the bitter debates over what policy England should adopt in the wake of the American colonies' furious resistance to the Stamp Act.

Also present was Charles Townshend. Chancellor of the Exchequer from 1766 to 1767, Townshend today is primarily remembered for the Townshend Acts, a series of attempts to raise revenue from the North American colonies after the repeal of the Stamp Act, but during his lifetime Townshend was considered among the most brilliant parliamentary speakers and debaters of his day. Defending England's position toward its North American colonies, Townshend had given a speech in which he referred to the American colonists as "children planted by our care, nourished by our indulgence . . . and protected by our arms."[3] This proved too much for Barré. "They planted by your care?" Barré exclaimed in indignation. "No! your Oppressions planted them in America. . . . They nourished by *your* indulgence? they grew up by your neglect of them. . . . They protected by *your* arms? they have nobly taken up Arms in your Defence, have Exerted a Valour . . . for the defence of a Country, whose . . . interior Parts have yielded all its little Savings to your Emolument. And believe me . . . that same Spirit of freedom which actuated that people at first will accompany them still."[4]

Perhaps it could be argued that because Barré had spent time in the American colonies, he had become prejudiced in their favor. But the same excuse could not be made for William Pitt, the first Earl of Chatham, who as prime minister was largely responsible for his country's immense imperial expansion during the war with France. He had never been to America, and yet he not only sympathized with the violent resistance of the colonists to the Stamp Act, he openly applauded it on the floor of Parliament. "I rejoice that America has resisted. Three millions of people, so dead to all feelings of liberty, as voluntarily submit to be slaves would be fit instruments to make slaves of the rest."[5]

Voluntarily submit to be slaves? By refusing to resist an exceedingly modest tax by today's standard? Perhaps such hyperbole could be understood if it had come from the mouths of some of the patriotic demagogues back in Boston, like James Otis or Samuel Adams, who were always ranting about the British conspiracy to enslave them. But what can we make of it when these words are spoken by one of England's greatest prime ministers? Men commissioned to collect a fiscally insignificant tax were intimidated by mob violence from performing the jobs that the British government had assigned to them—and William Pitt saluted them for it.

Lord Camden, chief justice of the Court of Common Pleas, went even beyond Pitt in his denunciation of Parliament's attempt to tax the American colonies. On the floor of the House of Lords, Camden rejected the very idea that Parliament possessed any such right to tax Americans. To tax the colonies at all would be, in his words, "absolutely illegal, contrary to the fundamental laws of nature and contrary to the fundamental laws of [the British] constitution . . . taxation and representation are invariably united; God hath joined them, no British parliament can separate them . . . there is not a blade of grass, which when taxed, was not taxed by the consent of the proprietor."[6]

It is one thing to understand how the American colonists, cut off from the motherland by a broad ocean, would become accustomed to the liberty of handling their own affairs and would naturally resent any attempt to take this liberty from them. But what made a British prime minister and a chief justice embrace their cause so zealously?

Pitt took care to explain why he willingly championed men who were rebelling against his own nation. In a speech delivered in January 1775, Pitt declared that the "glorious spirit of Whiggism animates three million Americans who prefer poverty with liberty to gilded chains and sordid affluence, and who will die in defense of their rights as freemen."[7] The American colonists were fighting the eternal battle of Pitt's own party, the Whigs, in their ongoing struggle against the ever-present threat of the recrudescence of governmental tyranny and imperial despotism. Indeed, the political labels that would be adopted by the American revolutionaries reflected this heritage. The patriots, or rebels, were the Whigs; those who remained loyal to England were Tories, the Whigs' political opponents back in Great Britain.

THE SLOGAN "no taxation without representation" is familiar to Americans as the ideological principle under which the revolutionaries operated. Less familiar is the British effort to get around the "taxation without representa-tion" issue, to which they were quite sensitive themselves, by offering the American colonies two different plans.

First, the British proposed that certain colonials, chosen by the Ameri-cans themselves, could travel across the Atlantic to represent their fellow countrymen back home. Americans would thus have representation in Parlia-ment, and hence it would be no indignity to be taxed by it—and it would cer-tainly not be slavery. Second, the British offered the colonies the option of volunteering to pay a reasonable share of the cost for their own defense, leav-ing it to the colonies to determine how this sum might be best raised by their own colonial assemblies—a very hands-off approach, much like that of today's enlightened parent who, in his handling of his teenage children, en-courages them both to make and *keep* their own rules, instead of high-hand-edly imposing his rules upon them.

The Americans didn't buy it. When presented with the first option, they pointed out, quite correctly, that the colonists could never hope to dominate Parliament; they would inevitably be in a minority and hence in danger of losing their already achieved independence in exchange for a mockery of representative government. Their position was simple: They already had governments that represented them—the colonial assemblies. They didn't need any more government than they had already. Indeed, for some, it was already too much. But whatever government they had, it must be firmly under their own control and not located an ocean away in the highly incon-venient age of sail.

When presented with the second option, that of making voluntary con-tributions, the American colonies instinctively recoiled from it. Yes, they would be raising money for their own defense, but this money would be used to pay British soldiers, or worse, German mercenaries, to defend them from their enemies. And since the French had already been defeated, what external enemies were left against which the American colonies needed defending? There were still the Indians, of course, who continued their own struggle for liberty against the encroaching newcomers, resisting the colonials as fiercely as the colonials resisted the Stamp Act and with far better reason. But there was no need of a professional army to fight the Indians—to keep them in check was work that many colonials believed could be easily handled by their own militias. Indeed, they had done this on innumerable occasions, not always to the credit of their slender humanitarianism.

Thus, there were many stingy American colonials and hard-pressed farmers and merchants who were unwilling to pay for an army when there was already a voluntary militia force that could be appealed to. Other colonials, less concerned with financial motivations, were deeply distrustful of the very idea of a standing army—and not just the standing army of foreigners, such as the British wanted to introduce, but even of standing armies of home-grown patriots. These colonials, like most people, had no interest in paying for something that they deeply feared, namely an army that could always be used to oppress them in the name of law and order.

The American colonials' dread of a standing army, however, was not a product of the New World. In fact, they had welcomed the army commanded by Wolfe when it had won French Canada for the British; but an army fighting a war was looked upon as a very different creature from an army that was just lolling around in peacetime, billeting itself in ordinary people's homes and conducting itself with bravado and bluster. Such armies were deplorable and dangerous—an attitude that the colonists had brought with them from England, where there had always been a negative attitude toward professional soldiers. This deep dread of a standing army was as unique a product of the English political tradition as cricket is of its sporting traditions. No one else would ever have come up with ideas so crazy. In a world full of powerful standing armies, like the superb French army, who else could be expected to defend your homeland?

A people who live in a violent world, in which aggressors are always on the march, have basically two choices. One is to be conquered and to submit; the other is to resist conquest by the same methods as those trying to conquer you. However much one might distrust standing armies as a general rule, a standing army that you pay for is a better alternative than a standing army that your enemy pays for; or, worst of all, a standing army that your enemy does not pay for but encourages its members to loot and pillage their way to personal financial compensation through your cities and villages and homes.

Seen in this light, a standing army is simply the lesser evil to the alternative of being maimed, murdered, and robbed by foreign troops. But in fact many nations went far beyond accepting such professional armies as a lesser evil and actually saw in them a positive good. The French, for example, tended to boast of their grand armies while extolling military glory as the noblest pinnacle of human ambition. But to "free-born Englishmen," as they liked to call themselves, the standing army was not seen as their protector but as a threat to their "ancient liberties." A king intent on achieving despotic authority could use such an army to impose his will, to take whatever he wanted by the sheer force of arms. He would not need to beg Parliament for money; he could abolish it with a wave of the hand and resort to the arbitrary method of tribute production that was the economic basis of all other great states and empires throughout human history, from the Assyrian, the Chinese, and the Aztec, to the French, the Russian, and the Ottoman empires.

Under a forcible tribute system, men not only had to give up single blades of grass without their own consent, they had to throw in their tables and chairs, their livestock, and their grain, and, of course, their money. (Hard cash was always best where it was available.) The only hope of tax relief, under such a system, was to lead an armed rebellion against the authorities, but since the authorities were in control of a fine standing army, what hope could rebels have of achieving their objectives? Even if those in authority under the present regime were vanquished by the successful rebels, it was more than likely that these rebels, once securely in the seat of power, would find themselves resorting to the exact same methods to expropriate wealth. People are inclined to make the rational choice when confronted with the classic challenge of the robber whose gun is pointed in their face: "Your money or your life!" So best not to start down that path at all is how many felt about standing armies.

Herein lies the problem with brute-force despotism: Once it has developed, it becomes almost impossible to resist. Few rebels in history have been a match for a well-disciplined professional army. Therefore, safety lies in refusing to let despotism get started, to prevent it from taking its first baby steps down the road to serfdom and ultimately slavery. The monster Tyranny must be strangled in its crib, long before it is allowed to become a raging full-grown Godzilla able to trample all in its way.

This explains why those who are jealous of their liberties, as the American colonists notoriously were, will be inclined to overreact to the slightest hint of oppression. They will behave as if they are in the grip of a persecution mania, reading even the innocent behavior of other people as evidence of a sinister conspiracy to rob them of their freedom. Their violent and exaggerated response to perceived threats will strike neutral parties as smacking of collective insanity, a monomania that is obsessed with seeing despots in perfectly harmless kings like George III and tyrants in well-meaning administrators like Charles Townshend. But the American Sons of Liberty, if they were collectively insane, had inherited their particular mania from the seventeenth-century Englishmen who had violently resisted what their generation saw as the sinister designs of Charles the First. This rebellious generation of Englishmen had passed their mania along to the Englishmen who had chased James the Second from the throne out of a paranoid fear of a vast Jesuit conspiracy to rob them of their religious liberty.

In trying to justify their passion for liberty, both the English and the American Whigs may have evolved a plausible ideology, and they were certainly fond of invoking nebulous abstractions. Lord Camden talked about the "fundamental laws of nature." Thomas Jefferson discoursed on the inalienable rights with which our Creator had endowed us. Thomas Paine pleaded eloquently for the rights of man. But there is a suspiciously metaphysical quality about these lofty slogans. What good, after all, is a fundamental law of nature that nature herself doesn't bother to enforce? No lightning has ever struck dead a tax collector for taking the last stick of furniture out of the hut of a starving peasant. And what cash value should we put on the inalienable rights assigned us by our Creator if he is willing to turn a blind eye to the horrors of the trans-Atlantic slave trade? And what slave merchant has ever been stopped from whipping a runaway slave to death by recalling that he is violating the rights of man by doing so? Wonderful sentiments, of course, and most noble—without a trace of realism to them. They are designed for a world not of this earth, one in which the lion is willing to lay down with the lamb and the lamb isn't fleeced by the tax collector.

These abstract phrases are misleading if we imagine that men became crazy for liberty because they had skimmed a pamphlet, or deeply perused a treatise, or heard a rebel-rousing speech or a fiery sermon. All that even the most compelling words could do was to arouse deep, visceral sentiments in the hearts and souls of men who were already crazy for liberty, and who were merely seeking a pretext to fight tooth and nail to defend their turf against the encroachments of those who sought, in even the smallest way, to diminish the personal freedom that they could exercise within it. Philosophers may have blown their hot air upon the spark of liberty, but they lacked the power to make it blaze.

To understand the political psychology of those individuals who had managed to escape their chains in colonial America, and who were determined to live free of all future chains, it is essential to grasp that their passion for liberty was intuitive and visceral. It was something that they felt powerfully at the gut level. They were what I have called "natural libertarians." Their resistance to chains had not come from reading books but from their own experience as individuals who had successfully managed their own affairs for as long as they could remember. They had created their wealth by their own efforts. The church they attended was of their own choosing—often they had created it themselves and were dead set on keeping it entirely in their own hands. Their political assemblies were largely under their control. Such individuals saw themselves as their own masters because, for the most part, they had always acted as their own masters. They did not know how to fawn, or to bend their knees before men with titles or power or wealth. They were their own men, and they intended to stay that way—and this has been the attitude of all those with a passion for liberty. Their independence of action had become a tradition that they found it virtually impossible to break.

Yet how did they get that way in the first place? If all were really born free, how did it come about that some had figured out a way to stay free, whereas others had not? Were perhaps some born freer than others?

Yes, in a sense, but not because some people have a freedom-loving gene that other people lack. Rather, a people's aptitude for liberty was the product of the kind of society they were born into. According to Thomas Paine, it was difficult, if not impossible, to be free under the despotic forms of government that existed in the Old World, unless you were the despot or one of his cronies. In Paine's inflammatory writings, such as *Common Sense* and *The Rights of Man,* he offers a radical deconstruction of the origin of European monarchies and aristocracies. They may claim to derive their power and authority from divine decree, but if you look at how they all started, Paine argues, you find that they are nothing more than glorified common thugs, which, historically speaking, was perfectly true. At best, the governments they created were like the protection rackets established by gangsters the world over. We will gladly protect you from gangsters—including us—but at a stiff price. In return for your money, we will not break your windows or your legs.[8]

Therein lay the beauty of the New World, as Paine saw it. There were no forms of despotism, political or religious, to rob the little guy of his freedom and independence. In America he didn't need to overthrow an existing tyranny—he simply had to declare his independence to be rid of it. Of course, this would cause fighting. But once this completely unavoidable violence had come to an end, then the men who had flocked to the New World to escape the despotism of the Old could start afresh, creating their own societies to their own tastes.

Here is one explanation for why some people appear to be born freer than others. They are born in self-made societies. They are the children of men and women who were not subject to any despotic or arbitrary force, because their forebears had gone to a place where they were compelled by circumstances beyond their control to make their own rules—born free, but only because their ancestors had been forced to be free.

CHAPTER 8

SELF-MADE MEN, SELF-MADE SOCIETIES

We can understand a lot about self-made societies by seeing them as analogous to self-made men. A group of people compelled by new circumstances to make up their own rules and routines become a different kind of people from those who inherit their rules and routines from unquestioned traditions, in the same way that the young man who struggles to achieve a position of wealth and high status will be fundamentally different from one who has his wealth and status handed to him on a silver platter. However reluctantly or unselfconsciously, members of a self-made society become innovators and creators. They do so not because they want to, but because they have no choice in the matter if they are to succeed in life.

Similarly, the self-made man is not preassigned a cozy place in the world. In most cases, he does not have the luxury of knowing beforehand what his ultimate place in the world will be. He may start out wanting to be a doctor, but circumstances beyond his control, such as poverty, may close this door to him, in which case he may change his plans and cast off in a new and unexpected direction. He learns to accept reverses, to start afresh with renewed optimism as if he has never known defeat. He is prepared to scrape and struggle to secure his place in the sun—to be a step ahead of his rivals, to outwit and outperform them. The classic self-made man patiently watches for opportunities to seize when they are present. He may lack the polish and the superb self-confidence of the well born; his grammar may be faulty and his table manners rough. And, he may be touchy and a trifle defensive about his origins, just as he is apt to be crudely boastful of his success. He may even be inclined to forget the gratitude he owes to those who helped him on his way. But the faults of the self-made man must be weighed against his virtues, and the same thing can be said of the faults and virtues of self-made societies.

Self-made societies are the creation of self-made men—or perhaps more correctly, of men who are also in the process of making themselves as they make their society. To say that these societies are self-made does not imply that they are made according to a preconceived plan that needs only to be faithfully executed to spring into existence. The men in such a society do make plans, but these plans are endlessly subjected to revisions and readjustments. Some of the plans may even have to be tossed aside and replaced with totally different ones—but these setbacks are taken in stride because the creators of a self-made society are not aiming to mirror some eternal truth; they simply want to achieve a society that suits their own purposes. If their needs and desires change, then what can be more appropriate than to change their rules and routines, in order to bring them in line? Because they are self-made, they have no established authorities that they must answer to.

The experience of making their own rules, their own customs, and their own institutions has a profound impact on the self-image of the individual members of a self-made society. Instead of looking upon their society as a *fait accompli* that has been passed down from time immemorial, they are bound to see it as their own creation. It is not an heirloom they have inherited; it is a living thing that they have constructed out of their own resources. They are dependent on themselves, which is simply another way of saying they are independent, and out of their practical day-to-day independence arises the most paradoxical of all human institutions—the tradition of independence.

IN 1848, with the discovery of gold in California, little clusters of self-made societies sprang up around the rivers and streams that flowed down from the mighty Sierras. These were the famous gold camps, whose homely names read like western fiction: Hangman, Dry Gulch, Git Up and Git, Roaring Camp. The men who came to California either as individuals or in groups found themselves facing a set of unprecedented challenges. Everyone was looking for the same thing—gold. Obviously everyone wanted to claim as much gold as quickly as he could, and thus every gold miner was potentially in conflict with every other gold miner. Indeed, we could imagine the great California gold rush as if it were a TV reality game show with an unlimited budget and an unusually spectacular stage set: What happens when you put thousands of young males together, most of whom are complete strangers to one another and all of whom carry at least one gun and one bowie knife, and then let them loose to grab up as much gold as they can, as quickly as they can, while drinking as much as they can. Those who stayed at home smugly predicted the outcome to be a catastrophic blood-letting due to brawls over competing claims—the kind of violent free-for-all that Thomas Hobbes envisioned as the natural state of man.

Such expectations were not fulfilled. Keen observers who made their way to the gold camps were uniformly astonished to find that the miners had spontaneously evolved sets of rules and regulations that they all accepted as binding on them. No government and no state set down these rules and regulations; the miners did it themselves. The details of these rules and regulations might vary from camp to camp given the different mining conditions, but they all aimed at achieving the same objective: the minimization of possible conflict due to competing claims over the digs. For example, each miner was permitted to stake a claim, but the size of the claim was limited—so many square yards for each man. In addition, there were rules that required a miner to actually be working the claim he had staked or risk losing it. This was necessary to prevent a single miner from laying claim to every patch of land in sight in the anticipation that one day, eventually, he might get around to working it. Over time, as the conditions of the mines changed due to further digging, these rules would be altered by the general consent of the miners themselves, allowing them to work larger and larger areas of the same field.

Just as the self-made young man may be crude and coarse, so too will youthful self-made societies be crude and coarse, though with the same mitigating circumstances: They are doing the best they can. This feature of mining life during the gold rush was epitomized by the frequent resort to lynching in order to punish men who grossly violated the fundamental laws of the camps. Though some thieves were often simply expelled, others were hung on the nearest tree—this is how the mining camp of Hangman acquired its grisly name. Yet in a remarkable number of such cases, records indicate that the miners insisted on going through the motions of formal justice as they understood it, appointing an impromptu judge and jury, and even assigning one of the more learned miners (of which there were a surprising number) to defend the accused against the charges.

In this respect the miners' camps functioned as many other self-made societies. When devising their own rules and routines, they found it advisable to borrow from traditions that they knew of. Back where so many of them had come from, along the eastern seaboard of the United States or from England, they had had firsthand experience with the basic principles of Anglo-Saxon justice, and they simply adapted these to their pressing needs. It was not because the miners had inherited this system that they turned to it, but because the system seemed to them to fit their needs better than any other. It worked, and because it worked, they adopted it in the spirit of pragmatic eclecticism, not out of blind obedience to tradition. And as happens whenever a self-made society adopts a tradition from elsewhere, the miners discovered that the tradition they had adopted was not exactly the tradition they had intended to adopt. The new circumstances that confront all self-made societies forced the miners to violate the letter of the rule of law in their very efforts to implement its spirit.

The rule of law means that people cannot take the law into their own hands. When confronted with a possible crime, they cannot select their own judge and compose their own jury; nor can they appoint counsel to the defendant they themselves have apprehended. Instead, they must turn these matters over to the proper authorities, that is to say, the legally established and recognized governmental agencies. But that was just what was lacking in California at the time. The proper authorities had been left back home, across a wide continent or an even wider ocean. Indeed, had the miners who made their trek to California discovered a set of proper authorities when they arrived, they would not have needed to make their own society—it would already have been established there. But along with the proper authorities of an established society, such as legislatures, law courts, and a police force, they would have discovered that other men had already preceded them in making rules and regulations by which they would have to abide—and it was unlikely that these rules and regulations would have been favorable to the influx of miners. Indeed, the main reason why the United States' government permitted the miners to make their own rules was that its presence in California was far too weak to effectively prevent the miners from doing more or less as they pleased—which explains why the federal government did not try to claim the enormous gold strike for itself. The government left the miners alone because it had no other choice.

Not all mining camps chose to adopt the Anglo-Saxon tradition of justice. Many preferred the tradition of justice prevalent in the Spanish-speaking portions of the New World. Here everything depended on the *alcalda,* the mayor of the pueblo who was given far more power to dispose of lives and property than any single man was permitted in either the United States or England. Certain camps adopted this tradition largely because it required far less day-to-day involvement on the part of the miners themselves. Instead of stopping work on their digs to attend a tedious trial, they turned all such matters over to the judgment of the man that the miners themselves had entrusted with the job of resolving disputes and finding suitable punishment for criminals. Such men were often ignorant of the law, capricious, arbitrary, and not terribly sober—but they got the job done to the general satisfaction of the community. And if they didn't, they could always be replaced. For here, too, the miners, in adapting traditions to suit their own novel circumstances, altered a central feature of this alien tradition. Whereas the real *alcalda* was routinely appointed by a central government, the miners' *alcalda* was ultimately their own creature.

The absence of previously established authorities forced the innovative adaptation of traditions to suit the miners' needs. What was true for the gold miners of nineteenth-century California—the so-called forty-niners— has been true of many other people who have been forced by circumstances to create their own rules and routines. Any time human beings find themselves faced with a radically new challenge, one which cannot be dealt with by their established traditions, they will find themselves in the same situation as the gold miners. But this is no guarantee that they will rise to the occasion with the spunk and gumption—the famous horse sense—of the forty-niners. The gold miners, we must remember, were an exceptional lot to begin with. While they were not yet self-made men, it was their ambition to become such. The very fact that they had spent months traveling from their native homes into an unknown region of the world amply proved their adventurousness. Individuals are not likely to undertake such risks unless they are convinced that they can be the masters of their own destiny. The men who came to California in 1849 believed that they were in control of their own lives and their fate, and they dismissed the notion that they were the helpless victims of circumstances, or of their society, or of the stars. Characteristic of all self-made men, they believed that they could improve their lot by their own efforts. While this trait was unusually prominent in the forty-niners, it has also been prevalent in virtually all those who decide to leave their place of birth in order to better themselves in a foreign land—as generations of immigrants to America have proven. Indeed, key to understanding the American national character is to grasp the fact that ours is a self-made society largely created by self-made men and women, who, like the forty-niners, were prepared to make their own rules and regulations to live by, but who were always willing to adopt for their own purposes the traditions of their homeland or, indeed, traditions they had discovered in the writings of the ancients. The pragmatic eclecticism characteristic of our nation-making was unconsciously imitated by those who created the mining communities of the California gold rush. That same kind of pragmatic eclecticism has also been practiced by other groups of immigrants lucky enough to find themselves on virgin soil and fortunate enough to come equipped with a rich legacy of human traditions—the richer the better.

When confronted with the problem of preserving order in the camps, the miners turned to two different traditions—the Anglo-Saxon system of justice with judges and juries and the Hispanic *alcalda* system. Each system had virtues that the other lacked. If the miners were more concerned with fairness, they might decide to choose the jury system; if they were more concerned with expediency, they might prefer to adopt the *alcalda* system. In either case, the tradition was adopted and subsequently altered by the miners to suit their own purposes, which was to advance their individual objectives as men striving to make themselves by striking it rich. Far from being slaves to a single tradition, they had become the master of several. The legacy of human political traditions was a smorgasbord from which the miners could pick and choose. It was no longer an incubus that held them in its grip.

In the case of the miners, it was in their interest to have at hand a number of traditions that had been devised by different people under different circumstances. In our reality TV show scenario, imagine that we have just thrown together thousands of young men who lack any experience or knowledge of a justice system—that is to say, thousands of well-armed males who have never heard of a judge or a jury or a law book, who have never had any experience of an *alcalda* or of any other figure of legitimate authority, but who do know how to resolve a dispute with a pistol or a knife. Even if one of them is gifted with the inventive genius attributed to the ancient sages, how would he persuade the others to accept an alternative to the Hobbesian war of all against all? It was tradition that came to the miners' rescue, but, as we have seen, a radically new sense of tradition as a pattern, a recipe that could be used so long as it served the particular purpose for which it was chosen and tinkered with or discarded the moment it ceased to play the role for which it had been chosen.

The miners were lucky in two ways. First, some of them were familiar with those European political traditions that had evolved precisely to avoid the Hobbesian condition of a war of all against all. Second, they knew what would happen to them if they did not adopt one of these traditions. They recognized that if they could not all agree on some system of justice, none of them would be able to fulfill their personal objectives in coming to the gold fields in the first place. Thus, while it is possible to argue that the miners had returned to a state of nature in the gold fields of California, they had brought with them something that gave them an advantage over the Hobbesian individual doomed to a solitary, nasty, brutish, and short existence—they were beneficiaries of a peculiar tradition that told them that individuals like themselves could pursue their own advantage without incessant conflict by behaving "reasonably" with each other, where behaving reasonably meant "I will respect your independence if you respect mine." Far from indulging in unbridled, anything-goes competition on the laissez-faire model, the miners recognized a collective need for their community to impose rules regulating the exercise of each individual's desire for acquisition of wealth.

Furthermore, it was only when something went wrong that the miners needed to call on either the Anglo-Saxon or the Spanish system of justice. As long as each miner respected the claims of the other miners and each worked his legitimate stake as recognized by the entire community, all went well. In part, this degree of mutual cooperation was achieved through the agency of good will and the principles of fair play that held such a prominent place in the miners' conception of proper behavior. But, as many earlier observers pointed out, the fact that every man carried his own pistol and bowie knife played a critical role in establishing a healthy respect for the independence of the other fellow. Even the biggest bully will think twice before trying to boss around a skinny kid toting a gun.

THERE IS a popular cliché that tries to solve the riddle of liberty by saying that one man's liberty ends when it begins to infringe on the liberty of others.

No doubt; but who is the person who gets to decide when there is such an infringement? If I am smoking a cigarette at my table in the restaurant, and there is no law to prevent me from doing so, then who is to say that I am infringing on your liberty—except you? You might tell me not to smoke while you are eating, but then I will argue that you are infringing on my liberty. It is no insult to human nature to observe that we are naturally more inclined to notice when other people are infringing on our liberties than we are to notice when we are infringing on theirs.

Herein lies the problem with any attempt to define rights in an abstract, once-and-for-all way. If an individual does not have the right to define what his rights are, if he must accept only those rights that others feel inclined to bestow upon him, then his rights are at the mercy of other people, and he will possess only so many of them as they permit him to possess. But if the individual is permitted to determine what his rights are, without consulting others, then he will invariably come into conflict with other people who are determining their own rights on the same basis. They will clash; but this clash does not prove that either of them is wrong to defend his rights as he has defined them. On the contrary, it is by virtue of this clash that we have an incentive to look for some means by which we can reconcile differing claims without dangerously escalating the conflict to the point where both parties have more to lose than either considers worth losing. It is only when we see that the other individual will stand his ground that we are tempted to give up some of our own.

If only one of the miners had been armed with a gun and a bowie knife, he could have played the tyrant over the others, forcing them to do his will. When the bully can boss everyone else around because they are afraid of him, there is nothing that will induce him to play fair with others, or to try to reach compromises with them. But when the would-be bully is confronted with a community in which everyone else is also armed with a gun and a bowie knife, he will recognize that he cannot hope to get what he wants simply by threatening others since they have the means to threaten him back.

A community that is trying to regulate everyone's conduct in accordance with a standard of fairness must have recourse to the threat of extreme measures against those who refuse to play by the rules everyone else has established. Otherwise, the community will be preyed upon by bullies and violent gangs. Many of those who obey the rules will do so because they recognize the justice of the rules. Others will be happy to live in a community with settled rules, even if they don't agree with some of them. Both groups, however, will recognize the fact that they must have some method of enforcing universal obedience to their rules, because if some can exempt themselves from their rules, the whole point of having rules will be lost and people will return to the law of the jungle.

The bully is always happy with the law of the jungle. It naturally favors the strong and the ruthless, the individual thug, or the violent gang. Thus, the only way the bully can be kept in line is through the ever-present threat of violent resistance on the part of those he desires to boss around, and the same principle operates in those cases in which the bully is a group as it does when the bully is a lone individual. The moment a certain group no longer fears another group, they will begin to rob the latter group of their freedom of action. The source of the fear may vary. In one age, the rulers may fear the pitchforks of the peasants. In another, they will fear the power of the ballot box. But in either case, the fear is salubrious insofar that it makes the governors more solicitous to gain the consent of the governed than they would be otherwise. So, too, in one age a man will fear the power of another man's dueling sword or pistol, while in another age he will fear the power of a lawsuit for libel; again, in either case, the fear makes us think twice before infringing on someone else's rights.

The capacity to make other people think twice before they try to bully and boss us around is a character trait shared by all self-made men. Everyone who is determined to remain in charge of his own life must develop a personal style designed to immediately warn off those who wish to manage and manipulate him. To borrow a word from the nineteenth-century American frontier where it originated, self-made men must become ornery.

CHAPTER 9

THE IMPORTANCE
OF BEING ORNERY

Since the rise of the Tea Party movement to political prominence, there have been many attempts to explain the movement purely in terms of ideology. But those who try to comprehend the meaning of today's populist revolt by examining its various slogans and ideals will invariably miss its whole point. The popular anger is not driven by intellectual arguments, which means that it cannot be brought to an end through intellectual arguments. Instead, it is deeply rooted in a specific human character type, which I have earlier dubbed the *natural libertarian*. Normally the natural libertarian simply wants to be left alone to pursue his own affairs. He only becomes rebellious when he believes, rightly or wrongly, that there are forces conspiring to rob him of his liberty. It is then, and only then, that he fights back and resists—but only in self-defense. Indeed, today's populist rebellion might be best understood in terms of what Freudian psychologists call a "defense mechanism." Defense mechanisms spring into play whenever an individual feels under threat psychologically, and they serve to protect his sense of identity. Often these defense mechanisms are immature and unhealthy, such as denial, fantasy thinking, and projection. Others are helpful and healthy, such as sublimation and humor. But the natural libertarian, whenever he feels that his self-image as a free and independent individual is under assault, will turn to a defense mechanism that is not listed in the classic Freudian inventory: he will become ornery.

Most languages have words that are difficult, if not impossible, to translate. I suspect *ornery* may be one of these. It first showed up in America around 1815, and it is said to be a contraction of *ordinary,* used in the invidious sense of vulgar and plain. Over time, however, *ornery* has come to have several other meanings. According to Webster's Third International, it can also mean "lazy, shiftless" as well as "independent and individualistic sometimes to the point of being eccentric." In addition, *ornery* can also mean "having a touchy disposition: inclined to be short-tempered: cantankerous."

At first glance, these definitions seem to be at variance with each other. Plenty of people have been shiftless and lazy without showing much independence of character, while people who are individualistic to the point of eccentricity have frequently been bundles of energy. Some eccentrics are touchy and short-tempered, but others are kindly and generous. Nonetheless, there is one quality that these different personality types have in common. They all resent being bossed around, and when confronted with those who try to manipulate them, they will all respond by acting cantankerous—that is to say, ornery.

Orneriness is often a highly effective defense mechanism against bossy people and bullies. Slaves in every culture have proverbially been accused by their masters of being shiftless and lazy, but in fact they were simply being ornery, and for the best of all possible reasons: They felt little inclination to do back-breaking labor so that someone else could live a life of luxury. Similarly, a person who has established his public credentials as an eccentric is immediately freed from the responsibility of conforming to the wishes and desires of other people. Every eccentric puts a placard around his neck saying: "I will behave as I want to behave. You cannot make me do a thing." And the people around him quickly adjust their expectations accordingly. They leave him be.

To be ornery is to maintain one's personal liberty, or at least a bit of it, even when it is being assailed by those around you—or, rather, especially then. Those passionate for their own freedom naturally identify with the hissing rattlesnake that graced many banners and standards during the American Revolution.[1] The snake's warning is clear: Don't tread on me, because if you do, I will bite you. Like the rattlesnake, orneriness often turns into truculence and outright defiance, even rebellion, when it is pressed against the wall and has no other option. Push an ornery man too far and he will revolt.

At the same time, one of the most striking characteristics of ornery people is that they don't want to boss other people around any more than they want to be bossed around themselves. In the golden age of American movies, the ornery man was often the hero, especially in Westerns. John Wayne's film persona was a man who would not let anyone else walk all over him but who had no desire to walk over other people. When Wayne's character saw other people being walked on, he would even rally to their defense. He often stood up to the bully to defend people he didn't know.

The ornery man's idea of liberty is the liberty to be left in peace, to tend to his own affairs, to pursue his business, make his home, raise his kids, without being told what to do or how to do it by other people. But there are also ornery men and women who want to be left in peace to go out to bars, to do drugs, and to watch dirty movies. There are ornery saints and ornery sinners, ornery heroes and ornery misfits.

DURING THE wee hours of June 28, 1969, a Saturday night, eight policemen, only one in uniform, raided the Stonewall bar in Greenwich Village, a notorious after-hours hangout for New York homosexuals and drag queens. This was not the first time the bar had been hassled by the cops, but something happened that made it the last time. That Saturday night, many of the bar's clients were escorted outside the bar; others were arrested. While waiting for the roundup to end, the gathering crowd got restless. They started shouting catcalls. They picked up rocks and bottles, and began throwing them at the police. The police tried to break up the angry crowd, but new protesters quickly swelled the ranks. The riot went on for days, making national headlines all around America. Instead of taking whatever was dished out to them, the drag queens fought back, and by fighting back they initiated a movement that would transform once despised "queers" and "faggots" into proud gay men and women, capable of claiming their fair share of human dignity. No one planned the Stonewall rebellion. Most rebellions, like this one, come out of the blue, often shocking the rebels themselves every bit as much as those against whom they are rebelling. Looking back, people often think: No one saw it coming. But in every case, it was coming. It was already brewing deep in the souls of those who were fed up with being pushed around and bullied.

On December 1, 1955, Rosa Parks was riding on the bus in Montgomery, Alabama. When the driver asked her to give up her seat to a white person, Rosa Parks refused. She would not budge, despite the Alabama law that clearly imposed this obligation on every black woman and black man of every age. The Jim Crow laws of that time were explicit: Whites came before blacks, everywhere, always. Rosa Parks was fully aware that she was breaking the law, but her orneriness told her that this was a law that badly needed to be broken. She felt, as ornery people so often do, that there was some kind of higher law that trumped mere man-made law. If she didn't have a legal right to keep the seat that she had chosen to sit in, then she had some other kind of right.

Like Rosa Parks, all ornery people have a quasi-mystical intuition of a higher standard of right and wrong than the positive law established by human institutions. They have tried to express this intuition in words and even in systems of philosophy. In contemporary jargon, the sense of a higher law is expressed in terms of moral rights or human rights, as if these were transparently self-evident concepts, which they certainly are not. In previous centuries the foundation of this higher law was a God-given faculty called conscience, or the authority of Nature and Nature's God that Thomas Jefferson invoked in the Declaration of Independence. The eighteenth-century

German philosopher Immanuel Kant believed he had discovered this higher law in the highest authority of all, Reason.

According to Kant, it was Reason itself that revealed to all human beings a set of strict ethical commandments called categorical imperatives, which must be obeyed unconditionally, without any regard for the consequences, even when they clash with man-made law. The basic principle behind these commandments was simple: Treat all human beings as ends-in-themselves, and not merely as means to your own end. Human beings are not objects to be used and bossed around, but persons whose individuality and independence must be at all times respected. Yet no thinker, however great, can adequately capture in mere words the ornery person's powerful intuition of what is just and fair *for him*. Perhaps children express this intuition better than philosophers when they protest to a playmate, "You can't have it. It's mine." This is in effect what Rosa Parks said: "You can't have this seat—it's mine." It is what the drag queens at Stonewall said: "You can't have this bar. It's ours." It is also what the Americans said to Great Britain during the War for Independence: "You can't have this country. It belongs to us."

ORNERY MEN and women who rebel are not revolutionaries. They don't want what other people have; they only want what is theirs. Revolutionaries try to change other people. Rebels try to keep other people from changing them. The Great English Rebellion of the seventeenth century was caused by people who thought, rightly or wrongly, that King Charles the First was conspiring to take away their ancient liberties and to rob them of their Protestant faith. The Soviet Revolution, on the other hand, was brought about by intellectuals who wanted to create a new man in a worker's paradise—a creature no one had ever seen, in a world that men had only imagined, and even then, not very clearly. Those who rebelled against King Charles were ornery. Those who embarked upon the disastrous Soviet utopian experiment were visionary ideologues.

Normally the ornery man is quite confident about his own wits. He may never doubt for a moment that he is smarter than most. Indeed, ornery people quite often suffer from this delusion, but they don't tend to act on it. Their often ill-founded self-conceit is merely protective—it keeps them from being suckered by charlatans who will not hesitate to use their superior smarts to take advantage of others. At the same time, ornery people don't think their smarts entitle them to control anyone else's life. They may give advice very earnestly but they will never attempt to force you to follow their advice if you have not been genuinely persuaded by it. Ornery individuals will often think that other people are complete jerks, totally lacking common sense; but they will never believe that it is their mission in life to set them straight. When seeing someone else act the fool, the ornery man will shake his head in dismay or disgust, and just walk away. He seldom tries to save people from themselves, as he certainly doesn't want them to try to save him from himself.

Common sense is the mode of intelligence favored by the ornery. It is what every man can see for himself without any scholastic training. You do not need to have a degree in anything in order to have it; and even the most exalted university degree cannot give it to an individual who doesn't already possess it. Indeed, ornery people who lack a college education will even suspect that too much education can damage a man's natural faculty of common sense—and they may have a point. They resent the idea that the "advanced" thinking of the highly educated gives them access to a special type of knowledge unobtainable to the average man, and that this knowledge confers upon the educated classes the right to make decisions for the entire society. Ornery people champion the truth revealed by common sense because it is an inherently democratic truth. It cannot be claimed as the monopoly of a cognitive elite. It belongs to everyone.

This explains why when an ornery guy cannot see the reason for something himself, his mind will not be changed when he is assured that so-called experts can see a reason he can't. The ornery man will greet the pontifications of Nobel Prize winners with the same skepticism he greets those of his barber. He will always inherently distrust those who claim to know something important that he doesn't. If he doesn't know it, it can't really be that important. And, as a corollary to this belief, it is the nature of ornery people that they would rather be wrong if being right requires them to ask another person for the right answer. This is why ornery men do not like to stop and ask directions. Instead, ornery men prefer to *explore* their way to their destination, often taking surprising scenic routes that open up unexpectedly glorious vistas. Better one or two extra hours of driving time than to put yourself in a position of cognitive inferiority to another man. Their thinking is, you may start by innocently asking what is the right way to get to Cherry Lane, but before you know it you will be asking what is the right way to raise your kids or get into heaven. The habit of relying on others to do your own thinking is an insidious one, since it is the surest way of losing the habit of thinking for yourself. Ornery people, therefore, nip this habit in the bud.

ORNERY MEN and women do not hold to abstract doctrines about equality. As long as society allows them and most everyone else to be in charge of their own lives, they are not concerned with others being richer than they are. As long as the other person's greater wealth does not translate into power over them, they have no complaints. It doesn't bother them that many worthless people make tons of money, though they may think them silly fools for the way they spend it. There are dozens and dozens of popular country and western songs that harp on this theme, celebrating a deep satisfaction at living the life of the average working-class guy, without much money, but with a wife who loves him and kids to have fun with. They speak the mind-set of the ornery in their attitudes toward those more favored by fortune than they are.

What bothers ornery people is when other people think what they have makes them better. Whether the snobbery is crass and materialistic, based on bank accounts, or whether it is more refined and ethereal, based on inherited status or college degrees or high IQs, ornery people hate it just the same. They don't like to be put down or looked down upon by anyone. But they are remarkably free from the curse of envy, mainly because they are too proud. To envy another would be an admission that they aren't happy to be who they are. The ornery man can appreciate the Latin poet Horace's admonition: *Nihil admirari,* admire or covet nothing. If you let a man know that you envy his lot, you will at once elevate him above you, while placing yourself beneath him. From envy it is often a short step to servility. And to ornery people, there can be no condition worse than servility. Their maxim is never grovel before any human being, figuratively or literally.

The picture that I have drawn of ornery people obviously represents a composite portrait, intended to highlight precisely those characteristics that are most relevant to understanding today's populist revolt. Taken on a case by case basis, it will become quickly apparent that not all ornery people will be ornery in the same way or to the same degree. But this is only to be expected when it is remembered that orneriness is a psychological defense mechanism. Different individuals will perceive different threats to their self-image as independent and autonomous agents, and they will respond to these perceived threats in a variety of ways, depending both on their own individual personalities and their cultural traditions. The orneriness for which frontier Americans were so notorious far exceeded the relatively mild degree of orneriness that the English gentleman felt the need to display, as the following examples make clear.

AT THE Sublime Porte at the Topkapi Palace in Istanbul, where the sultan of the Ottoman Empire traditionally held diplomatic audiences, anyone who approached him was required by strict court etiquette to perform a highly ritualized form of groveling at his feet. Those who routinely came before him thought no more about making their obligatory obeisance than Americans think of shaking hands—to humiliate yourself before the sultan was a way of confirming his position as the dominant alpha male without rivals in the world.

The court ritual of the Sublime Porte presented a considerable challenge to one of the first English ambassadors to the Ottoman Empire. As an Englishman, he had his national tradition of orneriness to uphold. He could not, under any possible circumstances, throw himself in abject servility before another man. It was unthinkable; he would feel the sting of the shame of it for as long as he lived. He also knew that if he went into the presence of the sultan, he could not go up to him and shake his hand, nor could he get away with making a respectful bow, such as he would make to an English sovereign. He had to touch the floor—that was the rule.

The English ambassador came up with an ingenious solution. Whenever he was presented to the sultan, he reached into his pocket, pulled out a handkerchief, and dropped it on the floor. When he "noticed" that it was on the floor, he did the most natural thing that anyone would do under similar circumstance. He reached down to the floor, and he picked his handkerchief back up. The trick worked. The sultan accepted it as gracefully as he could, no doubt because he knew of the English and their fanatical insistence of staying upright in the presence of the mighty. He knew the obvious charade was as much as he could get out of an Englishman, while the English ambassador looked upon his faux obeisance before the sultan as a necessary bit of playacting. He was not acknowledging the rightful authority of the sultan; he was merely humoring the man who held the title. For the Englishman, all legitimate authority required the consent of the governed. Mere brute power, such as the sultan possessed, could coerce others into obedience, but it would be the obedience of slaves and not of "free-born" Englishmen.

Yet, by and large, the English did not carry their orneriness beyond a certain point. An Englishman might refuse to grovel before the sultan, but he had no qualms offering a measured, stately, and dignified bow before his own monarch—indeed, it would have struck him as the coarsest insolence if he failed to do so. But his American cousins, once they broke away from their motherland, were quite proud to boast that they had no king before whom they needed to bow. Indeed, they made it a maxim not to bow before anyone. Furthermore, this proud attitude—one might even call it impertinence—was not limited to wealthy and powerful individuals in America. It could be found among all classes of American society, including the very lowest. In the United States, those whom Europeans frankly called "the vulgar rabble" thought of themselves simply as the people, and they showed not the slightest inclination to stay in their proper place at the bottom of the social hierarchy. In the Old World, the lower classes were expected to defer graciously and automatically to their betters, and many of them did just that. When French aristocrat Alexis de Tocqueville came to our shores in 1831,[2] he was struck by a culture in which the ideal of deference had completely disappeared. In France, as he later explained in his most famous book, *Democracy in America,* it was not at all rare for the servant of a great man to feel honored to wait and attend to him, and even to take pride in his display of deference to his superior. But in America, generally speaking, servants did not behave this way. They resented being servants, and when given the opportunity to become their own masters, they seized it with enthusiasm and never looked back. De Tocqueville accepted our rejection of the ideal of deference as simply an inevitable consequence of popular democracy, but other foreigners took a less charitable view, among them Frances Trollope, the mother of the English novelist Anthony Trollope.

Mrs. Trollope came to the United State in 1827, at the very eve of the Age of Jackson. She had hoped to start a department store in Cincinnati, Ohio, which at the time was still a bustling frontier town with around twenty thousand inhabitants. The store, called the Bazaar, was described as "a huge, fantastic structure that remained for years a marvel of the community."[3] Fortunately for us, Mrs. Trollope's get-rich-quick scheme failed miserably, and instead of becoming the founder of a great American mercantile family, she returned to England, after her nearly four-year journey in what was then the Wild West, to discover her true calling. Her first of many books appeared on March 19, 1832, and it was titled *Domestic Manners of the Americans.* No European traveler to our shores has ever written a more keen-eyed or delightfully wicked book about us. It is full of droll anecdotes, hilarious snippets of dialogue, and her own acerbic reflections on the coarseness and crudeness of

American life. The book was a smash hit in England, and despite the fact that she had started writing at the age of 52, she would go on to write 113 more books.

Mrs. Trollope did not like the way we lived back in the Age of Jackson. We were far too ornery for her. "The 'simple' manner of living in Western American was more distasteful to me from its leveling effects on the manners of the people, than from the personal privations that it rendered necessary; and yet, till I was without them, I was in no degree aware of the many pleasurable sensations derived from the little elegancies and refinements enjoyed by the middle classes in Europe. . . . The total and universal want of manners, both in males and females, is so remarkable, that I was constantly endeavoring to account for it."[4]

What perhaps shocked Mrs. Trollope the most was the compete lack of deference shown by the lower classes to their betters—namely, Mrs. Trollope herself. For example, one day two of Mrs. Trollope's children decided to explore some of the neighboring hills. When the boys did not come back when expected, Mrs. Trollope set off to find them with a few of her companions. On the way, Mrs. Trollope encountered a woman who generously offered her assistance in finding Mrs. Trollope's children. At first Mrs. Trollope recoiled in horror: "Her look, her voice, her manner, were so exceedingly coarse and vehement, that she almost frightened me," Mrs. Trollope recounted. Horror of horrors, the frontierswoman even put her arm in Mrs. Trollope's and commenced to drag her up the hillside, talking a mile a minute, as if they had always been the most intimate of bosom buddies. Despite the fact that the woman lived close by, Mrs. Trollope writes that "her violent intimacy made me dread to pass her door; my children, including my sons, she always addressed by their Christian names, excepting when she substituted the word 'honey'; this familiarity of address, however, I afterwards found was universal throughout all ranks in the United States."[5]

American egalitarianism in the Age of Jackson was not embodied in our national documents; it was embodied in our visceral covenant—in our manners or lack thereof. The woman who helped Mrs. Trollope find her children was a natural egalitarian—she did not need to read philosophic treatises that taught her all men were born equal. She had acquired her egalitarian spirit from her peculiar cultural tradition, that of the self-made man or woman. When she passed her arm causally through Mrs. Trollope's, she did not mean disrespect; she was simply being friendly. She didn't see any reason why she shouldn't have a neighborly relationship with the educated middle-class Englishwoman whom she startled with her uncouth familiarity. In a land where everyone is equal, not only in the eyes of the law but in the habits of their hearts, it is natural that everyone can be, and should be, friends. Deference divides. Friendship unites.

THE SPIRIT of fraternity is what makes a community of ornery men and women work successfully. Ornery people are willing to volunteer their help and their assistance to those who need it. It might seem a bit paradoxical that those who value their individualism and independence would be so quick to lend a helping hand, but my experience with ornery people has taught me that they are the ones who always turn out to be dependable in a pinch. When you drive your car off the road, they really do jump in theirs to come to your aid.[6] A little reflection again shows the logic behind this spirit.

By their willingness to help out their neighbors and friends, ornery people are protecting their own independence and individualism. Even ornery people realize that one day they may need help. If they did not have other people around who were happy and eager to help them out, who indeed absolutely insisted on helping them, they would be forced to ask for help; and whenever someone is forced to ask another person for help, he is immediately placed in the position of a suppliant. If he must ask for help, he will be giving up his independence as the price of getting help. He will become someone's dependent—and that someone now has power over him. If you must ask a man for something, which he has not cheerfully offered to give you of his own free will, then you will be in his debt. You will owe him. On the other hand, when you can't stop people from helping you, when they won't hear of you refusing their help, when they tell you, as you thank them, to think nothing of what they have done for you, then you can retain your independence and your dignity, beholden to no one. In a community in which everyone is so cheerfully helpful, a helping hand never seems like a handout. It preserves the dignity even of those who are down on their luck.

There was also a negative side to the frontier spirit of fraternity. Mrs. Trollope remarks that in Cincinnati "no one dreams of fastening a door. . . . I was told that it would be considered as an affront by the whole neighborhood."[7] The result was an intolerable situation in which Mrs. Trollope was "exposed to perpetual, and most vexatious interruptions from people" whom she scarcely knew. Unfortunately, the people who were most willing to offer unsolicited help to their neighbors often turned out to be people who were the most keen on sticking their noses, unsolicited, into their neighbor's business.

Mrs. Trollope even saw the negative side to the one feature that virtually all Americans were proud of, namely, the freedom that poor lads had to improve their lot in life through their own hard work. While Mrs. Trollope acknowledged that in America "any man's son may become the equal of any other man's son," this was not wholly a good thing in her opinion. Yes, the possibility of upward mobility was a wonderful "spur to exertion" for the poor boy, but it also was a spur to "that coarse familiarity, untempered by any shadow of respect" assumed by lower classes.[8] The country bumpkin, set on becoming a prosperous self-made man, might make his millions, but his manners would frequently remain that of a bumpkin. A society in which everyone knew his place and was content to stay there suited Mrs. Trollope's taste far more than a society in which ornery men and women refused to remain in the place their betters had assigned to them.

The startlingly uniqueness of American life during the Age of Jackson was also recognized by foreign observers who positively adored our democratic ethos, unlike Frances Trollope who clearly deplored it. When the English blue-stocking Harriet Martineau visited in the early 1830s, she could hardly find enough good things to say about us, and yet there was one aspect of American life that at first shocked and dismayed her—the enormous amount of unsupervised freedom that American kids of that era were permitted to enjoy. "It frightened me at first to see mere babies playing on broken wooden bridges, where the rushing water below might be seen through large holes; and little boys climbing trees which slanted over a rocky precipice; or getting into a canoe tossing on a rough river. But I find that accidents to children are rarely or never heard of. The obvious results of such training are a dexterity, fearlessness, and presence of mind, and aptitude for bodily exercises, which are of eminent use in mature life."[9]

No doubt Harriet Martineau was exaggerating a bit. Surely American children of that period were not immune to accidents, and some of them must have perished from their little adventures. Yet her basic sociological point remains valid. A culture in which children were left to their own devices, especially at a time when the vast majority of them did not attend schools, was almost predestined to be a culture rich in natural libertarians. As a matter of course, such children would grow up to be ornery adults, who insist on keeping control of their own lives and who will resist being managed and governed by their self-proclaimed betters. Whether this is a good thing or a bad thing is, of course, a matter of debate. But what is beyond debate is the decisive role that the ornery frontier ethos played in the populist revolt of 1828, when the people's hero, Andrew Jackson, was swept into the White House by a landslide, changing the nature of American politics forever.

CHAPTER 10

THE POPULIST REVOLT OF 1828— CAN IT HAPPEN AGAIN?

When trying to understand where current events are leading, people will naturally have recourse to history. They will seek out past events that most closely parallel those of the present, particularly during a period of crisis. Anyone trying to foresee where our current populist revolt may be leading will certainly gain some insight by examining the greatest populist revolt in our nation's history. Many features of that revolt mirror the features common to all populist upheavals—for example, the critical role played by a conspiracy theory. But the populist revolt of 1828 was unusual because it was not the result of a violent social upheaval, but of an uncontested national election.

The election of Andrew Jackson in 1828 might well foreshadow the presidential election of 2012 or 2016. Today we have a populist idol, Sarah Palin. Like Jackson, Palin positively delights in going rogue, in disconcerting the establishment, in displaying contempt for the "politics as usual" preferred by the upholders of the status quo. Like Jackson, she possesses an uncanny intuitive sense of the grievances, fears, and anxieties of the little guy—anyone who feels alienated and marginalized by a political system that has seemingly forgotten about them. She knows how to channel their visceral emotions into a grass-roots political movement capable of circumventing traditional party affiliations. Like Jackson, she displays no reluctance in trying to persuade the average man that a sinister conspiracy of wicked elitists is out to do him mischief. True, Palin talks about death panels while Jackson talked about corrupt bargains, but both charges were well suited to arouse and inflame the little guy's anxiety that his liberty and independence were on the verge of being taken away. Jackson's charges worked—they got him elected. Whether Palin's charges will be equally successful in getting her elected remains to be seen. But those who dismiss this possibility as too far-fetched should at least review the events leading up to Jackson's stunning electoral triumph.

In the election of 1828 twice as many men voted as did in 1824—that is a whopping increase, and it had nothing to do with the population growth of the United States during those four years. The landside of 1828 was the result of a serious charge that Andrew Jackson and his followers made against two of the most distinguished statesmen of that era, Henry Clay and John Quincy Adams. The charge was that these two men had conspired to defeat the people's choice in the previous election: Andrew Jackson, a hero of the War of 1812, celebrated for his astonishing victory over the British at the Battle of New Orleans.

In the election of 1824, Andrew Jackson had received more popular votes than any other candidate but fell short of the electoral votes needed to clinch the election. Because no one got enough electoral votes, the election was decided in the House of Representatives as the Constitution required. Henry Clay, a representative from Kentucky, had a powerful influence over the House, and was able to persuade enough members to vote for the candidate of his choice. When the representatives were polled for their vote, they elected not the man who had gotten the greatest percentage of the popular vote, Andrew Jackson, but John Quincy Adams, the son of the second president of the United States. Once he was president, John Quincy Adams appointed Henry Clay as his secretary of state.

Up until then in our nation's history, the position of secretary of state was the path to the presidency. Madison had been Jefferson's secretary of state.

Monroe had been Madison's secretary of state. John Quincy Adams had been Monroe's secretary of state, and, despite his lack of popular support, he too became the next president—thanks to Henry Clay who, upon being appointed Adams's secretary of state, doubtlessly thought he was assured of becoming the next president after Adams.

Shortly after the 1824 election, Jackson charged that Henry Clay had made a "corrupt bargain" with John Quincy Adams: Clay had promised to throw the election to Adams if in return Adams would make Clay secretary of state, thereby virtually guaranteeing that Clay would become the next president. Because everyone knew how badly Clay wanted the presidency, the rumor of the corrupt bargain seized the popular imagination, which is so often disposed to think the worst of those who hunger for power—not without cause.

Was there really a corrupt bargain? Henry Clay's admirers and defenders did not think so. They were sincerely convinced that Andrew Jackson would make a dangerous president, precisely because of his immense popularity with the uneducated masses. They agreed that Clay's decision to support Adams was based on what Clay genuinely thought was best for the country that he loved heart and soul. Adams no doubt thought that Henry Clay was far and away the best man for the job of secretary of state and the best choice to be the next president—certainly better than Andrew Jackson.

The theory of a natural aristocracy—rule by the better sort, based on merit and not birth—was the functioning political ideal of the American nation during the generation that preceded the Jacksonian rebellion of 1828. In effect, the presidents between Jefferson and Jackson were appointed, not elected. In choosing their secretary of state, each president was virtually allowed to select the man who would succeed him. Today we naturally tend to look on such a process as shockingly undemocratic. To us it is obvious that a president can only obtain office after he has been voted in by the people in a free and fair election. Under our current system, the Republican Party nominates one candidate while the Democratic Party nominates another, and we the people get to decide between the two. But the two-party system was no part of our Founding Father's plans for America. On the contrary, one of the few things on which all the Founding Fathers agreed was that a two-party system was a danger to be shunned by all patriotic Americans. Back then, a party meant a faction, and a faction was a collection of self-interested individuals pursuing an objective at odds with the general welfare of their society. Partisans, by definition, could not be patriots. The last thing the Founding Fathers wanted was for their fledgling republic to be divided between two rival factions, neither of which was capable of seeking the general welfare, each of which was solely anxious to gather to itself all the spoils of power and to promote the narrow and selfish interests of its own supporters, to the detriment of the national good. Two parties meant corruption, as in England. Or, it meant a constant flirtation with civil war. That had been the curse of the period in which the Federalists and the Jeffersonians had been at each other's throats. No one wanted that kind of disruptive political turmoil.

Far better to adopt the system by which Rome had been governed during the epoch that the eighteenth-century English historian Edward Gibbon had praised for its good and tranquil government in his masterpiece, *The Decline and Fall of the Roman Empire*. The system was simple, and it was designed to assure rule by the better sort. Each emperor would choose the man whom he thought most suitable to become the next emperor; he would formally adopt him and upon his death, his adopted heir would become the new emperor. No messy elections, no unseemly democracy to muddy the waters. And the system worked brilliantly—until the last emperor of the series, Marcus Aurelius, broke the rule, and let his idiot of a son, Commodus, step into his shoes. It was this Roman tradition that the administrations of Jefferson, Madison, Monroe, and Adams had in effect revived in the New World in order to avoid all the pitfalls of the vicious two-party tradition that had corrupted the British.

In addition, there were sound reasons why Henry Clay feared the presidency of Andrew Jackson. Jackson was both a general and a genuine military hero. He also had an unnerving admiration for Napoleon Bonaparte, whose cavalier contempt for legal procedures Jackson had emulated in virtually every position of authority with which he had been trusted. When Jackson heard that the French had turned against their former idol and abandoned Napoleon in 1813, Jackson thundered that if he had been in Napoleon's place, he would have burnt Paris to the ground. Clay was by no means alone in fearing that Jackson would become a Bonaparte-like tyrant if he assumed the office of presidency, and that is probably the best explanation of the so-called corrupt bargain. In the eyes of both Clay and Adams, if a little collusion between them was the only means of preventing the rise of an Old World tyrant in the New World, then that was a price both were willing to pay.

Jackson's many fans violently disagreed. They bought the corrupt bargain theory hook, line, and sinker. They believed there was a conspiracy against the people, as Jackson charged, and that an uppity elite had gotten power into their own hands, and that they were not about to let it get back into the hands of the people where it belonged. Jackson and his many vociferous and canny supporters played on the ornery Americans' visceral dislike of anything that smacked of elitism and snobbery. A great fuss was made out of the fact that John Quincy Adams had installed (at his own expense) a billiard table in the White House, billiards then being a snob's game, unlike the populist pool table of a later period. But then Adams was the perfect target of populist resentment. He was a cold fish. Many admired his sterling qualities among which was neither tact nor charm, and no one really liked him. He was superior to other people by birth, by intellect, by worldly experience, and he was completely incapable of disguising this fact from others or, more importantly, from himself. No one doubted that Adams was the better sort; least of all John Quincy Adams. Everyone who met him felt that he looked down his nose at them—because he did.

The people thought that Andrew Jackson was one of them, and so too did Jackson. He drank heavily, but drinking heavily was still a sign of robust masculinity, while teetotalers were generally held in contempt.[1] Jackson had fought several duels in which he had killed men. He had a passion for defending females whose virtue had been besmirched, including that of his dowdy but loyal wife Rachel, and the beautiful but scandalous Peggy Eaton. His famous nickname, Old Hickory, had been bestowed on him by his admirers, and it was an obvious tribute to his appealing frontier orneriness—hickory is a very hard wood that does not bend easily, and neither did Andrew Jackson. Despite his grand and well-deserved reputation as a war hero, Jackson was looked upon by the average man as one of their own. He had come from dirt-poor folks, and he had fought his way up in the world. Like so many of his supporters, he was a self-made man. Even after he became very rich, he always lived simply. His spelling was atrocious even in an era of bad spellers. But he could slap men on the back and tell them stories that made them laugh. John Quincy Adams, in contrast, was the bluest of American bluebloods and never smiled. Perhaps he didn't know how.

On winning the presidency, Jackson did not declare himself the Emperor of North America. He did not set up a military dictatorship. He was, no doubt, an immensely strong president, and he could be unforgiving and unyielding with those he regarded as his enemies—all the elitists who had control of wealth and power in the country. James Parton, who wrote Jackson's biography in the nineteenth century, complained that Jackson swept into office very much like a horde of conquering barbarians, interested primarily in spoils and plunder. Veteran administrators who had dedicated their lives to mastering the intricacies of a complex subject, such as Indian affairs, were summarily dismissed from office and replaced by ignorant oafs who knew nothing whatever about the department over which they had been put in charge. What counted was not a man's expertise but his loyal service to the cause of Andrew Jackson. Overnight the American government went from being a gentleman's club to a frontier saloon—at least in the eyes of Jackson's many detractors.

In retrospect most of us can agree that John Quincy Adams represented order and stability, civilization and gentility, whereas Andrew Jackson represented rebellion and turmoil, populism and orneriness. In the eyes of most men with property and education, Adams was obviously the best man for the office. Indeed, looking back at the populist revolt of 1828, it is quite possible to argue that America might have been better off in the long run if its government had remained a private club reserved only for the better sort, a self-appointing aristocracy that was largely exempt from democratic control by the masses. But it is equally possible, in retrospect, to argue that Jackson's rebellion was a necessary step in the creation of the world's first great modern democracy, liberating the ordinary—and ornery—man from governance by his self-proclaimed betters.

Today there are many Americans who would love to see a strong and tough president like Andrew Jackson, one who is willing and determined to shake up the status quo. But the problem is that in contemporary America the status quo has become so heavy and immense that it is difficult to see how it could be shaken up by the election of any single man or woman. The ornery Americans who lived on the frontier and who voted in droves for their hero Andrew Jackson represented an egalitarian culture in which individuals could live independently and self-sufficiently. Today, it is true, many Americans still continue to live like that, but they are most often found in what has come to be known as the "red states." It is no accident that Sarah Palin, the sweetheart of the Tea Party movement, hails from America's absolutely last frontier, the great, sprawling, and thinly populated wilderness of Alaska. In the eyes of her many admirers, Palin represents the opportunity to go back to an early and simpler era, in which the egalitarian frontier ethos of independence and common sense was the norm. In contrast, those who are most appalled by the prospect of a Palin presidency tend to come from those huge and sophisticated urban centers, such as Los Angeles and New York. In their eyes, Palin's appeal is, at best, simply a fantasy, a quixotic quest to revive a way of life that is no longer possible in the modern world.

It is entirely possible to feel a deep yearning to return to the simpler America of the past, while simultaneously recognizing that this is just not a realistic option in the twenty-first century. New York City cannot downsize to the scale of Sarah Palin's hometown of Wasilla, Alaska, and a glance at the skylines of the two cities reveals why. Like all major cites of the modern age, New York is full of sky-scrapers, while Wasilla has none.

Ever since the Woolworth Building was opened in New York City on April 24, 1913, the skyscraper has been the visible embodiment of the giant corporate entities that have come to dominate modern American life. At fifty-seven floors, the Woolworth Building was the tallest skyscraper of its day. Its monumental structure was entirely the product of the immense success of the Woolworth Corporation that financed and erected it, but this success had come at a heavy price—for the little retailers that Woolworth went into competition against. For most of the nineteenth century, the vast majority of Americans brought goods from their local county store, each of which was owned and operated by a lone individual or his family. But all this changed dramatically when Frank Woolworth began opening his own stores in the late 1870s. Applying the same monopolistic and predatory policies that had worked for Rockefeller's Standard Oil, Woolworth and his brother began to undercut the prices charged by the local merchants, either driving them out of business or absorbing them as partners. The result was the formation of one of the first giant American corporations, whose complicated organizational hierarchy was symbolically reflected in the majestic scale of the Woolworth Building.

At the heart of any large corporate enterprise stands a complex and elaborate hierarchy. Bob gives orders to Sam who gives orders to Sally who gives orders to Fred. Or Fred asks a question that Sally must take to Sam who must first find out the answer from Bob. Anyone who has worked in any sizable organization will know how this works. But this hierarchy has another important characteristic: It will invariably take the form of a pyramid. There will always be more people at the base of the pyramid than at the apex. In any pyramid-style organization, the VIPs, the movers-and-shakers, will be at the top, while the little guys and gals will be at the bottom. There is nothing deliberately sinister in the hierarchical pyramid of large-scale organizations. You obviously cannot have a huge corporation in which everyone thinks he is the boss. Nor can you have a huge corporation in which everyone is too ornery to take orders from those on the level of the pyramid above him. For "the system" to work, everyone must do his specific job, which is the task that has been assigned to him by those in charge of what he does. If you want an organization of human beings to be really big, then this is the system you must adopt. The only choice is whether you want something that big. If you don't, fine. You can go and start your own mom-and-pop business. If you can be content with small, you don't need a pyramid. But if you want huge, you must build one.

The American government started out much like a mom-and-pop business. At first it was very small. It was so small that it paid for itself out of custom duties—the amount the government charged for imports into the country—and it often ran a surplus. But today it has grown immense beyond what any of its founders could have imagined—a point on which the populist conservative dwells, and justly so. Yet the American government is not the only gigantic pyramid around. There are many others, in the form of huge financial institutions, enormous universities, titanic media conglomerates, and colossal industrial corporations. It is not just big government, it is this immense complex of pyramids, taken as a whole, that threatens the core American ethos of orneriness. By their very nature, all hierarchical organizations, be they state agencies or private corporations, succeed by reducing individuals to being cogs in a great machine that functions with a purpose of its own, which is simply to get bigger and bigger. Like all machines, it is disrupted when a cog falls out of place. A cog that acts ornery can shut down the whole operation. Those who tend the machine, whose job it is to keep it running smoothly, will be on the lookout for cogs that might start to act ornery and, to maintain quality control and stability, they will get rid of them when they see this happening. So, too, will social pyramids, those living machines made up of so many living cogs.

In an earlier chapter we made a thought experiment in which we assumed that our would-be utopian guardians were dedicated entirely to our best interests, and had not the least intention of manipulating us for their own purposes. Let us now give Sarah Palin the same benefit of the doubt. Assume that she is indeed the new Andrew Jackson: spunky, courageous, motivated only by the highest ethical ideals of patriotism. Could she really change anything? Barack Obama promised the change we need, but those who were formerly his warmest admirers are still waiting to see it. Can Sarah Palin succeed where he has failed? You betcha, her supporters claim, but there is little reason to think that she could reverse the deep currents of history that are leading us toward a post-American America. To acknowledge this is to cast no reflection on her individual capacity or dedication, but simply to point out that the task of turning back the clock may not be within the compass of anyone's gift. Pyramids are hard to build, but once they have been put in place, they are very hard to pull down. Yet that does not mean that we are condemned to be crushed beneath them. This dismal fate can be averted so long as there are men and women who refuse to be manipulated and organized by those who happen to stand a bit closer than they to the apex of the pyramid. Thus the importance of being ornery.

The enmity between the ornery and the huge is a natural and quite unavoidable conflict. It is simply part of how the world works. The struggle of the ornery to keep their domain from being invaded and taken over by the huge is at the heart of mankind's long rebellion. Each side, the ornery and the huge, have developed their own religions, devised their own gods, created their own political orders, come up with their own economies. They have written their own histories, have developed their own mores and manners, their own myths and their own philosophies. They represent two different ways of life, the way of the pyramid and the way of the covenant. It is out of the eternal conflict between the pyramid and the covenant that a just balance between freedom and civilization can be achieved, and by no other way.

IN THE Book of Genesis there is a famous story that tells of how Jehovah saw the people of Mesopotamia building one of their great towers, no doubt a ziggurat. They wanted something really big, so big that it would reach to heaven itself. Since people back then thought that heaven was not very far over their heads, this was an entirely plausible motive. But Jehovah did not like it and decided to thwart their grand ambitions. Instead of knocking down the tower, he made all those who were working on it speak different languages. Even those who struggled to do the task assigned to them and to finish the Tower of Babel could not find out what their supervisors wanted them to do. With the collapse of the social pyramid that had been organized to build it, the great tower stood unfinished, a monument to the foolish am-bition of those who thought that they could ascend to heaven, perhaps to enjoy the life of the immortal gods—for the urge behind all monumentalism is the insatiable craving for immortality.

Jehovah's motives in the story of the Tower of Babel have often been sus-pect. People say that he was jealous. But for once let us give him the benefit of the doubt. What if Jehovah simply did not like bigness? Suppose Jehovah didn't mean to create human beings who automatically obeyed the orders given to them by those in authority over them. Adam, obviously not created to be a robot, was made capable of disobedience. What if Jehovah wanted human beings to be ornery and had designed us that way?

When looked at from this perspective, Jehovah's decision to halt the con-struction of the Tower of Babel can be read in a more flattering light. He is not resentful of human technology. He is simply passing judgment on a form of social organization that will inevitably lead to oppression and bondage, in which human beings become merely units to be manipulated and managed by those who are higher up in the pyramid. In opposition to this model, Je-hovah is keen on covenants.

A covenant community is the antithesis of the pyramid society. Pyramid societies rank people in vertical space. A person's place in his society can be determined just as easily as a person's position on an Aztec pyramid. You look to see what story of the pyramid he is located on, who is below him, who is above him. In a covenant community, on the other hand, everyone is on the same level. No one is below and no one is above. When Jehovah makes his grand entrance in the Book of Genesis, it is for the purpose of inviting Abraham and all the males connected with him to enter into a covenant. The offer is egalitarian because he makes no distinction between slaves and masters. Biological lineage, too, is irrelevant. All males will be bound by the same covenant. But notice that Jehovah does not command Abraham to enter into a covenant but rather invites him. Abraham is free to refuse the offer or to accept it. Joining the covenant community must be voluntary. If someone is forced to enter the community created by a covenant, it ceases to be a covenant, just as when the gangster makes you an offer you can't refuse, it cannot be called a contract, since a contract can only be valid when all parties have given their free consent to it.

The voluntary basis of a covenant community is essential to preserving its egalitarian nature. When everyone signs off on a rule that they have promised to obey, someone may still break this rule, but when he does, he knows in advance that he will automatically incur the hostility of everyone else in his community. He has not broken *a* rule. He has broken *their* rule. He has offended each of his neighbors personally. He has broken his promise to everyone in his community. He will become their enemy, and they will regard him as an outlaw—a heavy price to pay for any crime. Of course, the community may also stone him to death, and that no doubt is an added incentive to avoid the crime. But shame is a far more effective deterrent, and it is the genius of the covenant to know how to harness shame and use it as a means of protecting egalitarianism in a covenant-based community.

If everyone were raised from an early age to feel a debilitating sense of shame at the very idea of committing a crime, there would be little need for a formal legal system. With everyone inhibited from crime by the mechanism of shame, little or no crime would exist, and there would be little or no need for institutions whose sole purpose is to catch and punish offenders. When a lot of crime exists, on the other hand, you must organize people to catch, judge, and punish the criminals—and this requires a break with the egalitarian spirit of the community. It must now be divided into two unequal groups. The first group is the elite that you entrust with policing your society and to whom you grant a monopoly of violence. You may not want to grant anyone such a monopoly but, if the crime gets bad enough, you will have no choice. Suddenly you are existing in a hierarchy. The legal elite commands the policing elite that punishes those members of the community that commit a crime, probably with more frequency and harshness than they would tend to punish each other or those they are closely connected with. There is now a serious form of social inequality, as anyone who has ever stood in court before a bully in a black gown knows—an inequality that wise men have complained of since ancient days. Insiders always have a considerable advantage over outsiders, while the cunning and crafty will inevitably begin to abuse the legal system to aggrandize themselves at the expense of others, manipulating the laws to take men's land and property and to secure their own. In short, the breakdown of a covenant community inevitably leads to the construction of a pyramid society.

By the same logic, the more strictly everyone in a community follows a covenant to which they have all agreed, the less need there is for a legal system and a police force: the nucleus of the state. Covenants are thus intrinsically egalitarian—not in the sense that they make everyone equal but because they minimize the need for a monopoly of the means of physical coercion placed in the hands of a few. Through shame, a covenant-based community can collectively police itself. Everyone already knows what is wrong and what is right, so there is no need to go to a judge for third-party justice. The community itself is the judge, and it renders its own rough form of justice—often quite brutally. And there is no appeal beyond it. Just ask those thieves caught red-handed in the mining camps of the California Gold Rush.

Ornery people clearly will wish to establish their social order on a voluntary covenant—what philosophers call a social contract. It is the form of organization that permits individuals to retain the greatest amount of freedom and independence. Hence, it is the kind of governance that the natural libertarian will be drawn to. A group of ornery individuals, who would instantly rebel at the thought of someone else forcing them to obey a law, can be persuaded to make up laws for themselves freely and by their own consent, to pledge to one another to obey these laws, and to regard as an outlaw and outcast anyone who, after promising to live by them, chooses to violate them for his own advantage. This, as we have seen, is precisely what the gold miners did. Finding no social pyramids in the wilderness of California, they set up their own covenant communities.

It's no surprise that so many self-made societies have venerated the idea of the covenant. A covenant is a contract among individuals who look upon themselves as being more or less equal; a strong man who can dominate his neighbors will see no need for a covenant or a contract. His will is law, and he sees no reason to change this arrangement unless forced to change it at the insistence of those ornery enough to resist him.

Philosophers such as John Locke have argued that all societies arose out of a social contract into which all the members of the social order entered by their free consent. We may leave aside the question of whether this is a valid historical account of how human beings first came to create societies. For even supposing that Locke was right and all societies started out in this manner, obviously most of them did not stay that way for very long. Search throughout history, and you will discover that most societies have been divided into two radically unequal classes—the small ruling class at the top of the social pyramid and the multitude of men and women at the bottom, whose sole function in life is to labor for the benefit of their masters.

It is relatively easy to see how people can live freely and independently under the egalitarian conditions present in all self-made societies. But it is very difficult to understand how those who have long been crushed beneath the weight of a gigantic social pyramid can hope to regain their lost freedom. Indeed, it even becomes difficult to imagine how those who have been subjected to such oppression over the course of many generations can even keep the memory of freedom alive. Yet certain people have managed to achieve this, and they have done it by repeating the stories of the strange god who hated all pyramids, and who instead of urging his followers to bow down before the high and the mighty, caused them to rise up in rebellion against their oppressors. The people touched by this strange god have belonged to every race and have occupied far flung corners of our planet, but they share the same fierce devotion to independence and self-government, even when it seems least obtainable—indeed, especially then.

CHAPTER 11

THE RELIGIONS
OF FREE MEN

The philosophers who told us that men are born free were optimists. Those born in self-made societies, or societies that have faithfully kept to the cultural traditions of self-made societies, may be said to be born free, but those who are born under a government that operates essentially as protection rackets do—one devised by the strong and powerful to oppress and exploit the weak and productive—may never have been given the opportunity to know what freedom is all about. Human beings who from birth have experienced only psychological humiliation and brutal subjugation—who are bullied and bossed, hoodwinked and preyed upon without any hope of improving their own lot in life—may even come to look upon slavery as their natural state.

It is true that men and women enslaved as adults or even as young people will retain a keen memory of their freedom and will yearn to regain it, often to the point of risking their own lives in acts of individual defiance and collective rebellion. In the Old South, runaway slaves proved their continuing desire for freedom, and slave uprisings have occurred in many societies across time. But these exceptions do not address the issue of the long-term effect of slavery on a people. The first generation to be enslaved will keep the idea of freedom alive, and they will try to pass it on to their children who are born in slavery; but over time, as the possibility of ever regaining their liberty dims, it will become more difficult to sustain interest in the idea. Worse, as each new effort to gain liberty is crushed more brutally than before, it is inevitable that the time will come when no such efforts will be made. For those societies in which the servile class has been kept in its place century after century, the social hierarchy will come to seem identical with the natural order of the universe. This will be especially true when the servile class has been taught a cosmic script that justifies their subjection.

A cosmic script is how the people in a particular society collectively *imagine* their place in the grand scheme of things. It is the biggest of big pictures. It is more than a myth, or an ideology, or a philosophy, or a theology, because the cosmic script does not merely make statements about the cosmos; it also includes everything that a dramatic script does. It lists all the actors in the drama and describes where the drama is set. It has a beginning, a middle, and an end. It contains a set of instructions telling people how to act in this drama and even what words to speak in certain scenes. In short, a cosmic script tells a story in which we ourselves are principal players.

In classical Hindu society, the cosmic script was centered on the drama of reincarnation and karma. During every person's life, he will do certain evil things and certain good things. Most often, as the Hindus realistically observed, the good is not always rewarded in this lifetime, nor is the evil invariably punished. Thus, in order to make the cosmos square with our intuitive sense of right and wrong, the Hindu cosmic script assures us that the wicked will eventually get their just desserts, not in this life but in their next one, and by means of the same mechanism by which the good will receive their rewards: karma. In his next reincarnation, a bad man will come back with a monstrous deformity, or he will be born an untouchable or a vile animal. Yet there is nothing to keep the bad man, in his new life, from turning over a new leaf. Hindu determinism is not continuous; it is more like the annual balancing of the books. After every cosmic accounting period, so to speak, the wicked man, having been reborn as a frog, might begin to do good deeds, in

which case, in his next lifetime, he will be equitably rewarded by being elevated to a more deserving species, like a cat. And if he is extraordinarily good,
then he might even aspire to be reborn into the priestly caste of Brahmins.
Therefore, we should all be content with our own lot and the lot of everyone
else, for when we survey the world, we see nothing but cosmic justice at
work. In the crippled beggar we can behold the terrible punishment that
karma has inflicted on the wealthy but wicked merchant, or in a child born
blind the fitting penalty for the previous life of a well-remunerated thief.

Among those who follow the cosmic script of reincarnation and karma,
each man, woman, and child knows exactly how to behave in the life he or
she is now leading. The stage directions are unambiguous: Accept with grace
all the afflictions that you must endure in this life because they are just what
you deserved for the way you lived in your previous life. Try to do good, in
order to improve your lot in the next lifetime. Accept the caste you have been
born into, because it was not an accident of birth, as it undoubtedly appears
to those who are going by a different cosmic script. Instead, it is a manifestation of cosmic justice and fairness, well concealed beneath the veil of Maya
known as biological reproduction.

By means of the cosmic script of reincarnation and karma, what appears
to outsiders to be a cruel and unjust social system based on inherited status
turns out to be a cosmic meritocracy, in which each person receives precisely
what he deserves based on his past merits or demerits. The Hindu cosmic
script therefore does several things. It allows those who follow it to imagine
that they are living in a thoroughly moral universe, in which no crime goes
unpunished and no act of charity goes unrewarded. It counsels us to resign
ourselves to our lot in this life, as cheerfully as possible, while offering an incentive to improve our status in the next life through virtuous actions. It does
not merely describe the world; it tells us how we are to perform in it.

The Great Chain of Being is another example of a cosmic script. It was
the metaphor that dominated European thinking from the Middle Ages
until the very verge of the modern world. Those who imagined the universe

through this model naturally looked upon its whole structure as having been intelligently designed and arranged by a God who obviously made everything for the best. Each link in the chain was therefore necessary. Most people must labor, and a ruling elite was necessary to keep them from rebelling. If you removed the ruling elite, everything would fall into chaos. There would no longer be any subordination, and the world would swiftly be turned upside down. Masterless men, to use the phrase of Thomas Hobbes, would run amok, and life would be miserable for all. Therefore, each link in the social hierarchy must be maintained at all costs. Unlike the eternal machine of karma that never needs to be adjusted and operates without our assistance, the Great Chain of Being requires each of us to discharge the duties and responsibilities of our respective stations in life, in order to keep the various links of the chain from snapping. For while it is impossible to rebel against karma, it is all too possible to rebel against the Great Chain of Being. That, after all, was precisely the crime of Satan. He could not accept subordination, despite his very high status in the celestial hierarchy, and he rebelled, with consequences that eventually brought us "all our mortal woes," as described in *Paradise Lost* by the seventeenth-century poet John Milton—who was himself, with curious inconsistence, a defender of both rebellion and regicide.

For those who followed the cosmic script provided by the Great Chain of Being, rebellion was not merely an act of insubordination to political authority, which was bad enough in itself; it was an attempt to topple the whole cosmic hierarchy, and hence it stood condemned by both God and man. For such rebellions endangered everyone by threatening the peace and stability of the entire social order. Rebellion was thus both a crime and a sin, an act of treason against the king, an act of blasphemy against the God who had appointed him to keep rebellion in check.

It should come as no surprise that those who are satisfied with the status quo will be attracted to cosmic scripts that justify preserving it, while condemning any effort to overthrow it. The beauty of such cosmic scripts is that they are designed to be convincing not only to the ruling class that most obviously benefits by it, but equally convincing to precisely those groups that are most abused and exploited by it. The European serf during the Middle Ages could imagine himself as being exactly where God intended him to be. The Hindu untouchable could imagine himself as suffering precisely the fate that he deserved, due to the sins of his earlier life.

Against this background, the cosmic script adopted by the ancient Hebrews becomes an extraordinary anomaly, because it is a celebration of defiance, rebellion, and revolt—the complete reversal of the cosmic scripts of karma and of the Great Chain of Being. Jehovah has chosen Hebrew slaves to be his people. He demands that they break the chains of slavery to which they had become accustomed in the land of Egypt. He instructs Moses to tell the pharaoh to set his people free. When the pharaoh fails to obey, Jehovah afflicts the land of Egypt with a series of horrendous plagues, culminating in the murder of the first-born of all living things. He is not merely encouraging a slave revolt; he is managing and directing it.

Once the Hebrew slaves have left Egypt, a new act begins. The Hebrews had been so accustomed to their chains that they had lost the desire to escape from them, and once in the desert they begin to clamor to return to the house of bondage. Slavery has so eaten into their souls that Jehovah sees no hope in making them free men, and recognizes that the old generation must first pass away, and that a new generation must be raised from birth to prize and cherish independence and freedom above all other worldly good and values. Finally, a new race of men is formed, whose passion for their liberty and self-determination makes them worthy of entering at last into the promised land, where they can create a new kind of society from scratch. It is so fanatically egalitarian that it refuses to accept a mere human being to rule over them. "In those days there was no king in Israel and every man did what was right in his own eyes."[1]

Here was a cosmic script designed for free men, for the natural libertarian who insists on doing what is right in his own eyes—a cosmic script that would have a profound effect on the history of freedom in two different ways.

First, during the many centuries in which the Jews found themselves forced to live under one or another of the great empires of the ancient world, and later when they were scattered in the Diaspora, they kept the memory and love of liberty fresh and alive by celebrating and retelling the story of Exodus to each new generation. Far from being ashamed to have once been slaves, they made the story of their liberation the center of their religion. The Jews were able to use their inherited cultural tradition to defend themselves against all the great worldly powers that wanted to break their spirit and to keep their spirit of rebellion alive across generations. Neither brute force nor adverse economic circumstances could rob the Jews of their longing for independence and self-determination—but only as long as they cherished and treasured the tradition of rebellion and defiance that had been passed down to them from their ancestors.

Second, the cosmic script of the Hebrews became part of the inheritance of the West through Christianity's adoption of the Old Testament.[2] Throughout the first fifteen centuries of Christianity, there was a tendency on the part of those in charge of the social order to minimize or utterly ignore the Hebrew cosmic script with its championing of rebellion and virtual anarchy. Upholders of the Great Chain of Being were apt to find the Hebrew story of their successful slave revolt too dangerous for the peasants to read about, which explains why Bible reading among the masses was not encouraged, and, indeed, prohibited. At the same time, it is little wonder that Protestant reformers rebelling against the Roman Catholic Church should want everyone to know the story of Exodus, and were eager to translate the Old Testament into the vernacular.

Karl Marx argued that religion was the opium of the people, and this was certainly true of the cosmic scripts offered by most religions of the world. But his collaborator and friend Friedrich Engels recognized that those religions that drew on the Hebrew cosmic script were in a different class altogether. Here was a cosmic script designed to appeal to those who were downtrodden and oppressed, but who were determined to retain a vision of their future liberation in a better world—a cosmic script that positively demanded the peasants to revolt, as they did in Germany from 1524 to 1525. The Puritans who came to New England in the 1640s saw themselves quite explicitly as the heirs to the Hebrew tradition: They had escaped the house of bondage of the Old World and were establishing a promised land of their own, taking their laws almost word for word from Leviticus.

Later, the Africans who were brought to North America as slaves quickly grasped the relevance of the story of Exodus to their own seemingly hopeless plight. African Americans aspiring to their fair share of freedom and equality have repeatedly appealed to the cosmic script handed down by the Hebrew tradition, from black spirituals like "Go down, Moses" to Martin Luther King's last speech, in which he declared that, like Moses standing on the top of Mount Pisgah, he had at last seen the promised land. In age after age, the Hebrew cosmic script has been the source of inspiration for the little guy who is determined to stand up against the bully. Whether it is the children of Israel leading the mighty armies of the pharaoh to their watery deaths in the Red Sea, or David knocking out the giant Goliath with his little boy's slingshot, Hebrew scripture has been there for the poor, the downtrodden, the outcast, and the marginalized.

Modern science and scholarship assure us, quite properly, that there is a great deal of stuff and nonsense in the Hebrew tradition. The parting of the Red Sea is hard to swallow, and even the most convinced Christian fundamentalist has trouble explaining how Joshua made the sun stand still on the hill of Gibeon. The myths and legends of the Bible clearly reflect a primitive view of the cosmos that is spectacularly out of date by modern scientific standards. The whole supernatural world that is the background to so many of the biblical narratives is alien to our modern sensibilities, and even those who claim to believe in them are privately troubled by their outlandishness. There are two popular, yet conflicting, ways of dealing with this dilemma. One is to simply discard the ancient scriptural traditions as fables no longer relevant to the present age. The other is to try your best to believe the unbelievable, which is the route taken by many modern fundamentalists.

But there is a third way of approaching the Hebrew tradition, which is to understand it as a cosmic script. A cosmic script is not a scientific treatise to be examined for its factual veracity, but more like a work of art to be evaluated for its moral depth and significance. A cosmic script requires the same "willing suspension of disbelief" that Samuel Taylor Coleridge expected of an audience watching a play by William Shakespeare. To object to the stories of Genesis because you don't believe in angels is as vulgar as objecting to the plot of *Macbeth* because you don't believe in witches.

In his famous lecture "The Will to Believe," published in 1898, William James offered a purely pragmatic defense of religious faith. James argued that those who seek to evaluate a man's religion by examining its doctrines and tenets in terms of their truth-value as judged by empirical science are really missing the whole point of what a religion is supposed to do. Do not ask, for example, whether there really is a Divine Providence—that is a mystery beyond the power of science or reason to solve. Instead, ask whether a belief in Divine Providence makes people happier or more successful. What needs to be considered, James said, is the impact that a man's sincerely held religious beliefs have on the quality of his life. If his faith makes him happier, more productive, better able to withstand temptations, capable of more heroic assertions, more loyal to the higher values of life, and more willing to espouse them when it is difficult or risky to do so, then his faith has produced a better man capable of creating a better world.

James was addressing the impact of religious belief on an individual; but the same pragmatic approach can be applied to the cosmic script that is shared by an entire society and culture. From the point of view of the pragmatist, the relevant question to ask is, What effect does belief in this or that cosmic script have on a society that subscribes to it? Obviously most cosmic scripts, like the Hindu ideal of karma and reincarnation or the Great Chain of Being, provide support to a social order in which virtually everyone will be content with or at least resigned to their place and rank in the established hierarchy. This hierarchy will not be looked upon historically, as the result of power struggles of the past in which a predatory band of warriors was able to subdue and enslave the general population—which is the way most such hierarchies have come about. Instead, it will be looked upon as right and necessary, eternally just and morally unimpeachable—the design of an omnipotent God or the Tao of an immutable natural order. On the other hand, the Hebrew cosmic script will have a radically different impact on the social order. It will make those on the bottom defy and rebel against those on the top—a fact that will not endear the Hebrew tradition to the ruling class but will make it of perennial relevance to those who only wish to rule themselves.[3]

A cosmic script can be shared by different religions. In this respect, it is similar to a movie script. When a director decides to do a remake of *Batman*, for example, there will be certain features that he will obviously need to keep. He can't have Batman dressed up like a duck. But he will be able to design different costumes for him and to portray Gotham City in a variety of ingenious ways, depending on his creative impulses. The Puritans' decision to reestablish the long-extinct Hebrew commonwealth on the inhospitable coasts of New England was like a decision to remake, in modern costume, an old favorite—namely, the story of Exodus. On the other hand, a religion can remain the same in name but undergo drastic revisions in substance, due to an underlying change from one cosmic script to another. The thirteenth-century Christianity of St. Thomas Aquinas reflected the cosmic script of the Great Chain of Being, while the Christianity of the seventeenth-century Puritans reflected the cosmic script developed by the ancient Hebrews over two thousand year earlier, at the very minimum.[4] This means that you have not really discovered much about what any individual believes if you only know of his nominal religious affiliation. By the standards of orthodox Christianity, Mormons are not real Christians—they do not hold the same theological tenets that all other Christian denominations share. Yet it is hard to imagine a religion that is more indebted to the cosmic script of the ancient Hebrews. Mormons use the same word, gentiles, to describe those outside their community of faith. They have their prophet, John Smith, who received divine revelation like Moses, and they can also boast their own Joshua, Brigham Young, who led his people into their promised land in the valley basin of the Great Salt Lake.

One of the perennial problems facing those intellectuals who wish to bring enlightenment to the people is that they grossly underestimate the degree to which people are attached to the cosmic script in which they have been raised. Such people will interpret everything that happens in their world according to this script and will know how to react to suffering, adversity, tragedy, and death based on how their cosmic script explains these misfortunes. Because science simply cannot answer the questions that haunt human beings most deeply, the vast majority of people will naturally gravitate to a cosmic script that affords them the psychological satisfaction of at least believing that they know the answers to those questions.

SCIENCE, PROPERLY speaking, does not offer man a cosmic script. It tells us about the universe but does not assign us a dramatic role within it. Nor does it aspire to answer questions beyond the realm of empirical verification—questions such as, What is the meaning of life? What happens to us after death? Is there something in the universe large and grand that truly cares for us and our individual suffering? Scientists who are aware of the limits of their discipline know that they cannot provide a scientific solution to these metaphysical riddles and therefore leave them alone. Some are agnostic, aware that they cannot prove or disprove the cosmic scripts offered by any religion; others may adopt the cosmic script of a particular religion, willing to live by its guidance and to imagine their place in the universe in terms of its teachings. They may even believe in God and angels, but, as scientists, they will certainly not claim to possess scientific evidence of their existence.[5]

Today the boundary line between science and metaphysics has been breached.[6] There is a rival cosmic script on the block, namely scientism, which is not content with the modest compromise offered by agnosticism. Scientism is championed by the Brights movement, which claims to base its worldview on naturalism and science. In one sense, the Brights have a point: They look on human beings as if we were the kind of objects that science normally takes as its subject matter. Like atoms, meteors, and comets, the material objects known as human beings are subject to the same universal laws as all other material objects. My actions and behavior are really no more free than those of the planets moving about in their predestined orbits. True, human beings have an illusion of freedom, and of consciousness, too, but ultimately this makes no difference to us, because we are all subject to the same impersonal forces that move and manipulate us as they move and manipulate all other material objects. The only difference is that we are *deluded* material objects.

Now it is of course possible that all of this could be true, though for some people the belief in the existence of deluded material objects ranks right up there with the belief in the existence of the Easter bunny.[7] But the pragmatist has the right to evaluate this cosmic script by the same standards that he evaluates competing cosmic scripts, namely by observing what effects the acceptance of this particular cosmic script might have on society in general. It is possible for the pragmatist evaluating the creed of scientism to subscribe to it personally and yet be wary of wishing to disseminate it to the general population. In particular, scientism has two features that are alarming to anyone who thinks that the illusion of freedom has been of great value to mankind.

First, while it is a creed that scientists might find uplifting or thrilling, the effect it would have on laymen who have little interest in or knowledge of science would be deplorable. There will be many people to whom such a cosmic script is simply a new form of fatalism, even more oppressive than karma or the Great Chain of Being. Many will come away from this bleak and uninviting cosmic script with the feeling that "all we are is dust in the wind."[8]

Here we are today, unable to control where we will be tomorrow, mere human debris thrown up by an inexplicable past, our brief life ending in a death beyond which there is the same nothing that there was before we were so pointlessly born. So, why bother to rebel against the powers that be? Resign yourself to the icy cosmic indifference revealed by modern science.

Second, just as the cosmic script of Hinduism seems perfectly designed to justify the rule of the Brahman class, it would be hard to imagine a cosmic script more perfectly designed to justify the rule of a scientific elite than scientism. For those of us living in the modern world in which we have been taught to respect scientists and science,[9] the cosmic script of scientism has something of the air of a revelation from on high. Respected scientists who also happen to be enthusiastic Brights have seen truths that laymen cannot see for themselves—and who are we to argue with them? If scientists say such and such is so, then this makes it a truth to which we must all defer, simply because as laymen we are in no position to challenge their judgment from a scientific point of view. Therein lies the danger of scientism. Because it is a creed being propagated by a cognitive elite whose authority cannot be intelligently challenged by mere laymen, this cognitive elite would in effect become a new priesthood. The priest-scientists would have access to special knowledge, knowledge that is vital to the laymen's welfare. The laymen would have no choice but to defer to the superior knowledge of these priests because they can never hope to possess this knowledge for themselves. They would have to take on faith what the priest-scientists know about the universe, in the same spirit that the peasant learned to repeat the words of the catechism administered by the Roman Catholic priests.

The scientific elite will naturally object that they are teaching not mystical nonsense but hard scientific facts. Still, for those who treasure their intellectual independence, it does not matter in the least whether the catechism being taught is true or false—what bothers them is that a catechism, by definition, is a set of questions and answers to be learned by mechanical memorization. Instead of encouraging people to think through questions on their own, a catechism is only concerned with the mass dissemination of "correct thinking" as defined by the priesthood in charge of administering it. Second-hand enlightenment is not enlightenment at all. It is indoctrination pure and simple.

IN CONTEMPORARY AMERICA the tradition of cognitive orneriness is still alive and well in the Tea Party movement and among the many Americans who sympathize with it. Often today, as in the past, this tradition leads to absurdity and nonsense. Yet it is a tradition that we should perhaps approach in the spirit of Burke's conservationism. Instead of trying to eliminate the tradition of cognitive orneriness by teaching everyone to accept the exact same truths about everything under the sun, we might be better off trying to preserve it as a national treasure, like the wilderness of Yosemite or Yellowstone. We desperately need to retain a large chunk of the population who will adamantly refuse to believe anything that they don't understand for themselves. Far better for children to reject Darwin's theory of evolution because they can't believe we came from monkeys than to teach them to repeat the theory by rote as if we were descended from parrots. Indeed, when faced with the prospect of mass indoctrination by a scientific priesthood, perhaps we need to actively encourage such contrariness in order to avoid the horror of mental servitude against which John Stuart Mill warned. The percentage of the population who will be able to see for themselves the more abstruse truths of science will never be very large. Hence, the only way to get the entire population to accept these truths is by a process of mass indoctrination, by which everyone in the society is trained and taught to take on blind faith the dictates of the cognitive elite. But once any elite has obtained this power over the masses, they will have achieved a degree of domination that no thuggish ruling class has ever possessed. They will literally be able to control what everyone thinks and believes. Now it may well be possible that an elite made up entirely of highly educated scientific minds would never dream of using their colossal power for their own selfish purposes, but the history of ruling elites throughout the ages is not exactly reassuring on this point.

It can be intelligently argued that we are all better off for having in our midst a large segment of the population who refuses to act intelligently—people who won't listen to what the scientists tell them even when the scientists are right. It may well turn out that their irrational resistance to a scientific outlook on life will prevent a world in which no other outlook is conceivable. If freedom depended entirely on rational actors making rational choices, it would have perished long ago. Sometimes the best way—indeed, the only way—to keep the love and passion for freedom alive by seemingly pointless and futile revolts.

CHAPTER 12

THE POINT OF
POINTLESS REBELLION

The populist revolt that put Andrew Jackson in the White House shared many of the characteristics common to other populist revolts. There was the paranoid fear that an aristocratic elite was conspiring to subvert popular democracy by corrupt means, the vicious caricatures of the motives of honorable men, a disturbingly blind hero worship of a man who went rogue at the drop of a hat. Yet, despite sharing in many alarming qualities of all populist rebellions, the Jacksonian revolt was remarkable in several ways.

First, it was successful. It was not a pointless uprising of the masses that was immediately crushed by the powers that be. On the contrary, for better or for worse, this time around "the people" won and "the aristocrats" lost—a fact that transformed the whole tenor and style of subsequent American politics. From that time forward, American politicians, including the elitist Whigs, recognized that the only way to gain power was through populist appeals. Often these appeals were carried to absurdly ludicrous degrees, as when Lincoln supporters at the Republican convention of 1860 created a tremendous hoopla by carrying around the rails that Abe Lincoln was alleged to have spilt with his own hands as a struggling young man. His supporters even celebrated his lack of formal education as a way of underscoring their main selling point: Lincoln was the classic American self-made man.

Second, the Jacksonian revolution demonstrated that populist democracy, at least in America, could avoid the perils and pitfalls that had wrecked previous experiments in populist democracy since the time of Athens' heyday. Poor men and women suddenly empowered in the Age of Jackson did not demand a redistribution of wealth, though they were in favor of cheap money—that is, an inflationary policy that would obviously help the debtor while injuring the creditor. Nor did the people crush dissent, as the Athenians did when they executed Socrates. Alexis de Tocqueville had been fearful that populist democracy would end by imposing a deadening conformity of manners and thought on the entire population, yet cranks and eccentrics of all sorts continued to abound in America.

Third, the Jacksonian revolution did not result in a national shipwreck. In their eagerness and hunger for new land, the supporters of Jackson became the most vocal champions of the doctrine of Manifest Destiny and eventually brought about an immense expansion of the territory of the United States. Today the doctrine of Manifest Destiny is reviled and derided—curiously enough by many Americans who are living happily in those regions that we "stole" from Mexico. But during and after the Age of Jackson, those who championed the interests of the people quite naturally supported their desire for more land and room. New territories permitted the creation of new self-made societies in which the frontier ethos of independence and orneriness could be kept alive.

Finally, as previously noted, the populist revolt that ushered in the Age of Jackson occurred without spilling a drop of blood. Other populist uprisings, like the French Jacquerie of 1361, were not only abysmal failures as rebellions; they were usually ghastly in their indiscriminate violence and slaughter.

THESE CHARACTERISTICS together make the populist rebellion led by Andrew Jackson every bit as exceptional as the nation in which it took place.

Had the vested interests of the time been more powerful, had the culture of corporate cash been as corrupting as it is today, the Jacksonian populist revolt might never have gotten off the ground. Indeed, by the time of the next great populist revolt, during the 1890s, the gigantic financial and corporate institutions of the East were able to use their vast wealth to depict William Jennings Bryan as a wild-eyed radical, socialist, and even communist, thereby denying him the presidency on three different occasions. In addition, had the general public of Jackson's age been educated, they might have turned up their nose at Jackson for his lack of education and elected the highly educated John Quincy Adams. Had they become used to getting their news and opinions about politics from powerful news monopolies that parroted a single party's script, they might have been easily persuaded that Jackson was a crude and coarse buffoon that no one in his right mind could take seriously. Instead, back then, every little town usually had a number of competing newspapers, each openly and often absurdly partisan in all different directions. In short, had the general population been less ignorant, less ornery, and less rebellious, they might well have been content with the continuation of the aristocratic tradition of government represented by Henry Clay and John Quincy Adams.

There is one last factor of enormous importance. The populist revolt of the 1820s was able to succeed without violence and bloodshed because of the weakness of its opponents. The people only needed to vote in order to achieve their success. They did not need to invade the nation's capitol, or fight off mercenary armies in the pay of the powers that be, or drag the elitists physically out of the halls of power, or execute them to keep them from plotting revenge. They didn't even need to riot, smash windows, and burn down mansions as the American Sons of Liberty had done sixty years earlier. Indeed, one might offer a general rule about the relationship of populist revolts to the degree of violence that accompanies them. The stronger and more ruthless the forces arrayed behind the status quo, the greater the violence that is required to defeat them, or even to merely shake them up temporarily.

It is not clear, however, what lesson should be draw from this general rule. One can argue that in those cases where the revolt is bound to be crushed by the overwhelming superior force of the established order, then there is simply no point in rebelling. Under such circumstances, the act of rebellion is irrational. Instead of leading to an improvement in the condition of the rebels, it leads to an overall worsening of their plight, even to their imprisonment or execution. From the point of view of cost-benefit analysis, this is utterly senseless. Therefore, the prudent policy is simply to accept one's lot until an opportunity arises when it is possible to attempt to improve it with a reasonable chance of success—although there is no guarantee that this opportunity will ever come. Indeed, if the oppressed victims of the established order decide their best course of action is to do nothing to challenge the status quo, then the status quo will be able to shore up its own power base without needing to worry about unpleasant upheavals from the masses. Its power will increase until the chances of a successful rebellion are reduced to zero.

Yet, the only alternative to this scenario is to engage in pointless rebellions that are bound to end in failure. To the rational individual, nothing could possibly make less sense than that. But fortunately for the development and spread of human liberty, the rebels of the past did not make rational calculations. They plunged into their revolts heedless of the consequences and sought to achieve their goals by what can only strike the modern observer as irrational violence.

Modern liberal societies are not friends to irrational violence. It represents an evil that they are determined to wipe out, like smallpox—and with good reason. But our horror of irrational violence makes us minimize the role that such violence has played in the creation of free societies. We prefer to think that our liberty was the gift of wise and benevolent men writing beautiful documents endowing their fellow citizens with a set of splendid rights. In grade school many Americans were once taught to look upon the document known as the Magna Carta as one of the great milestones in the creation of free societies like our own. But the true story of the Magna Carta is not the story of reasonable men seeking a compromise. Rather, it is the story of a power struggle between well-armed men who were quite prepared to use violence to obtain their objectives. It is also the story of a revolt that completely failed to obtain its stated objectives but nevertheless became a rallying cry for free men across the centuries.

THE MAGNA CARTA, or Great Charter, was signed by King John on June 15, 1215, in the meadow of Runnymede, not far from London. As the name implies, it was a written document—in essence, a legal contract. Its purpose was to limit the power of the king, to specify in great detail precisely those actions that the king promised he would never do again. Perhaps the most striking restraint on the king's freedom to act was clause 61, known as "the security clause." The longest and most elaborate part of the Magna Carta, the security clause set up a committee of twenty-five barons who could gather together whenever they thought best and were vested with the power to thwart the king's will by their collective veto. Furthermore, if they didn't succeed, the committee was authorized to restrain the king by force of arms, to seize his property and possessions, including his castles. By this method, it was thought, the king could not do anything offensive to the great barons. He could not go to war without their consent, and, perhaps most importantly, he could not take money out of their pockets without their declared permission—placing the king on a strict budget and a short leash.

In Anglo-American tradition, the Magna Carta has been looked upon as the inspiration behind all the subsequent written documents designed to guarantee the rights of the people against the power of the state, from the Petition of Right that Charles the First signed in 1628 to the Bill of Rights that was incorporated into the Constitution of the United States on December 15, 1791, after it had been ratified by three-fourth of the states. Out of the Magna Carta has come one of the most tenaciously held Anglo-American myths—the myth that the liberty of the subject can be both created and adequately protected by a written contract.

When David Hume wrote his *History of England,* he seemed to delight in exploding this myth. In his chapters on the Tudor monarchs, especially Henry VIII and his daughter Elizabeth I, Hume dwells at length on the despotism of the crown and the supine obsequiousness of the Parliament that, in theory, was supposed to keep the power of the monarch in check. In fact, he goes so far as to suggest that in terms of liberty of the subject, there was little to choose from between the rule of Elizabeth and the Grand Turk of the Ottoman Empire who, to the mid-eighteenth-century men of Hume's time, was the classic exemplar of arbitrary despotism. The Magna Carta (signed three centuries before the rules of Henry VIII and Elizabeth I) was supposed to curb the monarch's power, but under the Tudors you could not find twenty-five men willing to risk their necks in order to tell Henry VIII that he couldn't marry Anne Boleyn or who were crazy enough to threaten to seize the knives and forks of the king, much less his castles, in order to enforce their will against his.

The Magna Carta was itself a response to vigorous armed resistance to the king. King John did not wake up one fine morning and think to himself that he wanted to limit his power in order for his people to be guaranteed their liberty. On June 10, 1215, the powerful English barons, fed up with King John's misrule, entered London with their armed retainers. Though the barons were the elite class, there was widespread sympathy for their rebellion among the common people of London, who willingly opened the gates to let them in—a significant fact that gave the barons' rebellion a populist twist. King John was offered a stark choice: You will cease to be king or you will become a king who is subject to the contract that we have written for you to sign. By signing the document, the king saved his head but lost (temporarily) his sovereignty. He could now be overruled by his theoretical subjects, whose loyalty to him was made conditional on his upholding his end of the bargain.

But King John refused to honor his end of the bargain. As soon as the barons and their retainers had left town, he promptly renounced the security clause that would in fact have made him only an impotent figurehead, a mock king subject to the will of his barons. Pope Innocent III released John from the oath he had taken at Runnymede and annulled the Magna Carta on the recognized legal principle that no contract can be valid that has been made under duress. As the result of the king's renunciation of the Magna Carta, England was immediately plunged into a civil war known as the First Barons' War.

The revolt that led to the Magna Carta totally failed. It did not provide the powerful barons with a method of checking the ambitions of their king, and it certainly did not improve the condition of the English peasants and serfs, nor the independent artisans. By a cruel irony of fate, the little guy would acquire his first real taste of freedom as a result of one of the greatest disasters in the history of European civilization, the horrific outbreak of the bubonic plague that swept over England in the summer of 1348, commonly known as the Black Death.

THE BLACK DEATH, according to the most recent estimates, claimed somewhere between 47 and 48 percent of the English population. Precisely because of its cruel devastation, the English laborers who survived the plague found that suddenly, for the first time, the law of supply and demand was actually on their side. There was too much land and too few people to work it. The peasants had, through no virtue of their own, broken out of the population trap that parson Thomas Malthus later described in his famous book, *An Essay on Population,* first published in 1798 and subsequently revised through six editions.

One of Malthus's main points was that Nature had made it impossible to improve the condition of the servile or laboring class. If you paid them more wages, they simply had more children. When these extra children grew up, they swelled the ranks of the working class, and the law of supply and demand did the rest. Because new workers were competing to do the same amount of work as before, they could not expect to be paid the same wages. The wages of the average worker would drop and biology would return everything back to its "normal" place. Malthus recognized that there were ways out of the population trap. These were collectively identified by Malthus as Vice and Misery. Vice was man's way of dealing with overpopulation—infanticide, sodomy, war, genocide. Misery, on the other hand, was God's way of dealing with overpopulation, such as famine, drought, and plagues—like the Black Death.

The Black Death that swept over England and Europe in the fourteenth century temporarily turned the law of supply and demand very much to the advantage of the laborers. It freed them from the Malthusian trap that had held them down, and, more importantly, it offered them a glimpse of the possibility of self-improvement and a better life. For the first time, laborers felt that they had bargaining power, and they were willing to use it to gain some real control of their own destinies.

Malthus would hasten to point out that this was merely an illusion. Soon the population of laborers would increase to the point where they no longer had the same clout as when their numbers were much smaller. But, what is significant is that during the period in which their numbers were halved, they were able to rouse themselves from their norm of fatalistic apathy. They came to believe, however naively, that they themselves could be masters of their own fate. Thus, when the English government, urged on by the powerful landlords, attempted to turn back the clock and set wages to where they had been before the Black Death, by means of wage and price controls, the peasants no longer shrugged this off as a cruel act of nature. They resented it bitterly and eventually rebelled against it—and the great Peasants' Revolt of 1381 was the ultimate testament to their fierce determination to make the government respond to their wishes and needs. An ugly mob was the first stirrings of the free market.

The leader of the rebellion was Wat Tyler, after whom it is sometimes named. We know very little about Tyler; the best guess is that he had been a professional soldier, or perhaps a highway robber, or possibly both. Tyler became the chief over the great mob of armed men—peasants, ex-soldiers, landless laborers, artisans, and criminals—who made their way to London.

There, with the complicity of disgruntled or ambitious members of the city council, the city gates were thrown open to the rebels, forcing the young king, Richard II, and his counselors to seek shelter in the impregnable Tower of London. The rebels immediately went to the great houses of those powerful men and razed them to the ground. They also broke into wine cellars and got thoroughly plastered.

Up to this point, the English mob had not done much more damage than the American Sons of Liberty would do centuries later. But soon the rebellion became bloody with pointless violence. For example, the rebels turned on harmless Flemish merchants who were asked to pronounce the English words "bread and cheese." When the Flemings inevitably pronounced these words with their native accent, they were beheaded. Their crime was that they were foreigners—and populists, by and large, have never been fond of foreigners.

Soon London was full of the rebel forces under the increasingly dictatorial control of Wat Tyler. The rebels, however, were convinced that the fourteen-year-old king was on their side. They believed that he had been misled by his advisers, especially the archbishop of Canterbury. The mob demanded a face-to-face conference with Richard II to air their grievances and to present their demands.

The king then made the bold and heroic decision to meet the rebels face-to-face in the meadow known as Mile End, outside the walls of London. The rebels accepted these terms and the next morning Richard and his entourage rode out of the tower—both the king and his men were perfectly aware that they were stepping into a lion's den and might never return from their mission. Indeed, two of Richard's half-brothers, seeing the chance of escape, deserted him and galloped away to safety far from the city. When he met with the rebels, the young king acceded to all their demands, including the abolition of serfdom. He even instructed thirty clerks to write up formal documents giving freedom and amnesty to all the rebels who requested them. Many of the rebels were convinced that they had obtained all that they could desire and began to drift away. Back at the Tower of London that same afternoon, a contingent of insurgents entered the great fortress. For unknown reasons, the drawbridge had not been raised to keep them out, and the rebels rushed the guards, who offered no resistance. While the rebels fraternized with the soldiers, they did not feel brotherly toward the men in the tower whom they regarded as traitors. The hapless and well-meaning archbishop of Canterbury was dragged out of the chapel, carried to a hill outside, and beheaded. According to chroniclers of the time, the execution was badly done—it took eight strokes to separate the archbishop's head from his body.

The next day the king met the insurgents again. Wat Tyler apparently wanted to settle other matters besides the abolition of serfdom and manorial dues. Richard said that the people should have everything he could legally concede them short of giving up his crown. What happened next is not absolutely certain. Tyler became rude, asked for a flagon of beer, tossed it down, then jumped on his horse. A retainer of the king murmured that he had recognized Tyler and knew him to be a notorious robber and thief. Tyler, catching these words, became embroiled in a fight and within a few moments John Standwick, a squire of the king, plunged his sword into Tyler, who rode a little way crying (somewhat ironically) "Treason!"[1] He died in front of the enormous crowd of his followers, many of whom promptly began to get their bows and arrows ready for attack.

It was a critical moment for the young Richard II. Galloping on his horse toward the rebels, Richard yelled to them: "Sirs, will you shoot your King? I will be your chief and captain, you shall have from me that which you seek. Only follow me into the fields without."[2] Astonishingly, the armed rebels obeyed and followed him. There, for nearly an hour, Richard talked to the insurgents.

As often happens when apolitical men are confronted with the excess of anarchy, the men of property quickly rallied behind legitimate authority and soon a troop of 6,000 or 7,000 men had been gathered together to put down the rebellion. They hurried to Smithfield where the king was still talking to the crowd, and some of the loyalists urged Richard to seize the opportunity to rush upon and kill the rebels. But Richard was reported to have admonished those who gave him this advice, not wishing to have the innocent, brought there by fear and threats, to suffer with the guilty.[3] As a result, many of the insurgents were said to have fallen on their knees, offering the young king thanks for his clemency.

That same day, the head of Wat Tyler was brought to the king. It was taken to London Bridge to replace the head of the archbishop that the rebels had mounted there in their moment of bloody triumph. There would be more uprisings across England in the months to come, but the Peasant Revolt had been firmly put down. Richard II promptly took back the promises he had offered during the tensest moments of the rebellion. Serfdom, briefly abolished, was reinstituted; manorial dues, briefly canceled, were once again collected.

The revolt in 1381 failed to secure its immediate objective, the legal abolition of serfdom. The documents that the king had signed liberating the serfs swiftly became worthless scraps of paper. Yet the very fact that the peasants had been willing to rebel against the institution of serfdom inevitably did more to undermine that institution than any mere legal document could have done. So long as the peasants remained convinced that serfdom was simply part of the natural order of things, they would have remained in their servile state even if the king had sincerely intended to free them. It was by taking charge of their own lives through the act of rebellion that the English servile class convinced themselves of the injustice of their lot. If they were deluded in the belief that they could bring about the immediate abolition of serfdom through their rebellion, their delusion paid off for their descendants in the long run. For over the course of the next century and a half, a sweeping and revolutionary change would occur in the very structure of English society—the institution of serfdom would disappear. How precisely this extraordinary transformation came about is one of those tantalizing mysteries over which historians scratch their heads. Yet it is tempting to speculate that the road from serfdom was connected with the dramatic change in the self-image of the servile class brought about by their very willingness to rebel and to stand up for their rights. It was through their great revolt that individuals whose parents had accepted the status quo that made them laborious drones, stuck to the same spot of land to the end of time, began to see themselves quite differently, as human beings in charge of their own lives—at least, in charge enough to be able to move to greener pastures in search of higher wages or even to acquire a useful and well-paying skill. As a political movement, the populist revolt of 1381 had failed; but it had created a tradition of rebellion to which "free-born" Englishmen would continue to resort.

THERE WAS another interesting aspect to the Peasants' Revolt. Apart from Wat Tyler and Richard II, another famous person involved in the great revolt was John Ball, often known as "the mad priest of Kent."[4] Ball delivered sermons to the turbulent crowd in which he asked the provocative question, in the rhyming couplets in which he often preached:

When Adam delved and Eve span
  Who was then the gentleman?

To put it in contemporary English, Ball was saying that back when Adam was digging (delving) in the Garden of Eden and Eve was spinning, there were no gentlemen who lived off their labor. If that was how God meant it to be in the first place, then obviously the leisure class, the gentlemen who lived off the labor of others, had no right to exploit the hard work of their fellow men. As Ball put it: "In the beginning all men were created equal: servitude of man to man was introduced by the unjust dealings of the wicked, and contrary to God's will. For if God had intended some to be serfs and other lords, He would have made a distinction between them at the beginning."[5] Here was a cosmic script that clashed violently with the cosmic script of the Great Chain of Being. It was false that everyone was in their right place. The natural order, ordained by God in the Garden of Eden, had been violated by predatory men, and to make things right again, the wicked oppressors must be overthrown. Rebellion is neither a crime nor an act of sacrilege: It was the duty of all Christians who wished to restore the social order to the original plan that God intended.

At one time it was generally supposed that the contemporary religious movement known as the Lollards, founded by John Wycliffe, had played a role in the Peasants' Revolt. In fact, there was no formal connection between John Wycliffe and John Ball although they shared a common aim. They despised the cosmic script of the Great Chain of Being for justifying the iniquitous hierarchies that dominated European civilization during the Middle Ages, and both were keen on reviving the egalitarian cosmic script developed by the ancient Hebrews. John Ball quoted the Hebrew story of creation to prove that God had not intended the unjust and unequal social order that reigned throughout England and Europe. Instead, he blamed it on wicked men who had clearly disregarded God's plans, and who had unjustly set themselves up in power over their fellow men.

In England the enthusiasm for the religion of the ancient Hebrews began in the fourteenth century with Wycliffe and Ball. Within centuries it would become one of the most dynamic forces in English politics, until the Puritans of the seventeenth century, under the brilliant leadership of Oliver Cromwell, seized power for themselves and immediately showed their contempt for the Great Chain of Being by committing an act that horrified the rest of Europe and their own non-Puritan countrymen. On January 30, 1649, after a brief and pointless trial, the Puritan leadership executed King Charles the First, God's anointed, personal choice to stand at the head of the human segment of the Great Chain of Being. At that time a Puritan custom was to raise their mugs of beer—for the Puritans were not teetotalers—and quote their favorite verse from the Book of Judges: "In those days there was no king in Israel and every man did what was right in his own eyes."

THE ENGLISH Civil War, which had begun when Parliament attempted to assert its ancient rights and privileges against the king, became a horrible and bloody affair, ending in a military dictatorship under Cromwell's New Model Army. In the end, the project of recreating the ancient Hebrew common-wealth on English soil was abandoned, and the Englishmen pleaded with the rightful heir to the throne, Charles II, to resume his place at the head of their nation. The experimental republic had failed. Once again a rebellion had seemingly proved futile and pointless. Yet that is far from being the whole story. For the Great Chain of Being was never really restored to its original place in British thought. Too many Englishmen had formed the habit of feeling themselves entitled to judge their king, and in the bloodless revolution of 1688, they chased James II both from his throne and from England.

Americans tend to be fond of this rebellion, agreeing with the English Whig historians in calling it the Glorious Revolution. For one thing, it was successful. For another, it was carried out without violence. James II was allowed to keep his head, and Louis XIV even permitted him to live in his favorite palace at St. Cloud for the remainder of his life, where he was always treated with the proper dignity due to the lawful king of England. Yet, as we have seen, not all rebellions have the good fortune to be as glorious as this one. Despite this fact, even the most inglorious rebellions have contributed their share to the cause of human freedom.

AN OBVIOUS problem with the tradition of rebellion remains. Although the revolts of the past were necessary steps on the road from serfdom, all these revolts came at a high cost in terms of other significant human values. These are the values that we naturally associate with the ideal of civilization, namely, stability and order, peace and harmony, respect for the rule of law and a refusal to use mob violence to gain one's objectives. The English peasants who beheaded the Flemings simply because they were foreigners who spoke a different language may have been promoting the cause of liberty, but they were also behaving like utter bloodthirsty hooligans.

Most modern Americans have been taught to think of the march of liberty as a stately progression that in no way poses a threat to civilization. Yet the Peasants' Revolt of 1381 and the great English rebellion of the 1640s amply demonstrate that the clamor for freedom, even if it is justifiable, has too often ended by lowering the standards of civilized life, degenerating into outrageous mob rule, and tearing the community into bitterly feuding camps, plunging what was once an orderly and stable society into the gruesome ordeal of civil war. Civilization can pose a threat to freedom, but freedom can also pose a threat to civilization.

CHAPTER 13

LIBERTY VERSUS CIVILIZATION

I n the West and particularly in the United States, liberty has often been championed as an absolute good in itself. Indeed, there is a tendency among modern Americans to believe that liberty is not only compatible with all the other things that men hold dear in life, but that liberty is an indispensable precondition of the emergence of other desirable human values, including the economic prosperity that improves the quality of life of most people. But there are simply too many counterexamples to this thesis for it to be accepted without serious qualification. Consider just two contemporary cases. In his book *From Third World to First: The Singapore Story (1965–2000)* Lee Kuan Yew describes how as the leader of his tiny nation of Singapore he was prepared to abridge the freedom of the press in the interests of what he considered more important values, such as social stability and rapid economic development. "Freedom of the press, freedom of the news media," he argued, "must be subordinated to the overriding needs of Singapore, and to the primacy of purpose of an elected government."[1] An even more startling example that a lack of liberty does not pose a threat to a nation's economic well-being comes from the People's Republic of China. Despite the brutal suppression of the democracy demonstrations in Tiananmen Square in 1989, communist

China has experienced one of the most astonishing economic growth rates in history, raising vast numbers of its citizens out of the most abject poverty.

On the other hand, there have been many freedom-obsessed people—the Spartans and the Iroquois come to mind—who have demonstrated zero interest in material prosperity, seeing wealth as a threat to their liberty. In the sixteenth century, the Italian political thinker Niccolò Machiavelli even argued that the citizens of a republic could only keep their liberties so long as they remained relatively poor. In his *Discourses,* he wrote that "it is of the greatest advantage in a republic to have laws that keep her citizens poor. . . . poverty produces better fruits than riches,—[poverty] has conferred honor upon cities, countries, and religions, whilst [riches] have only served to ruin them."[2] Furthermore, in making this observation, Machiavelli makes no claim to originality, noting that he is simply adopting a thesis that many earlier thinkers embraced as well.

It is relatively easy to shrug off the examples of Singapore and China. After all, the United States has demonstrated that it is possible for a nation to achieve great prosperity while maintaining the proper respect for the liberty of the press and the freedom of assembly. Perhaps it is even true that, due to their different cultural and economic circumstances, nations like Singapore and China really needed to curtail the liberties Americans have traditionally enjoyed, but this is not an issue that confronts America today. The case is quite different when it comes to Machiavelli's pessimistic assessment of the influence that economic prosperity has on the amount of freedom that a society can enjoy, because it raises a profoundly troubling question: Is it possible that American's spectacular worldly success is the real threat to our traditional liberty, and not a sinister cabal of godless liberals?

As we have seen, the early American republic, to which today's populist conservatives often imagine they would like to return, was not an economic superpower dominating the world stage, nor did it aspire to be. Those who swept Andrew Jackson into the White House in 1828 agreed with him that a national bank would be a horrid evil, threatening to crush the little guy with its awesome concentration of wealth. Today we are a superpower beyond the wildest dreams—or nightmares—of our Founding Fathers. The Federal Reserve system of regional banks has become an accepted part of our lives that we implicitly have relied on to maintain sound monetary and credit positions for our nation. Yet the Federal Reserve Act was not signed into law until 1913, and only after the hero of the agrarian populists, William Jennings Bryan, had given it his imprimatur, a fact that clearly demonstrates the great reluctance with which the bank-hating Americans of the nineteenth century accepted our transformation from a land of yeoman farmers into the financial center of the world. Ironically, in the aftermath of our latest financial crisis, many twenty-first century Americans have come full circle, and are once again suspicious of big banks and their supposed regulators. They are especially furious that it was the little guy, in the form of the ordinary American tax-payer, who was forced to come up with the money to bail out colossal financial institutions and mega-corporations on the principle that they were "too big to fail." Perhaps, the average person can't help thinking that corporations too big to fail are simply too big to begin with and should be brought down to size. Yet a downsizing of American institutions, economic and governmental, would involve a massive and radical transformation of contemporary America that few are willing even to contemplate. Our bigness is a fait accompli, and there is simply no realistic way of undoing what has been done.

America's rise to an unprecedented scale of bigness has inevitably had a profound impact on our traditional conception of freedom. Lee Kuan Yew, when justifying his suppression of certain newspapers in Singapore, offered an argument that goes right to the heart of the issue. "I do not subscribe to the Western practice that allows a wealthy press baron to decide what voters should read day after day."[3] Back in the nineteenth century, when there was a myriad of different newspapers, even in small-towns, freedom of the press possessed a quite different function and meaning than it does today, when a handful of wealthy and powerful individuals control not only chains of newspapers, but various other media outlets. The freedom of a small-time editor to try to persuade his tiny readership to accept his political views is an altogether different thing from the freedom of one tycoon to impose his ideas on millions and millions of newspaper readers and TV viewers. And this is only one example of how what we call "modern progress" has dramatically altered the ideas of freedom that once flourished in simpler times.

SINCE THE time of the Founding Fathers, we have lost all sorts of freedoms, but like the freedom of a man to spit wherever he wants, the loss of many of these is not greatly regretted. Today the question that faces us is whether we have lost too many freedoms, even if this loss has been compensated by an increase in our wealth, power, and influence. The issue is not a simple-minded choice between being pro- or anti-liberty, as many spokespersons of today's populist revolt claim. Instead, the choice is one of balancing two often conflicting values: the freedom to do whatever you want to do on one hand, and the order, stability, and comfort of civilization on the other. In many instances, a compromise can be reached. But not always. If we want to dine in a smoke-free environment, we must take away the liberty to enjoy a good cigar after a fine restaurant meal—a liberty that meant a great deal to Americans not so long ago. Here there can be no compromise. Today there are some Americans who would like to take away the freedom of other Americans to buy guns, arguing that this would lead to vastly fewer violent crimes in our society, which, if true, would certainly represent progress in the direction of a higher stage of civilization—assuming, of course, that it didn't lead to a mass uprising of gun-loving Americans. Here, too, it is hard to see room for compromise.

Freedom is by no means the only value that people have tried to maximize. There are many other valuable things that individuals have sought to secure as well, such as economic growth, political stability, and a civilized lifestyle, but these other ideals are not always compatible with a society that gives everyone the unchecked liberty to do pretty much as they please. When human beings, either as individuals or as groups, have been forced to choose between liberty and other incompatible goods, the choice they face is inescapably tragic. There is nothing tragic about choosing between good and evil, since no one regrets the loss of the evil. But there is something inherently tragic about a choice between two incompatible goods. It is true that by selecting one of the two goods, you are not choosing an evil—but you inevitably take the risk of rejecting a genuine good in the pursuit of an even better one.

Consider the risks run by the Sons of Liberty. Not only were they imperiling their own necks, they were risking retaliation upon their community by the greatest power in the world, their own motherland, Great Britain. In addition, there were more subtle risks. A society in which mob action becomes accepted is a society that will forever be threatened by the specter of anarchy, chaos, and civil war. If everyone developed a habit of inciting mobs to air their daily grievances, what society could maintain even the minimum degree of stability? The passion for liberty has more than once degenerated into a license to run amok, resulting in civic upheavals and anarchy. The town hall revolts of 2009 are only a very gentle wake-up call from our anarchic past.

Our most difficult challenge today is to decide whether our contemporary populist revolt is championing human freedom or endangering it. This challenge is not a new one. It was faced by the Founding Fathers when a group of disgruntled farmers in rural western Massachusetts decided to stage an armed rebellion under the leadership of Daniel Shays, a veteran of the American Revolution who had fought at Lexington, Bunker Hill, and Saratoga. The rebellion—known as Shays's Rebellion after its leader—began in 1786 and ended a year later.

The rebellious farmers no doubt thought of themselves as the new Sons of Liberty, and not without reason. They had the same grievances—taxation without representation. Right before the revolt, the state government, located in urban eastern Massachusetts, passed a grossly unfair tax apportionment that penalized farmers for owning their wealth in land, but left the merchants' buildings, personal property, and physical inventories untouched by the expropriating hand of the tax man. The already debt-ridden farmers, out-raged at what they rightfully saw as a rigged political system, a plutocracy sucking their life's blood, took the law into their own hands—and on several occasions even took the officers of the law and judges into their own hands.

To many of the Founding Fathers, including George Washington, Shays's Rebellion was the harbinger of an impending social breakdown, the first sign of the slide of the newly minted republic into anarchy. The original Sons of Liberty had been patriots fighting for the independence of their na-tion, but the rebellious farmers, whose behavior was not nearly as violent as the Sons of Liberty, were agents of sedition. Something had to be done—and something was done. Those concerned that populist democracy was about to get out of hand gathered in Philadelphia in order to create a new and stronger system of government than the weak Articles of Confederation al-lowed. One of those peculiar ironies of history is that without the populist re-volt in western Massachusetts—a revolt that made many wealthy men anxious about the security of their property—the United States would proba-bly not have its present Constitution.

The document composed in secrecy in Philadelphia in 1787—the year Shays's Rebellion ended—had no impact on the fate of the rebels. Even if their methods were unruly, their cause was so just that they received the supreme vindication of having the hated urban merchants' and bankers' laws stricken from the books and their own farmer-friendly laws written. Yet surely the Founding Fathers had a point. What happens to a society that per-mits judges who deliver unfavorable verdicts to be threatened with death by enraged mobs of violent men? The rule of law must be respected, even when we disagree with its verdict. And yet we Americans are not entirely one hun-dred percent convinced of this. Certainly, respect for the rule of law is a good rule of thumb, but do we really want to argue that the rule of law must always be respected, even when it clashes with basic human rights? Should the Sons of Liberty have accepted the Stamp Tax? Should Rosa Parks have given up her seat on the bus?

Most Americans today, looking back a half century, feel that Rosa Parks was right to disobey the law; she was asserting through her civil disobedience a higher law. But who should decide when it is okay to break a law? Morally right or morally wrong, segregation was still the law of the land in the South. Like many other laws, the segregation laws were unjust, a fragrant violation of the rights of blacks in the states of the old Confederacy, but we have been taught that the way to deal with unjust laws is to change them through the appropriate legal procedures, not to violate them. Even if the violation is intended merely to be a symbolic protest against the law, it will undermine the all-important respect for the rule of law. But is respect for the rule of law all-important? Can it not be trumped by higher values?

Here we come to something that might be called the internal contradiction of naïve liberalism, the dominant political philosophy of our era. Naïve liberalism assumes that respect for the law and enthusiasm for liberty are compatible values. Sometimes they are. Sometimes they aren't. That is why those who are passionate for liberty must inevitably be prepared to obey the call of a higher law. They may well grope vainly for a way of expressing their unconditional loyalty to this higher law. They may devise different metaphysical systems as a way of explaining to themselves why their insistence on their own liberty must trump every other good that men hold dear, including life itself—otherwise what is the point of the passionate outburst "Give me liberty or give me death"?

All these attempts to justify the passion for liberty are, at best, only clumsy efforts at rationalizing what is at bottom an utterly irrational drive—the urge to be masters of our own fate, despite the abundance of evidence demonstrating that we are merely the victims (or the beneficiaries) of circumstances beyond our control. If, as science tells us, we are determined to behave in a certain way and cannot behave otherwise, then freedom does not exist—not at any level of consciousness, except as an odd kind of illusion, viscerally compelling but cerebrally specious. Because all of us suffer from the illusion that we are free, we are forced to undergo much wholly unnecessary and pointless suffering. We strive for what we cannot obtain. We seek to change in ourselves that which cannot be altered. We work to improve human beings instead of trying to program them to respond to their real and evident needs. Get rid of the illusion of freedom instilled in us by our cultural tradition, and all will be equally happy—the very position that B. F. Skinner advocated in his book, *Beyond Freedom and Dignity*.

Like Skinner, I have argued that the illusion of freedom is instilled in us by certain cultural traditions, but not by others, and that there is no need for human beings to have an illusion of freedom at all. We are not born with this illusion—it is entirely the result of certain traditions of cultural programming. For example, those human populations that have been condemned to live century after century as the serfs and slaves of a despotic ruling class will have a difficult time even imagining themselves as free, and this will be especially the case when they have been raised to accept a cosmic script that justifies their own subjugation even in their own eyes. But it is precisely because the illusion of freedom can be so completely extinguished by certain regimes and certain religions that it is necessary for those who champion the cause of freedom to protect and defend those rare traditions that are able to keep the longing for liberty alive even under the most adverse circumstances. Obviously, those who find the illusion of freedom to be a handicap to human progress, as Skinner did, will disagree. They will want to eradicate all memory of those freedom-friendly traditions, seeing in them the source of endless human misery.

How do you make a choice between these two positions? For the pragmatist, this involves a judgment about whether the illusion of freedom has been more of a benefit to the human race or more of a curse. But who can possibly make such a sweeping judgment and call it a logical conclusion, no matter how much evidence he appeals to? One person can point to where the illusion of freedom led to folly or disaster, while another to where it led to virtues and blessings. The point will be forever debatable and can ultimately be decided only by our temperament. Some people are viscerally horrified by the very idea of living in a world without even the illusion of freedom. Even a hardened determinist, if he is a pragmatist, may prefer to live in a community in which the illusion of freedom is widely shared, as long as he is convinced that the illusion of freedom brings important ethical values to the community that nothing else can provide.

For the pragmatist, there is nothing astonishing about an illusion yielding good fruit—it happens all the time. Hence, even the pragmatic determinist may want to keep the illusion of freedom alive and well. Furthermore, he will also approve of those inherited cultural traditions that have helped to promote and to preserve this illusion. He will want his society to keep these traditions alive, passing them on to the next generation, not because they are true in any sense, but because they have proven themselves to be useful in creating free and open societies. For the pragmatist, in short, the argument simply comes down to the question: Is the illusion of freedom good for us? If it is, then we must also support the cultural traditions that have given rise to it.

The pragmatic approach also permits us to take a fresh look at the influential distinction between negative and positive liberty that the philosopher and historian of ideas Isaiah Berlin developed in his essay "Two Concepts of Liberty," first published in 1958.[4] The concept of negative liberty can be traced back directly to the seventeenth-century English political philosopher Thomas Hobbes, who wrote in his masterpiece *Leviathan* that "a free man is he that in those things which by his strength and wit he is able to do is not hindered to do what he has the will to do."[5] Isaiah Berlin argued that negative liberty was the essence of the Anglo-American tradition of liberalism: It is the freedom to do what you please and to be left alone while you are doing it, both by the government and by other people. Today this concept of freedom has come to dominate our culture in the form of a *carpe diem* ethos that is intent on liberating individuals from the constraints of social custom and inherited cultural traditions—it is the freedom to do your own thing and to follow your bliss. Yet, when pushed too far, this ideal of freedom can easily become a pretext for selfish and irresponsible behavior that can be self-destructive as well as harmful to the community. The heroin addict who throws his life away shooting up drugs is doing his own thing. So, too, is the guy who drives drunk, and the mother who neglects her children. But is this kind of liberty really desirable?

Thomas Hobbes, who originated the idea of negative liberty, did not think very highly of it. Indeed, he thought that too much negative freedom was quite dangerous. If everyone was free to do his or her own thing, there would be a constant struggle among them, that perpetual war of all against all that is the essence of lawlessness and anarchy. Under these circumstances, individuals can have only as much freedom as they can claim and defend for themselves. According to Hobbes, to create an orderly and stable society, men have to relinquish this dangerous kind of freedom. That is the only path by which they will be able to enjoy the blessings of civilization—by surrendering as much of their natural liberty as is required by society.

Here is the problem with negative liberty: If its value lies simply in the fact that there is no one to keep you from pursuing some external good, then negative freedom is not an end in itself but merely a means to an end. If someone gave you the good you were pursuing, you would no longer need the freedom to pursue it on your own. In addition, the value of your freedom to the other people in your community would depend entirely on what you did with it. If you used it to get drunk all the time and raise hell in the streets, then your liberty would appear to them to be mere license—something that they would have every right to take away from you.

This argument can be pushed even further. The abuse of such license would permit a paternalistic government to justify a radical curtailment of people's personal liberty for their own good. Citizens would be permitted the freedom to do those things that are genuinely valuable actions, while they would be denied the right to do anything that was deemed to be injurious or even merely worthless. Men would be at liberty to do good deeds but would be restrained from doing bad ones—and no genuine good would be lost by this limitation of our liberty. Indeed, it might well be argued that limiting our liberty in this way is a positive good, because it prevents the commission of positive evils. Men would no longer be free to get drunk or gamble or commit adultery—and the world would be better off for it. Hence, if negative liberty is merely the liberty to sin, then we may still be willing to fight for it, but can we do so with a clear conscience?

In the face of these objections, it is still possible to argue that negative liberty is an end in itself, a supreme good, despite the fact that its exercise so often results in terrible evils. But there is another way of approaching this question, and it is the one taken in this book. Negative freedom—the freedom to make your own choices and decisions without the interference of other people—is not an end in itself. It is valuable not because it lets people do what they want, but because it is the indispensable condition for creating a certain kind of human character type, as Harriet Martineau recognized in the nineteenth century. Reflecting on the abundance of negative liberty that we gave our children on the frontier, she recognized that the only way of creating adults who were capable of self-government was by permitting kids the freedom to make their own decisions and to take their own risks. Just as nursemaids are not good for the development of free-spirited boys and girls, so too a nanny-state is not good for the development of self-reliance, autonomy, and intellectual independence.

In this interpretation, negative liberty, the lack of restraint, is merely a means to an end, but it is an unavoidable means to this end. Only those who have de facto control over much of their own lives will be able to display the spirit of independence—and this de facto control can only exist when a large latitude for the exercise of negative liberty also exists. When children are not allowed a healthy degree of independence in their daily lives or when the state behaves like a nanny micromanaging the behavior of adults, it will be difficult for the social psychology of the natural libertarian to flourish; and when natural libertarians do not flourish, free societies are in peril. The natural libertarian, because he values his own freedom to do as he judges best, will automatically resist the attempts of those who might wish to take his freedom of action away. Thus, by fighting to preserve his own narrowly defined negative liberty, the natural libertarian benefits the society as a whole, much the way Adam Smith argued that the baker and the candlestick maker do not benefit society by pursuing the general welfare, but by seeking their own self interests, both guided, as it were, by the same invisible hand.

The independent man and the ornery rebel are character types that have proved to be of solid value—a community is better off when it has a sizable number of such individuals. Whatever conditions are required to create such individuals must therefore be embraced, even if this means embracing the unavoidable harm that comes from negative liberty. Because negative liberty remains a means to an end, it can still be legitimately checked whenever its exercise is found to undermine and subvert the objective that alone justifies its existence, namely, the creation—or social construction—of the kind of independent human beings that have proved uniquely valuable. This caveat provides us with a kind of rule of thumb by which we can judge when paternalism has gone too far: When the paternalistically inclined government begins to infantilize its citizens, to rob them of their desire to control their own lives, then it has gone too far, and must be checked.

On the other hand, when the Chinese government in the early nineteenth century attempted to prohibit the importation of opium into their country, they were acting paternalistically because their aim was to keep their population from becoming hopelessly codependent on opium, as millions eventually did. They were fearful that cheap and easily available opium would prove too much of a temptation, and that by giving into this temptation, millions of their citizens would be diminishing their capacity to be in charge of their own lives and destinies. Their overindulgence in negative liberty would result in a total loss of practical autonomy in their daily lives. They would be the slaves of their addiction—a consequence of unbridled negative liberty that the libertarian John Stuart Mill cheerfully accepted, but which most of us would intuitively reject.

Libertarianism, when pushed to its logical conclusion, not only permits us to become metaphoric slaves to opium addiction, but genuine slaves who must submit to real human masters. If no one has the right to interfere with our decisions regarding our own life and liberty, then who is to prevent someone from selling himself into slavery? The twentieth-century American libertarian thinker Walter Block argued that in a truly free society, constructed on purely libertarian principles, a man should be allowed to exercise this freedom.[6] But here again our rule of thumb tells us that a government that forbids such a transaction may well be interfering with our negative liberty, but its interference is justified because it is aimed at conserving the spirit of independence in the community, which the introduction of slavery is bound to erode along with the dignity of labor. In such cases, the state has both the right and the duty "to force men to be free," as Jean-Jacques Rousseau paradoxically maintained in his eighteenth-century work *The Social Contract*.

When Isaiah Berlin came to speak of the concept of positive liberty in his essay, "Two Concepts of Liberty," he had in mind Rousseau's claim that men sometimes needed to be forced to be free. For Berlin, the tradition of positive liberty, which he identified with such continental European thinkers as Rousseau and Hegel, was a threat to true freedom. By handing over to the state the power to coerce citizens "for their own good," the champions of positive liberty were justifying an unwarranted and dangerous interference in citizens' lives and robbing them of their independence of both thought and action. Better to keep the state out of the business of making men free, Berlin warned; they are free enough already.

Yet consider the outcome of a society in which individuals are free to become addicted to drugs and to sell themselves into slavery—perhaps for a desperately needed fix. The extreme libertarian might be willing to live in such a community, but ordinary Americans are not. When populist conservatives rage against the modern state, they are complaining about a state that is becoming too intrusive and too bossy. But not very many of them wish to abolish laws against slavery or overturn laws that prohibit the sale of highly addictive drugs, like crack, morphine, or heroin.

The populist conservative may be a natural libertarian, but he is far from being a doctrinaire or ideological libertarian. The ideological libertarian holds that all governments are, by their very nature, both the enemy of liberty and a threat to all that is glorious in civilized life—a condemnation that would apply to the government of the United States. Yet deep within the American political psyche, especially among conservatives, there has always been the profound sense that our nation is different. Yes, it is a state, but it is a different kind of state. It has not been the enemy of the people. Instead, it has, by and large, promoted liberty and the general welfare. Even if libertarian scholars can go through history documenting the horrors committed by the state in its various incarnations, our government in the United States is somehow exempt. Here, too, we have been exceptional.

To take but one shining example, back in the fifties, when the United States government decided to wipe out polio among American school children, it acted promptly, efficiently, and effectively. Everyone was thankful. No one regarded the polio vaccine as a sinister conspiracy to inject communist bacilli into our unsuspecting kids. In the early nineteenth century, people expressed genuine alarm at the idea of using federal government money to build a bridge, a canal, or a turnpike. Today, not even the most right-wing, antigovernment fanatic avoids driving on the interstate.[7] In the late nineteenth century, it was the American federal government that stepped in to preserve and protect our great wilderness areas like Yellowstone and Yosemite by creating national parks. Today few complain about this high-handed act of government interference, though there were many at the time who bitterly resented it—namely, those individuals who wished to use these national treasures for their own purposes, such as grazing and mining.

Those government programs that fail receive much attention while those that succeed are all too often taken for granted. At a 2009 town hall meeting, for example, many of those who spoke out most vociferously against socialized medicine were asked if they were on Medicare. Yes, they were—but Medicare was different, they argued: It wasn't socialized medicine; it was their right as Americans, conveniently ignoring the fact that Medicare is paid for by the American government, acting, in this role at least, much more like a solution than a problem. This is not to say that our federal government has not at times infringed on people's liberty, for obviously there are many lamentable occasions when it has done so, such as the internment of American citizens of Japanese descent during the Second World War. Yet, when seen against the grand perspective of world history, we tend to believe that our track record is better than that of other nations. Today's populist conservatives, far from disputing this claim, are among its most enthusiastic champions. They are deeply patriotic. They regard the role that America has played in world affairs as altruist and benevolent, unlike their opponents, the liberal statists, who are usually highly critical of America's past conduct.

There is, however, another reason why the populist conservative has good reason to be wary of doctrinal libertarianism. In the eyes of the ideological libertarian, big government is the root of all evil. But what about big media conglomerations that permit a handful of influential individuals to control and even dictate what news is to be printed and what movies and TV shows our kids will watch? Today much of the anger of the populist conservative is directed against what they perceived as the liberal elite's arrogant domination of America's popular culture, influencing what news is channeled through the mainstream media, and deciding what kind of messages will be conveyed by popular movies and TV shows. Yet this media-dominating liberal elite was not appointed by the government. They obtained their positions of power and influence through their success in the free market. The populist conservative is equally outraged by the bailout of big corporations, and he is particularly galled by the fact that the well-heeled executives of these corporations were awarded spectacular bonuses, apparently for their skill at driving their colossal enterprises to the verge of insolvency. But here again it is idle to pretend that big government was the cause of high level executive incompetence or that it was directly responsible for the wanton excesses of corporate greed. Doctrinal libertarianism, by concentrating exclusively on the evils of big government, is strangely oblivious to the host of other ills that are brought about by big media consortiums or big financial institutions—but the populist conservative, precisely because he is the little guy, needs to recognize that any kind of bigness poses a threat to his freedom and independence. Ideological libertarianism, on the other hand, has zero interest in leveling the playing field for the little guy. It is perfectly willing to accept the most extreme degrees of inequality, allowing the big to get bigger and the powerful to become more powerful.

Ultimately the natural libertarian must part company with the doctrinal libertarian over the very question of freedom. Going by strictly libertarian principles, it is inevitable that some individuals will turn out to be "freer" than others, just as in George Orwell's *Animal Farm* some animals turned out to be more equal than others. In the libertarian community advocated by Walter Block, as we have seen, some men would not be free at all, having made use of their freedom to enter into slave contracts. Most people would no doubt choose to remain free, but no one would be forced to stay free. By this process, it would be entirely possible for a libertarian community to be divided into free men and slaves, just like so many despotic societies of the past. Yet this is precisely the kind of social order that ordinary Americans have instinctively rebelled against. Our operating maxim has been "Liberty for all." But the only way that liberty for all can be achieved is through a government that is prepared to stand up for the rights of everyone, including the weak, the poor, and the oppressed—indeed, especially them. Such a government must possess far more power than the ideological libertarian is prepared to give it. Yet the American government has repeatedly demonstrated that it is possible for the state to protect and defend liberty not just for some, but for all, and to achieve this noble objective without crushing the spirit of independence essential to the preservation of a free and open society.

CHAPTER 14

CONSERVING
THE SPIRIT OF LIBERTY

On May 21, 1944, the distinguished American jurist Learned Hand gave a speech in New York City's Central Park as part of the annual patriotic event called "I Am an American Day." At the time, Hand was a judge on the United States Court of Appeals for the Second Circuit, but his reputation as a judicial philosopher of the first order was universally recognized by others in his profession. The brief remarks he gave that day in 1944 quickly made the shy and retiring judge famous throughout the nation, as many compared his speech with Lincoln's Gettysburg Address.

The huge crowd Hand addressed included 150,000 new American citizens who had come to swear their oaths of allegiance to their new homeland. The speech was entitled "The Spirit of Liberty," and it was consciously and unavoidably set against the backdrop of America's struggle against the sinister forces of European fanaticism and totalitarianism. D-Day was only two weeks away. Yet there was nothing jingoistic about his address.

Learned Hand began by telling the massive audience that he could not define the spirit of liberty: "I can only tell you my own faith. The spirit of liberty is the spirit which is not too sure that it is right; the spirit of liberty is the spirit which seeks to understand the minds of other men and women; the spirit of liberty is the spirit which weighs their interests alongside its own without bias."[1] After reminding his audience that all Americans started out as immigrants who came to the United States in search of liberty, Judge Hand warned them not to be lured into believing that courts, laws, and constitutions could protect or guarantee the liberty they sought. "[B]elieve me, these are false hopes. Liberty lies in the hearts of men and women; when it dies there, no constitution, no law, no court can save it; no constitution, no law, no court can even do much to help it."[2]

Liberty, Hand explained, was not "the ruthless, the unbridled will," nor was it the "freedom to do as one likes. That is the denial of liberty, and leads straight to its overthrow. A society in which men recognize no check upon their freedom becomes a society where freedom is the possession of only a savage few, as we have learned to our sorrow."[3]

In Hand's judgment human beings needed to recognize a check upon their own ruthless and unbridled will; but this recognition could not be imposed on them from the outside, by laws, or courts, or constitution. The recognition had to come from within—from their character, and not from their reason. Hand realized that all too often our reason acted merely as a slave to our passion, or worse, as the handmaiden to our ruthless and unbridled will-to-power. For Hand, liberty could only be secured by becoming "a habit of the heart" operating throughout an entire community. It had to become second nature to the members of the community to refrain from being too sure that they were right. They had to guard against being swept away by their own strong convictions.

Hand's speech was a great triumph. An edition of it was bound as a pamphlet and sent to American servicemen fighting overseas as part of the war effort. Later, during an interview about his speech, Learned Hand quoted with approval the words with which Oliver Cromwell challenged his enemies before the Battle of Dunbar in 1650, "I beseech thee, in the bowels of Christ, Think that ye be mistaken."[4] In the interview, Hand said that he wished that these words would be inscribed "over the portals of every church, every courthouse and at every crossroad in the nation." He added that "it seems to me that if we are to be saved it must be through skepticism."[5]

To many of us today, "saved through skepticism" might sound like a strange paradox. In the eyes of cultural conservatives especially, skeptics are the people who use critical reasoning in order to question the traditional values of their community; they are the relentless critics keen on revealing the fallacies of traditional faith and the absurdities of society's system of government. Nor is the skeptic's job particularly challenging, since every faith has its sacred fallacies and every system of government its equally sacred foibles. Thus, for many who value the inherited traditions of their culture, skeptics are the enemy, intent on subverting and undermining the intellectual and ethical foundations of their own society—a dangerous threat to the stability of the entire social order.

But what Judge Hand was recommending was not this kind of destructive skepticism. Rather, what Hand called for might best be termed *constructive skepticism*—a skepticism that, instead of dissolving the basis of the community, holds it together through a collective process of systematic self-doubt. Hand's constructive skepticism, in sharp contrast to destructive skepticism, starts at home. It begins not by challenging the opinions of other people—which is always a pleasant enough recreation—but rather by challenging the opinions we hold ourselves, which is a far more demanding task.

Skepticism may seem like the luxury of philosophers who have nothing better to do with their time than to doubt things that no one in their right mind would ever think of doubting. Yet there are many quite ordinary people who have never picked up a book of philosophy and are still capable of questioning someone who tells them something that defies their own common sense. What ordinary Americans call "healthy skepticism" is itself a form of constructive skepticism, because it reminds us that we have a duty to think about important questions for ourselves, and not simply to take the word of experts on faith. We are right to respect the advice of experts, but we have a duty to check out for ourselves, to the best of our abilities, the evidence that the experts adduce in support of their expert advice and opinion.

This is where ornery men and women can play a critical role in maintaining the spirit of liberty and independence in their communities. By refusing to recognize the authority of a cognitive elite to make decisions for them, they are guarding all of us against the danger of bureaucratic totalitarianism. Even if the bureaucrats who are micromanaging our lives are the best of all possible people to run a nanny-state, those with a passion for liberty will reject their well-intentioned paternalism.

This suspicion of those who claim cognitive authority is simply one particular manifestation of that blanket skepticism that ornery people have about power. They simply do not trust it, and history has shown them abundant reasons why their skepticism is well founded. We ourselves may not share this skepticism, but we are the beneficiaries of those who do.

IN THE nineteenth century the German philosopher and economist Karl Marx developed a philosophy of history that continues to have a profound effect on how many practical-minded men think about the world. Marx ranks among that group of deceased economic and political thinkers whose influence, as the economist John Maynard Keynes said, is all the greater for being wholly unsuspected. According to Marx, history is the conflict of economic classes; therefore, if there were only one class, the proletariat, history would come to an end. There would be nothing more to struggle over. Power would simply disappear as the central problem of politics, since everyone would have as much as they want and no one would have too much. Marx should have known better. He believed in technology, just as most of us do. And he knew that a society that lives by technology will be a society in which economies of scale will dominate. The big will get bigger, and they will tend to crush the small. The pyramid will arise, even if it is made out of microchips, and the specter of power, vast and baffling, will return. And with that return of power will come the return of the quarrel between big and small, the little guys on the periphery and the big guys at the core. The struggle for power can never be abolished, and it is political utopianism to think that it can be.

The same point was made by the American thinker Murray Rothbard, one of the most brilliant representatives of modern libertarianism in the twentieth century. Like Marx, Rothbard saw the broad outline of human history in terms of an ongoing and unending conflict. But for Rothbard, the struggle was not between different economic classes or different ideologies, but rather between power and liberty. Furthermore, unlike Marx, who believed that the conflict between classes will eventually terminate in a worldwide revolution ushering in the end of history, Rothbard argued that the struggle between liberty and power will continue without ceasing. On this point, I agree with Rothbard, and not Marx. That is why I have stressed the need to conserve the American heritage of orneriness. No matter who has the power and however benignly they intend to use it, there must always be a sizable segment of the population that resents and resists their power. It does not matter greatly whether the resentment and resistance makes sense logically or is backed by solid evidence: It may well be the result of paranoid fantasies. All that matters in the long run is that there is an effective check on the accumulation of too much power in the hands of any single group of people.

Libertarianism as a philosophy suffers from many defects, but as an attitude it makes perfect sense. To keep liberty alive, there must be enough people around who will instinctively act to curb and check those with power from abusing it. The problem with libertarianism arises when it assumes the rigid and doctrinaire form of an ideology. All ideologies fail to grasp that sometimes less is more. All aspire to conquer the hearts and minds of the whole world, and all set about with missionary fervor to do just that. Paradoxically, when natural libertarians make the transition to doctrinaire libertarians, they often forfeit their most attractive characteristic: resistance to indoctrination by others. Ayn Rand's many followers and devotees all yearn to live like her Nietzschean supermen and superwomen, yet most of them end up sounding like parrots endlessly repeating the same monotonous cate-chism. That is what ideology does to the soul.

It is undesirable for all of us to be natural libertarians. But it would be a catastrophe if the spirit of the natural libertarian vanished from the landscape of American culture: A robust supply of ornery men and women protects us all. Therefore, those of us who differ from them, both in ideology and atti-tude, should recognize that we need them even if we don't agree with them—even if we find them as annoying as hell, even if we think their ideals to be shabby, selfish, and materialistic, even if we loathe the misguided pettiness of so much of their political agitation, even if their beloved conspiracy theories are often totally whacko, we still need them. Therefore, we must all be willing to allow them to play a vital role in the public forum. We must put up with them for our own good—just as they must put up with us for their own good.

VIRTUALLY ALL ideologies work on the principle that a society would be better off if everyone shared the same ideology. But one size doesn't fit all. We need genuine diversity, not pseudodiversity, a real diversity of tempera-ment, of attitudes, of character types. The only way that America can remain rich and powerful and free, all at the same time, is by means of a carefully balanced and continually refreshed civil ecology. Just as any ecological system is the interplay of a number of different forms of life that have come to har-monize together in the life of the system, so too is a successful society. Take away one element in the system, and it can go into a tailspin.

In 1985 the government of Australia decided that it would intervene to save the population of seabirds on Macquarie Island, located halfway be-tween New Zealand and Antarctica. The feral cats on the island took a tremendous toll on the native bird population, killing approximately 60,000 of them each year. The government figured that the seabird population could be saved simply by eliminating the cats. By 2000, the last of the roughly 2,500 cats had been removed from the island. At first, the absence of the cats seemed to work, and the population of seabirds began to increase. But this trend was soon reversed by an explosive increase in the island's population of rats and rabbits, whose numbers had previously been kept down by the cats. The rats fed on the seabirds' chicks, while the rabbits' habit of nibbling on grass caused the erosion and the collapse of the shoreline, where the seabirds were accustomed to building their nests. The removal of the cats did not help the seabirds. On the contrary, it threatened their continuing survival.[6]

Now imagine trying to explain to the birds that they really need the cats on their island. This might be almost as difficult as explaining to Rush Limbaugh and Ann Coulter why we need knee-jerk liberals in our society, and nearly as daunting as trying to explain to the editors of the *New York Review of Books* why we need Rush Limbaugh and Ann Coulter. Yet all of these things, I am convinced, are true. The bloodlessly abstract checks and balances provided by our beautifully drawn up Constitution may get all the credit for the fact that the United States has managed for a long time to remain rich, powerful, and free; but the real credit goes to the delicate balance of our civil ecology, in which different personality types, different life styles, different ways of making a living, different religious views come together and clash. We were not meant to all get along. We are far better off keeping our differences and sincerely, vigorously pushing our own agendas based on these differences. It is folly to try to aspire to the Roman ideal of a virtuous patriotism that looks only for the good of country. If it were absolutely clear what this good consisted in, then it might make sense. But nothing could be less clear. Hence, it is better that we fight about what is good, to put our all into the struggle to realize our cherished values and ideals. If compromise comes too easily, it will not be taken seriously. A little stubbornness is a good thing.

Our society will be better off if we all remain loyal to those values and ideals that we naturally represent and embody. College professors should be detached and aloof. They should not have the narrow prejudices of the person who has worked to build up a little blue-collar business. The professors' perspective should be broader, more nuanced, less crude. But the people who have successfully figured out a way to make a good living by their own wits and who don't have an advanced degree, their two cents are important too. They need to represent the plainer and more down-to-earth truths that their own experience has disclosed to them. They have come to know things in the same way they have made their fortunes—the hard way, by firsthand personal experience, the famous school of hard knocks. If they do not insist on raising their voices in the public forum to defend the values and ideals they are loyal to, then we will all, the college professors included, be the worse for it.

Each of us should be true and faithful to what is deepest in us, and loyal to our own ideals. But we need to respect the loyalty that other people show toward their own ideals, not out of courtesy, but out of our commitment to maintaining our civil ecology. The bird must learn, however grudgingly, to accept the cat. Some of us should even learn to treasure our own divided loyalties.

Most people are firmly committed to their own values and ideals. They simply do not see even a glimmer of truth in their opponent's position. But there are some people who are divided, who often find themselves hesitating between two different and incompatible ideals. One moment we might find ourselves taking the side of those natural libertarians who are passionate for liberty and who will raise holy hell if others try to take it from them. The next moment we are in sympathy with those whose job it is to impose order and stability on those who are raising hell. Reading one book, we find ourselves in sympathy with the rebels, like Robert E. Lee, who chose his loyalty to his state of Virginia over his loyalty to the United States of America. Reading another book, we find ourselves admiring the radical republicans, like Charles Sumner, who championed the cause of the emancipated slaves. But how is it possible to reconcile, logically and ideologically, an admiration for two such entirely different men?

The American philosopher Josiah Royce had an explanation. A colleague of William James at Harvard during the late nineteenth-century, the golden age of American philosophy, Royce had been greatly influence by James's philosophy of pragmatism. Yet Royce ultimately felt that pragmatism was simply not enough. For the pragmatist, all that ultimately mattered was whether beliefs and ideas were actually successful in promoting a better world. For James, a good belief had a "cash value" in the sense that it changed and improved the lives of those who subscribed to it. But Royce felt that there was something missing in James's picture. For Royce, much of the nobility of human life comes from the capacity to be loyal to a lost cause, to stick with our convictions and ideals even when it becomes painfully obvious that we are on the losing side. For the Jamesian pragmatist, the solution to this problem is simple: There is no place in pragmatism for loyalty to a lost cause; you simply discard the beliefs that aren't working for you and adopt those of your opponent, which are working for him. If Robert E. Lee had been a strict pragmatist, he would simply have switched sides once he recognized that the Confederacy was doomed to defeat. The Yankees might have accepted his military advice, yet none would have admired him for being a turncoat.

Royce dubbed his philosophy the philosophy of loyalty and he made it his fundamental maxim, Be loyal to loyalty.[7] In order to admire other men, it is not necessary that we agree with their ideas and convictions. Instead, we can admire the loyalty that they display toward ideals that are different and even incompatible with our own. What we are admiring are not their ideals, but the devotion and sacrifice they bring to the defense of their ideals. Loyalty to any ideal higher than our own narrow personal interests will always command the respect of a generous heart, even when our minds cannot endorse the action taken in the name of the ideal. Soldiers have often been moved by the heroism of those who were trying to kill them. Even a fanatic like John Brown, whose attack on Harpers Ferry was lunatic and reprehensible, achieved an aura of weird sanctity due to the dignified nobility with which he died for his sins.

Can we admire the orneriness of the natural libertarian? Because populist conservatives today sometimes seem intent merely on serving their own grubby material aims, by screaming whenever someone tries to reach into their pockets, we have a tendency to withhold our admiration, precisely because we do not see in this response any loyalty to a higher ideal, such as we find in solders who are willing to die for their country, or a mother who will sacrifice herself for the welfare of her children, or a martyr preparing to die for his faith. There is no glamour in the vulgar motives of men who are staging a tax revolt. True, they often try to impart a sense of heroism to their activities by spouting slogans about liberty, but what is liberty to them except the desire to keep control of their purses?

In fact, this dismissive attitude to the motives of natural libertarians is a very serious mistake. Sometimes the natural libertarians seem to get carried away with their rhetoric. They have a tendency to go soaring off into vague abstractions and windy platitudes whenever they try to justify their positions. Thus, it is necessary to bring them down to earth, which is what I have tried to do. Yet behind every supposedly grubby tax revolt there is a genuine struggle for human dignity. The fact that it is inevitably a first-person struggle in no way diminishes its grandeur since it is always the struggle of the little guys against the big guys, and thus it invariably takes on the drama of a David versus a Goliath. The big guys can hire armed men to defend their interests, lawyers to protect their wealth, and priests to sanctify it. They can even retain philosophers to explain that it is eternally right and just that their interests should prevail over the paltry and trifling interests of the little guys. That is why the only way the little guys can resist being bullied by the big guys is if they are willing to get down and personal, to make the fight a fight not about ideals, but about the realest of all things in their eyes, namely, their own lives, their own liberty, their own things, their own pursuit of happiness.

It is unfair to demand a higher ideal of the little guys when they are defending the very highest ideal of which they are capable—the ideal of preserving their ability to be masters of their own fate, and to resist those who could rob them of the most essential attribute of human dignity—the freedom to be in charge of their own lives. When the little guys rebel against the big guys, they are forwarding the cause of liberty and dignity in the only way they know how. But in the process, they cannot help but achieve a much higher end than any for which they are aiming. It has not been the writing of august philosophers that has made men free, but the rebellion of little men up in arms over the tyranny of the big—rebellions that must be carried out again and again, because otherwise the big never stop growing. There is no more dangerous delusion than to imagine that men can become free once and for all. Each generation must earn its freedom by taking charge of its own destiny, and by the adroit application of the principles of pragmatic eclecticism. Some generations will have to rebel—perhaps only to remind those with power that they cannot push too far.

TODAY AMERICA is facing such a rebellion—a populist revolt against the liberal elite. The question before us is whether we can still find the wisdom and the good sense to strike a satisfactory balance between liberty and civilization when confronted with the unprecedented challenges of the twenty-first century. For it is an illusion to think that the tension between civilization and liberty can ever be fully resolved, or that there is some method by which we can settle once and for all exactly how much liberty we must give up for the sake of civilization, or how much civilization we must forgo for the sake of liberty. That is a conundrum that each generation must puzzle out for itself—not at the level of theory but at the level of day-to-day practical reality.

The freedom crisis we face today is the most perplexing of all possible crises—a philosophical crisis that leaves us confused and divided about even our most basic values and ideals. We can no longer agree on what freedom means, though we have all been raised to think it is something we should care about intensely. Some Americans want to go back to the good old days when every man could do what was right in his own eyes. Some Americans want to go full speed into the future, discarding the outmoded delusion of liberty and deploying the most up-to-date techniques in cultural engineering to produce a utopian society in which, through proper management, we can all be wealthy, healthy, and happy.

There are dangers on both sides of this conflict. If the American tradition of liberty is to survive, it cannot be by turning back the clock and ignoring the history that has brought us to our present state of affairs. Political nostalgia, if pushed too far, can become a dangerous form of ideological escapism. Yet those who warn of a threat to our liberties, though often shrill and paranoid, have a point that deserves much more serious consideration than has usually been granted by their liberal opponents. When they talk about the march of socialism under the Obama administration, however, they are indulging in self-defeating rhetoric. Worse, they are indicating that they do not grasp the real threat to liberty today.

As I have argued in this book, the threat to liberty does not come from the sinister machinations of power-hungry socialists. It comes from the very nature of modern advanced civilization, from impersonal forces operating beyond the control of any individual or set of individuals, from the economies of scale that have provided us with our prosperity and affluence, from the very hugeness of our nation, of our government, of our corporations, of our media. The American meritocracy has provided us, in abundance, with so many of the blessings of civilization that we have come to take for granted. This same meritocracy, however, has the potential to create a new ruling elite as indifferent to the needs and anxieties of the average person as the various ruling classes that have exploited and oppressed their perceived inferiors in the past.

The current populist revolt, including the Tea Party movement, could well have a healthy effect on our society, by forcing our cognitive elite to take more seriously than they now do the fears and aspirations of ordinary men and women. But this revolt also contains the seeds of potential catastrophe as long as there are populist demagogues willing to exploit popular discontent with the meritocracy for their own narrow and self-serving agendas. In short, America's freedom crisis may turn out to be the proverbial blessing in disguise or it could degenerate into a new hi-tech civil war between Blues and Reds— a conflict for which we are no more prepared than those of our ancestors who woke up one day to find their nation divided between Blues and Grays.

CONCLUSION

ADVICE FROM
THE PHOENIX

Looking back over the rise and fall of earlier civilizations, thoughtful people may well be excused from wondering whether our own society, despite its prosperity and success, can avoid the fate of all its predecessors. There is no truer philosophy of history than the maxim, Nothing fails like success. And we have been wildly successful. No civilization, if it is successful, can avoid the problem of decadence. On this point, the historical pessimists are right. But they overlook an aspect of Western civilization that has already demonstrated its remarkable power to revive and revitalize.

It is only in the West that a tradition has developed that instills a passion for liberty in the hearts and souls of men. Because the passion for liberty inevitably clashes with the status quo, it will first appear in a negative light, as resistance to authority, as rebellion against the forces of law and order. It will start by destroying and tearing down—often quite literally. But this negative beginning is simply the prelude to the period of positive construction, much like dynamiting an old building in order to erect a new and improved one. This is because those with a passion for liberty will insist on taking charge of their own lives, and if the only way they can do this is by remaking their social order, then that is the task they will set themselves.

Often this process of remaking society will go dreadfully astray; it will lead to violent tumults, the murder of innocents, the disruption of the social fabric. Too frequently the forces of social inertia will simply be too great to overwhelm, and the passion for liberty will then appear in the light of a suicidal madness; but the same passion, when it flares up in a more favorable environment, will succeed in reshaping the social order in a way that maximizes the opportunity for individual men and women to make and to shape themselves, which is the whole point of the strange passion for liberty.

No culture has a monopoly on visionaries and reformers. Confucius, Zoroaster, Buddha, and Muhammad all offered their world what they saw as a better path and a higher truth, but each of them ultimately sought to establish a new order that would be fixed and permanent. Their mission was essentially constructive. True, it may have required the overthrow of the old order, but the goal was to create an ideal community that would have no need of future rebels. The Western tradition of rebellion, on the other hand, assumes that all social orders will inevitably become unjust over time and that the only way to check their inherent tendency to injustice and inequality is through acts of defiance and rebellion. Needless to say, many in the West have not shared this tradition and have vigorously opposed it. Nonetheless the West has been distinguished by its unusual willingness to harbor dangerous ideals that radically challenge the supremacy of order and stability as the highest political goods. Other civilizations have essentially justified themselves by arguing that they represent order; the alternative to us, they each declare, is chaos and anarchy. Be loyal to the status quo and you will have peace. Oppose it, resist it, and you will have war. So which do you chose? In the West, many individuals have quite deliberately chosen chaos and anarchy. They have resisted and opposed, and instead of being regarded as madmen or villains, they have been celebrated as heroes, or patriots, or martyrs to the cause of liberty. In the West, the heretic has become the founder of a faith, and the traitor, the father of his country. These paradoxes, incomprehensible in other civilizations, have become commonplace in ours.

All of which leads us to the greatest of paradoxes: If the West is to escape the fate of all other civilizations, it will only be because, and as long as, it is eternally willing to raise the question, Is civilization enough? Are peace and order, stability and prosperity all that people yearn for? Or is there a higher ideal beyond all that even the best of civilizations can provide? And if there is such an ideal, how much of the undoubted blessings of civilization should we be prepared to sacrifice for it?

Many in the West have believed that there is such an ideal. In a lecture delivered at the Bridgnorth Institution in England, on February 26, 1877, Lord Acton gave eloquent expression to their shared belief: "Liberty is not a means to a higher political end. It is itself the highest political end."[1] And to make it clear, he spelled out the implications of putting liberty first. "A generous spirit prefers that his country should be poor, and weak, and of no account, but free, rather than powerful, prosperous, and enslaved. It is better to be the citizen of a humble commonwealth in the Alps, without prospect of influence beyond the narrow frontier, than subject of the superb autocracy that overshadows half of Asia and of Europe."[2] Acton believed that those who championed liberty above all else must be prepared to sacrifice all other political goods and ideals if it was only by this means that their liberty could be preserved. But how many among us today would be willing to go to the extreme of sacrificing our power, security, and prosperity—the preeminent values of civilization—to safeguard our personal liberty and independence of spirit?

Too often today we believe that no such sacrifice is necessary. It has become an article of collective faith, both in the United States and in the other democratic nations, that we can be rich and strong *and* free. Indeed, many would argue that we have become rich and strong because we are free. But even if we accept this optimistic thesis—that freedom is the cause of our prosperity and power—we must still ask which freedom is responsible for our happy state. As we have seen, there are many senses to the word *freedom*; some of which contradict each other.

WE HAVE recently lived through a period that defined liberty in terms of Horace's maxim *Carpe diem!* Freedom meant the freedom to seize the day and to do whatever you wanted to do with it. But the *carpe diem* ethos is the enemy of the tradition of independence. When it rules, the future of freedom is jeopardized precisely through an excess of the desire for too much freedom. The visceral covenant that underlies all genuine communities of free and independent individuals strictly bans the policy of that naked self-assertion. The strong cannot butt in front of the weak, nor can they rob them of the fruit of their labor. The clever may not use their wits in order to perpetrate fraud on those with simpler and more straightforward minds. No Ponzi schemes, no pyramid sales. No stealing from those who have trusted you with their money.

When individuals are given the freedom to violate the visceral covenant of their community at will, the covenant is destroyed. There is no longer that automatic degree of trust that exists among people who are genuinely bound together by the same unquestionable visceral covenant. If an honest man sees that the thief is being rewarded for taking someone's money, he will began to wonder whether honesty is the best policy. He may conclude, Yes, if everyone is honest, but no, if only some are. Thus, those who find themselves caught up in the *carpe diem* ethos of the people around them discover that it wears off on them, often no matter how hard they fight to resist its infection.

Today, we are sobered by the recognition that our embrace of the *carpe diem* ethos came at a terribly high price—it led to an economic crisis and crash. But with the economic crash came an even more profound crash—namely, the crash of the high hopes of the libertarian tradition. Many of those who deeply admired the ideas of Adam Smith suddenly remembered what he really said about the invisible hand. He never claimed that it was always in operation whenever men pursued their economic self-interest. Instead, he wrote in *The Wealth of Nations,* published in 1776, that men were "frequently" led by the invisible hand to do good for their community at the urging of their narrow self-interest—and frequently is far from always.[3] Adam Smith recognized that the unbridled pursuit of narrow economic self-interest was not necessarily a panacea, that it could go wrong.

It is often forgotten that before Adam Smith wrote *The Wealth of Nations* he had written a book entitled *The Theory of Moral Sentiments*.[4] The earlier book was not dedicated to praising "the virtue of selfishness" that became the mantra of those free market libertarians inspired by Ayn Rand.[5] On the contrary, Smith praised those unusual individuals who could raise above their own narrowly self-interested perspective in order to make decisions based on the view of the matter that would be taken by "an impartial spectator." We should ultimately judge our actions, including our economic decisions, not only by what we have to gain or lose by them, but from the perspective of a neutral observer. Of course, Smith recognized that this is not the way that most human beings normally judge their own actions, but he believed that an ethical community required a sizeable number of individuals who are capable of passing an impartial judgment on their own conduct. The invisible hand can do a great deal, but it cannot provide the indispensable foundation of a genuinely ethical community.

Smith's point is more relevant to our day than to his. In the eighteenth century, unbridled selfishness was still something people were taught to be ashamed of. But in our era the triumph of the *carpe diem* ethos has led far too many of us into thinking that selfishness really is all the virtue that a materially prosperous society needs.

Today's populist conservatives overwhelmingly tend to agree with Adam Smith that society needs solid moral foundations, and they find these foundations in the various political, cultural, and religious traditions that they have inherited from the past. Much of the anger of today's populist revolt stems from the belief that the liberal elite is systematically undermining the very traditions that are most indispensable in preserving the delicate balance between liberty and civilized order that has made America so exceptional among nations. As I have argued in this book, the populist conservatives have a valid point—there are certain traditions that, when examined from the perspective of the pragmatist, have proven themselves to be invaluable in the creation and conservation of free societies. To toss these traditions into the trash-bin of history before we fully grasp the role that they have played in sustaining our free and open society is exceedingly dangerous. Indeed, it may well turn out to be that many of these traditions have been indispensable in preserving our collective sense of national identity despite the various contending forces that have so often threatened to tear us into hostile and warring camps in the past, and which are again threatening us today.

THERE IS an alternative to escalating civil breakdown, but it is one that may well be much harder to achieve, since it involves nothing short of a moral reformation of our society. Throughout this book I have argued that it is impossible to turn the clock back to earlier days. Even if we were willing to try the experiment, we could not shrink present day America back down to its early nineteenth-century scale. Yet it is always possible to revitalize traditions from the past, updating them, as need be, in the spirit of pragmatic eclecticism.

To begin with, we might consider raising our children today a little bit more as children were raised in the Age of Jackson. Let them have more say in the management of their lives. Permit them more free time. Have them do less homework. But also instill in them the ethos of the impartial spectator. Insist that they play fair, and to be decent and civil in their encounters with other people—even on the Internet. Teach kids that they have duties and not merely rights. Teach them, in fact, that they only have rights because their ancestors were willing to do their duty, and that we of this generation must learn again to do the same. Tell children to stand up against bullies. Teach them that there is a difference between the bully's violence and the righteous violence necessary to put the bully in his place. Teach them all about the heroes of the tradition of independence, putting special emphasis on precisely those who have stirred up trouble, like our own American Sons of Liberty.

Teach them that men can only have enough freedom when they begin by asking for too much of it, but they can only retain it if they can learn to use it wisely, to preserve and maintain their independence, and not to betray their self-control. Teach them that freedom creates unpredictability. Free markets soar too high, creating bubbles and busts, unleashing panics and causing crashes. But out of these panics and crashes come new opportunities. When the forty-niners ran into trouble, they simply went back and made new rules, in the hopes that these might prevent the future return of the same trouble. Yet even when they were successful in averting one kind of trouble, others were always brewing. None of the miners felt less free because he and his fellows made new rules for themselves; these rules were what in fact guaranteed the preservation of their freedom. It is simply a false dichotomy to pit the free market against governmental regulations, for as we have seen, the freedom of the individual flourishes most in an ethical community that abides by inflexible visceral covenants.

Teach our children the truth about freedom—strip it of its sentimental associations. Tell them how those with the passion for liberty have often run amok, overturning the hard work of ages in their pursuit of impossible dreams, but tell them that without this quixotic streak in the soul of those passionate for liberty, there would be no liberty at all. Teach them, too, that it is not enough to fight for their own independence; if they wish to live in an ethical community that secures their liberty, they must promote the spirit of liberty in their fellow citizens. The welfare and the dole cannot create independence of spirit—they are the means by which the independence of spirit is most effectively undermined—but poverty and ignorance devastate the foundation of the ethical community.

Our enlightened elite must remember that it is difficult to persuade a man to accept your ideas while you are sneering at his. Yet this is a message that some of the brightest of our elites just don't seem to get, causing a neutral observer to wonder whether they are interested in enlightening the people or simply annoying them. In addition, the progressive elite has too often focused on the question, How can we use government to create a better society? Those who genuinely desire to use government to improve society must do more than merely examine the intrinsic merits of their proposed reforms and programs. They must ask, What kind of people are we trying to govern?

Here is a fact that all of us are familiar with in our everyday life: Some people are far easier to manage and to govern than others. There are some children, for example, who readily do whatever mom asks of them. There are other children who are in a continual state of defiance and rebellion. If the progressive elite genuinely wishes to improve society, it must, at the very least, learn something about the care and handling of those ornery natural libertarians who are most resistant to the liberal elite's ideas of progress, otherwise even the best designed programs will be doomed to failure. If America cannot solve its health care crisis, blame should be placed not only on those populist demagogues who spread rumors of death panels, but also on those progressives whose complete failure to understand the social psychology of the ornery American made them gape and gasp at the inexplicable populist explosion of the town hall revolts. They must begin operating by the maxim: Know those you wish to nudge, and when you must nudge, nudge them very carefully.

Most importantly, our liberal elite must liberate itself from the condition of historical amnesia. Our own freedom was not the creation of the orderly and the well bred, of the educated and the upper class, but of the rowdy and the unruly, of the ignorant peasant and the illiterate laborer. Wise philosophers did not free the serfs—the serfs freed themselves. The liberty that we enjoy today emerged out of the defiant "Don't tread on us" attitude of all the ordinary people in the past—people who knew what it was like to be tread upon because they had often felt the heel of their superiors on the back of their necks, and who were determined that no one would ever tread on them with impunity again.

It is true that the rowdy and the unruly can evolve in the direction of civilized values—they can become less addicted to violence, less feisty, less touchy; but they can preserve their liberty only as long as they remain just ornery enough to resist forcefully those who try to control them, as the big and powerful always and inevitably will try to do. Admittedly their resistance will most often be for purely personal reasons, to maintain the control over their lives that they have always enjoyed; but if there are enough ornery men and women in a society, they will be able check any force that aims to subdue and tame them. By doing so, they will hold back, at least for another day, the dusk of decadence that comes whenever the forces of order have triumphed too completely over the anarchic will of free men. Even those who think ornery individuals tend to go too far are ultimately the beneficiaries of their sometimes excessive orneriness. Because no one dares tread on them, they make it far more difficult for anyone to tread on us.

The Dutch-born orientalist Henri Frankfort once praised the civilization of Egypt because, during the course of three thousand years, there had never once been a popular rebellion against the established order represented by the pharaoh, that god on earth. Against this model of millennial tranquility, Western civilization—with its rebellions, its reformations, its revolutions, its civil wars, its continual turmoil—cannot but appear to be a prodigy of mayhem, a bedlam that fancies itself a civilization. Yet if the West has any chance of doing what no other civilization has ever done, it will be only because, like the mythical Phoenix, it has learned that the true secret of eternal life is the ability to set yourself ablaze and then to rise up from your own ashes.

ACKNOWLEDGMENTS

A number of people have helped me through the various stages of this project and I would like to take this opportunity to acknowledge them.

First of all, I want to thank my agent Andrew Stuart, without whose guidance, tact, and persistence, this book could never have been written. Like a great coach, he has unfailingly given me encouragement when I was most in need of it.

Second, let me express my deepest gratitude to my wonderful editor at Palgrave Macmillan, Alessandra Bastagli, both for championing the book and for inspiring me to make it the best book I could. Working with her has been among the most stimulating experiences in my life. Thanks also to Colleen Lawrie, her assistant editor, and to Alan Bradshaw, the production manager at Palgrave, both of whom have made my task much easier than it would have been otherwise. Indeed, it has been both a privilege and a pleasure working with the entire staff at Palgrave.

My warmest appreciations go to Lee Smith and Tod Lindberg for their patience in reading the manuscript in its earlier stages and for their generous moral support, and thanks to Barry Rubin for encouraging me in this project.

Much thanks to Ellen Vivet, for generously offering her good judgment and advice during every stage of this process.

In addition, I would like to acknowledge the many helpful conversations I have had with my friends in Georgia, including Michael Lynch, Wesley Brookshire, Sundown Walker, Stacey Parr, and Sid Gough.

Lastly, I could never thank my partner Andy Fuson adequately for the patience and love he has shown during the twenty two years that we have shared our lives. That is why I keep dedicating books to him.

NOTES

INTRODUCTION

1. "Obama Gets Voters' Message: It's Jobs, Jobs, Jobs," Associated Press, January 21, 2010.
2. "Scott Brown Drives His GMC Pickup to U.S. Senate Victory," *USA Today*, January 20, 2010.
3. The line is from Ralph Waldo Emerson's "Concord Hymn" of 1837.
4. "A Revolution Begins," *Boston Herald*, January 20, 2010.
5. Rasmussen Reports, June 29, 2009. "Many surveys have documented the fact that . . . people are generally in the mood for improving the health care system," but the report goes on to note that nevertheless "most of those with insurance are happy with the coverage they have."
6. Paul Krugman, "The Town Hall Mobs," *New York Times*, Aug. 7, 2009. Needless to say, the view that the protestors were "mobs" was disputed by many conservatives, who noted that by classic mob standards, the protestors were reasonably well-behaved. No one got killed or even slugged. Indeed, as my friend Bob Hessen reminded me, no one even had a pie tossed in his face.
7. Rasmussen Reports, August 7, 2009.
8. Rasmussen Reports, August 10, 2009.
9. Thomas Paine, *Collected Writings* (New York: Literary Classics of the United States, 1995), 6.
10. Thomas Paine made this point in his pamphlet "Common Sense," in reference to the liberty enjoyed by the average Englishman of his own time, "laying aside all national pride and prejudice in favour of modes and forms, the plain truth is, that *it is wholly owning to the constitution of the people, and not to the constitution of the government* that the crown [i.e., the state] is not as oppressive in England as in Turkey." Ibid., 11. (Emphasis his.)
11. The Italian Renaissance thinker Niccolò Machiavelli put forth this conception of freedom in his *Discourses on the First Ten Books of Livy*, Book One, Chapter Four. Responding to the classical tradition that lamented the perennial conflict that existed in ancient Rome between the people and the elite, Machiavelli argued that "those who criticize the clashes between the nobility and the populace [are attacking] the primary factor making for Rome's continuing freedom. They pay more attention to the shouts and cries that rise from such conflicts than to the good effects that derive from them. They do not take into account the fact that there are two distinct viewpoints in every republic: that of the populace and that of the elite. All the laws made in order to foster liberty result from the tension between them, as one can easily see was the case in the history of Rome. . . . The demands of a free people are rarely harmful to the cause of liberty, for they are a response either to oppression or to the prospect of oppression." Niccolò Machiavelli, *Selected Political Writings* (Indianapolis/Cambridge: Hackett Publishing Company, Inc., 1994), 94–95.

12.   This is an adaptation of the famous line from the move *Network*, released in 1976, and origi-nally uttered by the character of TV news anchorman Howard Beale in the form: "I'm as mad as hell, and I'm not going to take this anymore."

CHAPTER ONE

1.   Rasmussen Reports, August 15, 2009.
2.   John Maynard Keynes, *The General Theory of Employment, Interest, and Money* (New York: First Harvest/Harcourt, 1964), 383.
3.   Thomas Paine, *Collected Writings* (New York: Literary Classics of the United States, 1995), 6.
4.   Aristotle discusses natural slavery in *The Politics*, Book One, Part Five. The Benjamin Jowett translation of *The Politics* is available online at http://classics.mit.edu/Aristotle/politics.1.one.html. Here is the relevant quote: "Where then there is such a difference as that between soul and body, or between men and animals (as in the case of those whose business is to use their body, and who can do nothing better), the lower sort are by nature slaves, and it is better for them as for all inferiors that they should be under the rule of a master. For he who can be, and therefore is, another's and he who participates in rational principle enough to apprehend, but not to have, such a principle, is a slave by nature. Whereas the lower animals cannot even appre-hend a principle; they obey their instincts. And indeed the use made of slaves and of tame ani-mals is not very different; for both with their bodies minister to the needs of life. Nature would like to distinguish between the bodies of freemen and slaves, making the one strong for servile labor, the other upright, and although useless for such services, useful for political life in the arts both of war and peace. But the opposite often happens—that some have the souls and others have the bodies of freemen. And doubtless if men differed from one another in the mere forms of their bodies as much as the statues of the Gods do from men, all would acknowledge that the inferior class should be slaves of the superior. And if this is true of the body, how much more just that a similar distinction should exist in the soul? but the beauty of the body is seen, whereas the beauty of the soul is not seen. It is clear, then, that some men are by nature free, and others slaves, and that for these latter slavery is both expedient and right."

CHAPTER TWO

1.   When we listen to the uplifting music of Aaron Copland's *Fanfare for the Common Man*, we naturally think of the phrase *the common man* as referring to a grand and noble element of our species. Yet the English word *common* in the context of the Greek and British attitudes is a syn-onym for *vulgar*, and is intended to convey a put-down, not a compliment.
2.   The analogy is taken from Plato's *Republic*, Book VI, 488b-e. In the original version, the cap-tain is "slightly deaf and of similarly impaired visions," while it is the ordinary sailors on the ship who are "wrangling with one another for control of the helm, each claiming that it is his right to steer though he has never learned the art." *The Complete Dialogues of Plato, Including the Letters,* ed. Edith Hamilton and Huntington Cairns (Princeton: Princeton University Press, 1961).
3.   Fareed Zakaria, *The Future of Freedom: Illiberal Democracy at Home and Abroad* (New York: W.W. Norton, 2003), 240.
4.   The United States has had several important political dynasties, such as the Adamses, the Roosevelts, the Kennedys, the Bushes, and the Clintons. But the successful members of even the strongest dynasty still needed to go through the formality of being elected by the people. None could simply inherit office from a family member.
5.   A cognitive elite is any managing or governing class whose authority is based on their claim to possessing superior knowledge, intellectual powers, or mastery of classical texts. It is irrelevant whether the cognitive elite really know more than the masses. It is their claim to know more that defines them. The cognitive elite may be quite conservative, and even reactionary. Indeed, this was generally the rule before the European Enlightenment. The explanation of why today's cognitive elite is an emphatically liberal elite will come in Chapter Five, "Enlighten-ment in Power."

6. Henry Ford exercised a high degree of paternalistic control over the employees of his corporation. He frowned on both smoking and drinking among his workers.

CHAPTER THREE

1. Alexander Stephens, vice president of the Confederacy, had originally opposed the secession of his native state of Georgia. After the Civil War, however, he wrote a two-volume justification of the southern cause, *A Constitutional View of the War between the States.*
2. Members of Roosevelt's original Brain Trust included Raymond Moley, Rexford Tugwell, and Adolf Berle. Felix Frankfurter joined the Brain Trust later in FDR's administration. Before joining the Roosevelt administration, Moley had taught at Barnard College, and became a law professor at Columbia University in 1928. Rexford Tugwell had earlier taught at the University of Washington and Columbia University. Adolf Berle became a professor at Columbia Law School in 1927. Frankfurter was given a law chair at Harvard Law School in 1921. Moley eventually turned against the New Deal and wrote a devastating critique of it entitled *After Seven Years* (New York: Harper & Brothers, 1939).
3. Mark Levin, *Liberty and Tyranny: A Conservative Manifesto* (New York: Threshold Editions, 2009), 4.
4. Mark D. Shear, "Rift Between Obama and Chamber of Commerce Widening," *Washington Post,* Oct. 20, 2009.
5. For Marx, the last stage of capitalism, in which big corporations would come to dominate the economy, was progressive because it was a necessary step in preparing for the advent of socialism. Just as a single big corporation could operate more efficiently and economically than a host of small businesses irrationally competing with each other, so the transition to socialism would constitute the final phase in the rationalization of economic life.
6. The case is *Pollock v. Farmers' Loan & Trust Company.*
7. According to www.ourdocuments.gov, "in 1913, due to generous exemptions and deductions, less than 1 percent of the population paid income taxes at the rate of only 1 percent of net income."
8. Edmund Burke, *The Writings and Speeches of Edmund Burke, Volume III, Party, Parliament, and the American War* (Oxford: Clarendon Press, 1996), 119–21.
9. Once the United States joined the war against Germany, William Jennings Bryan fully supported the American war effort.
10. Republican Senator Arthur Vandenberg is perhaps the most outstanding example of an isolationist who abandoned his position when faced with the threat of Soviet expansion.

CHAPTER FOUR

1. A story line, in my sense of word, is related to the concept of the "mobilizing myth" that Georges Sorel developed in his book *Reflections on Violence,* originally published in 1908. The purpose of the myth is not to reflect reality accurately but to give people a cause worth fighting for.
2. The Pew Poll for December 26, 2009.
3. Jonathan Alter, "Polls: The Education Gap," *Newsweek,* Nov. 8, 2004.
4. Jon Cohen, "Behind the Numbers," *The Washington Post,* Feb. 15, 2008.
5. The motto is offered in Immanuel Kant essay of 1784, "What is Enlightenment?" (*Was ist Aufklärung?*), but the Latin phrase, *Sapere aude,* has been traced back as far as the first century B.C. to the Roman poet Horace.
6. James Boswell, *The Life of Samuel Johnson* (New York: Alfred A. Knopf, 1992), 279. The direct target of Johnson's attack was the Scottish philosopher and skeptic David Hume, but Johnson would certainly have included Voltaire, Rousseau, Diderot, Holbach, d'Alembert, and other leading figures of the Enlightenment in the class he dubbed "skeptical innovators." Johnson would not have been terribly impressed by our contemporary tendency to distinguish a prudent and sensible Scottish Enlightenment from a reckless and radical French Enlightenment.

CHAPTER FIVE

1. French thinkers like Voltaire, Diderot, and Condorcet are often designated by the French term for philosopher, *philosophe,* but, rightly or wrongly, the French label has come to mean something akin to an amateur meddler in philosophy. For a more comprehensive view of Condorcet's ideas and his life, see my discussion of him in *The Suicide of Reason* (New York: Basic Books, 2007), 139–54.

2. Merle Curti, *The Social Ideas of American Educators* (Totowa, New Jersey: Littlefield, Adams & Co., 1935, 1968), 107.

3. Cf. Curti, ibid., 79–80. "Anxious to wring support for public schools from propertied interests then opposed to taxation for such a purpose, educational spokesmen warned them of the dangers to property rights from universal suffrage, Jacksonian democracy, and even, possibly, revolution—any of which might result if the masses were left undisciplined by education. . . . [I]f they were to curb 'men of warm passion and little reason,' vindictive and dangerous workingmen, restless and vicious frontiersmen—they could do no better than to lend support to the movement for free public schools."

4. Johann Gottlieb Fichte, *Addresses to the German Nation* (Chicago and London: The Open Court Publishing Company, 1922), 21.

5. Daniel C. Dennett, "The Bright Stuff," *New York Times,* July 12, 2003. The article is available on The Brights' Net, which includes Dennett in the list of "enthusiastic brights," along with Richard Dawkins, Steven Pinker, James "The Amazing" Randi, and many others. There are influential atheists today who reject the Bright label as a bit too self-consciously smug. Christopher Hitchens, for example, has rejected this label. Dennett himself has argued that the label Bright should not be taken to imply that religious believers are "dim"—but the implication is hard to resist.

6. The phrase "evangelical atheist" is not mine. There is a website called "The Evangelical Atheist," the stated mission of which is "helping mankind overcome religion." The phenomenon of evangelical atheism is also witnessed by the number of books written explicitly to spread the gospel of atheism, among them *The God Delusion, Breaking the Spell, God Is Not Great, The End of Faith,* and *Letters to a Christian Nation.*

7. Both Thomas Hobbes and David Hume were atheists. Both recognized the danger to society from unbridled religious fanaticism. For both, the solution was not to convert the masses to their own view, which they regarded as impossible, but to impose a uniform and bland faith on the masses through an established church controlled by the state. Religion, in short, should not be abolished but rather made an instrument of social control.

8. William Cobbett, *Political Works,* vol. II (London, 1835), 289. For this quote I am indebted to John W. Derry, *The Radical Tradition: Tom Paine to Lloyd George* (New York: St. Martin's Press, 1967), 69. Derry's discussion of the problem of education with the English tradition of radicalism is extremely illuminating.

9. John Stuart Mill, *On Liberty,* ch. 5, "Applications," *The Utilitarians* (Garden City, NY: Doubleday, 1961), 587.

10. The quote is from the Fairy Queen's curse on the House of Lord in the finale of the First Act of *Iolanthe,* first performed on November 25, 1882.

11. James Boswell, *The Life of Samuel Johnson* (New York: Alfred A. Knopf, 1992), 485.

12. These remarks were made during a fundraiser speech in San Francisco on April 6, 2008. A fuller version of the quotation is: "You go into some of these small towns in Pennsylvania, and like a lot of small towns in the Midwest, the jobs have been gone now for 25 years and nothing's replaced them. And they fell through the Clinton administration, and the Bush administration, and each successive administration has said that somehow these communities are gonna regenerate and they have not. So it's not surprising then that they get bitter, they cling to guns or religion or antipathy to people who aren't like them or anti-immigrant sentiment or anti-trade sentiment as a way to explain their frustrations."

13. Edmund Burke, "Speech on Conciliation with America," *The Writings and Speeches of Edmund Burke, Volume III, Party, Parliament, and the American War* (Oxford: Clarendon Press, 1996), 119.

CHAPTER SIX

1. I have borrowed the phrase "cake of custom" from Walter Bagehot, *Physics and Politics; or, Thoughts on the Application of the Principles of "Natural Selection" and "Inheritance" to Political Society* (New York: D. Appleton, 1875).
2. James Cook, *Voyages of Discovery* (Gloucester: Alan Sutton, 1984), 343.
3. The original "admirable Crichton" was James Crichton (b.1560), a Scottish polymath celebrated for his linguistic abilities and his knowledge of the arts and sciences. He died at the age of twenty-two in a duel.
4. In fact, the slaughter was not carried out thoroughly; Joshua 6:22–25 describes how the Hebrews spared the family of Rahab the prostitute, her family and "all who belonged to her." More tellingly, there is the opening sentence of the Book of Judges: "After the death of Joshua the Israelites enquired of YAHWEH, which tribe should be the first to attack the Canaanites?'" (Judges 1:1) Obviously, if the Canaanites had all been slaughtered by Joshua and his forces, there would be no Canaanites left to attack after his death.
5. Samuel Johnson, *A Johnson Reader,* ed. E. L. McAdam Jr. and George Milne (New York: Modern Library, 1966), 213.
6. Hume and Smith both believed that the loss of the unbridled license of their barbarian ancestors represented progress, because civilized manners replaced a way of life that was coarse and brutal. Rousseau feared that when men become too civilized, they lose those manly and heroic virtues that keep them free. Vico believed that the transition from the freedom-loving barbarians of the Heroic Age to the civilized manners of the Age of Reflection was a pattern that all societies inevitably went through—a recurring cycle which inevitably ended when a society became too civilized and too intellectualized, at which point it would be overrun by barbarians who were still in the midst of their Heroic Age.
7. Thomas Jefferson to James Madison, Paris, January 30, 1787. Jefferson was referring to Shays's Rebellion, which we will discuss in Chapter Thirteen.

CHAPTER SEVEN

1. Edmund S. Morgan and Helen M. Morgan, *The Stamp Act Crisis: Prologue to Revolution* (Chapel Hill: University of North Carolina Press, 1953), 21.
2. Cf. Lawrence Henry Gipson, *The Coming of the Revolution, 1763–1775* (New York: Harper, 1954), 115.
3. Robert Middlekauff, *The Glorious Cause: The American Revolution, 1763–1789* (New York: Oxford University Press, 1982, 2005), 78–80.
4. Ibid., 79.
5. William Edward Hartpole Lecky, *A History of England in the Eighteenth Century,* vol. 4, (New York: D. Appleton, 1878–1890), 90.
6. Gipson, *The Coming of the Revolution,* 112.
7. Lecky, *A History of England in the Eighteenth Century,* 337.
8. Thomas Paine, *The Collected Writings* (New York: The Literary Classics of America, 1995), 16. Dismissing the idea that "the present race of kings in the world" had "an honorable origin," Paine writes that "could we take off the dark covering of antiquity, and trace them [i.e., European monarchs] to their first rise, that we should find the first of them nothing better than the principal ruffian of some restless gang, whose savage manners or pre-eminence in subtility obtained him the title of chief among plunderers; and who by increasing in power, and extending his depredations, overawed the quiet and defenceless to purchase their safety by frequent contributions."

CHAPTER NINE

1. Modern scholarship tells us that there was no hissing snake on the early Continental Navy jack, but the rattlesnake, known not to attack unless threatened, appeared in cartoons and illustrations published in the colonies, including a famous image, drawn by Benjamin Franklin, of a snake cut in thirteen pieces to represent the colonies and the need for unity. The coiled snake with the "don't tread on me" legend was often used as a symbol of resistance to Britain during colonial times.
2. Alexis de Tocqueville, along with Gustave de Beaumont, had been sent to America to study our prison system, which was then considered a model for the rest of the world. His visit eventually led to the publication in 1835 of the first volume of *Democracy in America.*
3. Donald Smalley, Introduction to Frances Trollope, *Domestic Manners of the Americans* (New York: Vintage Books, 1960), vii.
4. Frances Trollope, *Domestic Manners of the Americans,* 44–45.
5. Ibid., 99–100.
6. This is theme of the popular country and western song, "Find Out Who Your Friends Are" by Tracey Lawrence. I am indebted to Stacey Parr for this reference.
7. Trollope, *Domestic Manners of the Americans,* 100.
8. Ibid., 121.
9. Harriet Martineau, *Society in America* (London: Saunders & Otley, 1837; reprint, New York: AMS Press, 1966), vol. 3, 174.

CHAPTER TEN

1. "Ardent spirits, though lamentably cheap, still cost something, and the use of them among the men . . . is universal." Frances Trollope, *Domestic Manners of the Americans* (New York: Vintage Books, 1960), 117.

CHAPTER ELEVEN

1. Judges, 21:25, *New English Bible with the Apocrypha* (Oxford, 1976).
2. The incorporation of the Old Testament into the Christian tradition was by no means an inevitable step, though it may seem that way to us now. One of the foremost expounders of Christian doctrine in the second century A.D. was Marcion who urged that Christians reject the Old Testament in its entirety. He was declared a heretic by the Roman Catholic Church, decisively closing the door to the idea of a Christianity cut off from its Hebrew roots.
3. Here I am adapting an idea put forth by Thomas Huxley known mainly today for his defense of Darwin's theory of evolution and for coining the word *agnosticism.* In the prologue to his book *Science and the Christian Tradition* (New York: D. Appleton, 1898) Huxley wrote: "So far as . . . equality, liberty, and fraternity are included under the democratic principles which assume the same names, the Bible is the most democratic book in the world. As such it began, through the heretical sects, to undermine the clerico-political despotism of the middle ages . . . ; Pope and King had as much as they could do to put down the Albigenses and the Waldenses in the twelfth and thirteenth centuries; the Lollards and the Hussites gave them still more trouble in the fourteenth and fifteenth; from the sixteen century onward, the Protestant sects have favored political freedom in proportion to the degree in which they have refused to acknowledge any ultimate authority save that of the Bible. . . . I do not say that even the highest Biblical ideal is exclusive of others and needs no supplement. But I do believe that the human race is not yet, possibly may never be, in a position to dispense with it." (58).
4. Modern scholarship places the scriptural version of Exodus to the middle of the fifth century B.C., but certain parts of it can be traced back as far as the ninth or tenth century B.C. Oral versions may have long preceded written ones, as in the case of the Homeric epics.
5. This interpretation of the term *agnostic* is perfectly in line with the interpretation offered by Thomas Huxley himself. An agnostic may believe in elves, God, and the Easter bunny all simultaneously; as long as he does not claim to have scientific knowledge of their actual existence.

Huxley, as a boy, had taught himself German, and he was familiar with Kant's *Critique of Pure Reason.* Kant had argued that science could only provide answers to empirical questions and therefore could tell us nothing about God or the immortality of the soul. Huxley always respected the line that Kant drew between scientific knowledge and faith. Huxley would obviously have been disturbed by the creationists who are trying to pass off their faith as scientific knowledge, but he would also have been disturbed by the Brights who claim that scientific knowledge requires men to cease to have faith in God.

6. The origin of this breach can be traced back at least to the nineteenth-century French thinker August Comte, who argued that the advent of modern science rendered all previous religions and philosophies obsolete. His contemporary Thomas Huxley, who disliked Comte, warned that his attitude toward science would lead to the establishment of the kind of all-dominating scientist-priesthood that would end by stifling individual thought and innovation. In fact, Huxley coined the term "agnosticism" as a way of distinguishing his own philosophy from Comte's positivism.

7. A deluded material object is a contradiction in terms; the Easter bunny isn't.

8. A line from a popular song of the same name by the group *Kansas,* released as a single in 1977.

9. It is a mistake to think that Christian fundamentalists do not respect science as much as everyone else. In fact, their peculiar doctrine known as creationism is a bizarre testament to their belief in the importance of science, as paradoxical as this might sound. Their forefathers were perfectly happy to assert, as a truth of revelation, that God had created the universe in six days, and that he had formed man out of a handful of dust, into which he breathed life. The modern creationists, however, are not satisfied with the old time religion of their fathers and seek to establish God's creation of the world, not terribly long ago by their accounts, on scientific principles. They would be wiser to stick with the simple and beautiful tradition of the forefathers.

CHAPTER TWELVE

1. Charles Oman, *The Great Revolt of 1381* (Oxford: Clarendon Press, 1906), 75.

2. Ibid., 76.

3. Ibid., 78.

4. The designation comes from the French chronicler of the times, Jean Froissart.

5. Oman, *The Great Revolt of 1381,* 51–52.

CHAPTER THIRTEEN

1. Lee Kuan Yew, *From Third World to First: The Singapore Story: 1965–2000, Singapore and the Asian Economic Boom* (New York: HarperCollins Publishers, 2000), 190.

2. Niccolo Machiavelli, *The Discourses on the First Ten Books of Livy,* Book III, Chapter XXV, "On the Poverty of Cincinnatus, and that of many other Roman citizens." Available online at http://www.marx.org/reference/archive/machiavelli/works/discourses/ch03.htm#s25.

3. Lee Kuan Yew, Ibid., 190–91.

4. Cf. Isaiah Berlin, *Two Concepts of Liberty* (Oxford: Clarendon Press, 1958).

5. Thomas Hobbes, *Leviathan* (New York: Penguin Books, 1985), 262.

6. Walter Block, "Privatizing Rivers and Slave Contracts," LewRockwell.com. In this piece Block defends slave contracts, but he notes that the "the case for legalizing voluntary slave contracts is held by a minority of libertarians. Indeed, until recently, only Nozick and I held this position, and, according to my friend and colleague David Gordon, Nozick had renounced this viewpoint before his death."

7. Walter Block, however, has advocated the privatization of roads and highways. Cf. Walter Block, *The Privatization of Roads and Highways: Human and Economic Factors* (Lewiston, NY: Edwin Mellen Press, 2006).

CHAPTER FOURTEEN

1. Gerald Gunther, *Learned Hand: The Man and the Judge* (New York: Alfred A. Knopf, 1994), 549.

2. Ibid., 548.

3. Ibid., 548–49.

4. The quote is from Oliver Cromwell's *Letter To the General Assembly of the Kirk of Scotland; or, in case of their not sitting, To the Commissioners of the Kirk of Scotland,* dated 3d August 1650. It appears in Thomas Carlyle, *Oliver Cromwell's Letters and Speeches: with elucidations,* vol. III (New York: Scribner, Welford, and Co., 1871), 15.

5. Quoted in Irving Dillard's Introduction to Learned Hand's book, *The Spirit of Liberty* (New York: Knopf, 1952), xxiv. The remarks were originally made by Learned Hand to Spencer R. McCulloch, special writer for the *St. Louis Post-Dispatch*.

6. Michael Casey, "Removing cats to protect birds backfires on island," *San Francisco Chronicle,* Jan. 13, 2009. Also see the article on Macquarie Island on Wikipedia.

7. This is the basic theme of Josiah Royce's book, *The Philosophy of Loyalty* (New York: Macmillan, 1911).

CONCLUSION

1. John Emerich Edward Dalberg-Acton, *The History of Liberty and Other Essays* (London: Macmillan, 1922), 22.

2. Ibid., 23.

3. Adam Smith, *An Inquiry into the Nature and Causes of the Wealth of Nations,* par. IV.2.9. Here is the full quote: "As every individual, therefore, endeavours as much as he can both to employ his capital in the support of domestic industry, and so to direct that industry that its produce may be of the greatest value; every individual necessarily labours to render the annual revenue of the society as great as he can. He generally, indeed, neither intends to promote the public interest, nor knows how much he is promoting it. By preferring the support of domestic to that of foreign industry, he intends only his own security; and by directing that industry in such a manner as its produce may be of the greatest value, he intends only his own gain, and he is in this, as in many other cases, led by an invisible hand to promote an end which was no part of his intention. Nor is it always the worse for the society that it was no part of it. By pursuing his own interest he *frequently* promotes that of the society more effectually than when he really intends to promote it." (Emphasis added.)

4. The reference is to the title of Ayn Rand's book, *The Virtue of Selfishness, A New Concept of Egoism* (New York: New American Library, 1964).

5. Cf. Adam Smith, *The Theory of Moral Sentiments,* (Indianapolis: Liberty Classics, 1982), *passim.* "The propriety of our moral sentiments is never so apt to be corrupted, as when the indulgent and partial spectator is at hand, while the indifferent and impartial one is at a great distance." (154).

INDEX